Praise for

CANNING AND PRESERVING
WITHOUT SUGAR

"Persons who are trying to avoid sugar will welcome this book with its tempting recipes for canned and frozen fruits, jams, jellies, pickles and relishes which can be prepared without sugar or artificial sweeteners . . . a valuable resource for diabetics, hypoglycemics, and persons without those metabolic disorders who simply want to eat a more healthful diet."
—*Provident Book Finder*

"'The key is making a test batch of the syrup and heating the fruit in it,' says Norma MacRae, a registered dietitian. . . . 'Don't just daydream about flavors; taste them,' she urges."
—*Rodale's Organic Gardening*

"A book for anyone who wants to avoid refined white sugar. Good-tasting reliable recipes . . . special nutritional information provided with each recipe—calorie count, sodium content, and diabetic fruit exchange."
—*National Gardening*

"An excellent book about preserving without sugar. For the most part, concentrated fruit juices are used for sweetening, but there are some recipes for using honey. Information about date sugars and dried fruits as sweeteners are given, too."
—*Journal of the American Dietetic Association*

"This guide, written by a registered dietitian, will appeal to those interested in eliminating sugar from their diet. After providing basic preservation tips, MacRae follows with assorted recipes for preparing a variety of jams, jellies, pickles, and fruits in this sugarless manner."
—*ALA Booklist*

"Along with the recipes . . . is considerable information on fruits and vegetables and on canning techniques."
—*Santa Cruz Sentinel*

"Helpful for people on restricted diets (medically or self-imposed), hypoglycemics, as well as diabetics. Year-round recipes are included, from Peach Butter and Celery Chutney to Herb Jelly and Winter Corn Relish."
—*The Bloomsbury Review*

CANNING AND PRESERVING WITHOUT SUGAR

Third Edition

by Norma M. MacRae, R.D.

The Globe Pequot Press

Old Saybrook, Connecticut

Illustrations by Kathy Michalove

Library of Congress Cataloging-in-Publication Data

MacRae, Norma M., 1924-
    Canning and preserving without sugar / by Norma M. MacRae. — 3rd ed.
    p. cm.
    Includes bibliographical references and index.
    ISBN 1-56440-163-4
    1. Canning and preserving.   2. Sugar-free diet—Recipes.
I. Title.
TX603.M23   1992
641.4'2—dc20   92-21478
                         CIP

Manufactured in the United States of America
Third Edition/Fourth Printing

---

*To my good friend Josephine Krezak Phillips, Lifelong Canner,
Master Gardener, and Master Friend!*

*"Jo" has been a constant source of encouragement and help
with each of my books. My especial thanks for the recipes she
contributed and for testing new recipes for this edition.*

CONTENTS

TABLES

ACKNOWLEDGMENTS

The author wishes to acknowledge the expert assistance of Jan Grant, B. S., M. A., King County Extension Agent for Washington State University. Her suggestions and help to the author in determining new processing times to conform with the latest United States Department of Agriculture canning recommendations were invaluable and greatly appreciated. Special thanks to copy editor Norma Ledbetter, whose many hours of hard work have helped to bring this edition into existence.

INTRODUCTION

This book is for everyone who wants to avoid sugar—people who are aware of how much sugar they've been eating, how harmful it can be, and who want to cut down—diabetics, hypoglycemics, natural food enthusiasts, and anyone concerned about good nutrition, good taste, and good health.

Traditional canning methods call for large amounts of sugar. Juice-canned fruits and jams made with fruit sweetening are available commercially, but often they cost so much that many people are reluctant to buy them and many others refuse. A cookbook was needed that would show how to preserve fruit easily at home, without sugar, for a reasonable price. This book was written to answer that need.

These recipes took many hours to test and involved a fair number of failures. Fruit juice sweetened recipes were not easy to develop, and it was difficult to create mixtures using honey without overpowering the natural flavor of the fruit. Here, then, is a collection of good-tasting, reliable recipes for canned fruits, jellies, jams, pickles, and relishes the whole family will enjoy. Best of all, they are made without adding table sugar (or, if desired, salt).

BEFORE YOU BEGIN

WHAT TO USE FOR SWEETENING

Liquid must be added when canning fruit. Early diabetic fruit was packed in water, but the fruit tasted just as it sounds—watery! To process fruit this way, be sure it is eating-ripe, and pack it into jars in slices or other small pieces so that little liquid is needed. This gives almost a juice pack but, without any added sweetening, will not enhance the fruit flavor.

Several liquids can be used to make syrup, including natural fruit juice, concentrated fruit juice, honey-sweetened water, and actual fruit such as thin applesauce. To make the most of the natural sweetening in ripe fruit, pack it in small slices or pieces to allow more of the fruit's sugar to go into the liquid and more of the liquid's sweetening into the fruit. The result is most tasty!

When selecting fruit juice, use natural juice, if available—apple juice with canned apples, for example. This will give the most natural fruit flavor; adding a small amount of lemon juice will enhance the flavor even more. Try small batches using various juices. What sounds good doesn't always taste as good; you may find that adding a spice helps perk up the flavor. Whole cloves, grated fresh ginger root, or whole cinnamon sticks can work wonders. Although the Washington State Extension Service does not recommend it, I like to add a *few* fruit pits to various canned fruits to give a pleasant, slightly almond flavor. Remember to save and freeze apricot, peach, and plum pits for use with apple slices, fruit cocktail, and pears. A few cherry pits added to canned cherries also enhance their flavor.

FROZEN JUICE

Concentrated apple juice, orange juice, and pineapple juice are all available in the freezer of your grocery store and should be used as soon as possible after thawing for best flavor. Most frozen juices are meant to be diluted with three volumes of water. Used undiluted or partly diluted, they make a concentrated sweetener for canning or preserving. Just be sure they are labeled "pure juice."

FRUIT JUICE CONCENTRATES

Cooperatives and some health stores sell fresh or frozen fruit juice concentrates. These are much more concentrated than regular frozen juices and are excellent to use in cooking and canning. Fresh juice concentrates taste the most natural, frozen are almost as good, and canned least desirable. Taste any of these products before using as there is considerable difference in taste and desirability among brands.

I suggest that you buy the smallest size available when trying any new fruit concentrate. Test it by actually canning one jar of any fruit before using it for further canning. Let stand at least 12 hours so that it's completely cool and the liquid has had a chance to permeate the fruit—then taste-test.

CANNED JUICE

Canned or frozen concentrated juice may not be just as it comes from the fruit (with only water removed prior to freezing). If it says "pure" juice, it must legally be just that—no sugar or other substance added. Read labels carefully to be sure you are getting pure juice with no sugar added. A number of juice combinations are now appearing on the market. Apple-pear would be an excellent choice for canning pears, and pineapple-grapefruit a possible choice for freezing grapefruit and/or fresh pineapple. Keep watching to see what new mixtures are introduced that might be good to use.

DATE SUGAR

Date sugar can be added to sweeten jam and preserves. This is a pure, natural product made by drying and grinding dates. It has a distinctive, slightly acidic taste and must have lemon juice added as part of the liquid called for in the recipe to help mask this flavor.

OTHER DRIED FRUITS FOR SWEETENING

Commercially dried fruits (available in the grocery store) are treated with sulfur dioxide to prevent darkening. Untreated dried fruits will be much darker and probably a bit lower in moisture (some may be a lot lower). If you plan to use home-dried fruit for preserves or cooking, allow extra moisture in the recipe unless it is one that you want to simmer down for reduced volume. Allow at least 1 tablespoon extra liquid per cup of dried fruit. The color of the finished food will be more intense (darker) with home-dried or unsulfured dried fruits, but this substitution should not affect the taste.

The best way to use dried fruit is to place dried fruit equal to $1/2$ the volume of fresh fruit called for in the recipe in a large crockery bowl. Cover fruit with boiling water, loosely cover, and allow to stand overnight. Drain (save liquid) and measure. You should be able to use this soaked fruit in the same amount as fresh fruit. Substitute the drained liquid for as much of the recipe's liquid as possible so that you won't lose any of the fruit's natural sweetness.

HONEY SYRUP

Any fruit can be canned with honey syrup; there need be no change in directions given for both hot pack and cold or raw pack when it is used. I have not emphasized its use because those who do not want to use refined sugar may not want to (or cannot, in the case of the diabetic or hypoglycemic) use honey either. (Although a naturally occurring sugar, honey still adds highly concentrated sweetening to the natural sweetness of fruit.)

Fruits canned with medium-strength honey syrup are very good if enough lemon juice is added to disguise the taste of the honey. With honey, the sugar content will be greater than with juice pack (and the calories greater), the color won't be as apt to fade (as it will using juice), and the taste will be more satisfying to the sugar user than the less sweet fruit-juice pack.

SPECIAL INGREDIENTS

LEMON JUICE AND DRIED CITRUS RIND

Many of these recipes call for lemon juice. Frozen lemon juice can be used with complete satisfaction; ideally, however, use fresh juice and strain it to remove seeds and pulp. Grate the rind before squeezing the lemon and dehydrate or freeze the grated rind for later use. Commercial orange and lemon peels all contain sugar, but it is very simple to dry your own. Follow the instructions given below and store in a closed container in a cool, dark place. (I have kept home-dried rind for more than two years and found it just as good as when first prepared.)

If you don't want to dry the grated rind, place it in a small freezer zip bag, squeeze out all air, zip, and sharp-freeze until needed. Use same amount as fresh as called for in the recipe.

DRIED CITRUS RIND
Lemons, oranges, grapefruit (or mixed citrus fruit) 1 or more

Using a fine grater, grate rind onto nonstick cookie sheet, spreading over sheet to give even grating without lumps. Place sheet on top rack of oven preheated to 200°. Turn down to 150° when you put in rind, and leave to dry for $1\frac{1}{2}$ to 2 hours until rind feels dry—and not sticky. Remove from oven; allow to cool. Break up lumps with the bottom of a glass tumbler. Place dried rind in tightly covered jar and store in cool, dark place.

Note: Color will fade if left where rind gets light. A brown bottle will help prevent this. Rind will dry to about half the volume of fresh. *Use half the amount of fresh lemon rind called for in a recipe,* slightly more than half the amount of orange rind and slightly less than half the amount of grapefruit rind (stronger flavor). Or let dried rind soak in warm water for 20 to 30 minutes and use as fresh.

FOOD COLORING

A few of these recipes suggest adding vegetable food coloring. Colors sold in grocery stores are artificial colors, not from vegetable sources. If you don't want to use anything that is manufactured like this, a totally natural color can be obtained with the use of items found in most kitchens (see suggestions below).

Red: Rhubarb and berries tend to fade when cooked without sugar.

To restore the color naturally, take beet liquid and simmer it down to half the original volume. Add the concentrated beet liquid to the mixtures you wish to color (1 tablespoon liquid will color 1 cup or more), but be sure to add spices or extra lemon juice to help disguise any flavor carried over from the beets.

Yellow: A number of spices will give yellow color, including saffron, mustard, turmeric, and cumin. Since saffron is so costly, mustard and turmeric have strong flavors that are hard to disguise, and cumin also has a flavor that some people notice, none of these is ideal. If you can afford it, saffron is most useful, and a minute amount will give concentrated color. Cumin is probably the next best choice, unless you have a strong ingredient such as vinegar to help disguise the mustard or turmeric taste.

Green: Peelings of zucchini squash have an intense green color. These can be cooked until soft and pureed for use as a coloring agent. Again, you may have to adjust the recipe with lemon juice or additional herbs to cover any taste that the peel may have added.

SALT AND SALT SUBSTITUTES

Table salt (sodium chloride) is usually processed to add iodine for prevention of goiter. It does not make a good pickle; get *noniodized* or *pickling* salt—a coarse salt ideal for pickles. This is for sale in most large groceries during canning season.

Sea salt contains chemicals other than sodium chloride and is not a good choice for pickling, although kosher salt will work. A salt substitute can be used in any of these recipes, provided it is acceptable to your taste. I have found only one I think good enough. It can be obtained by mail order from Johnny's Enterprises, Inc., 319 East 25th Street, Tacoma, WA 98421 (800–962–1462 to order). It is called "Healthline Salt Replacement" and contains potassium, but it does not have the bitter aftertaste of most salt substitutes. I have used it in pickles and sauces with success. Use this salt substitute as you would use salt called for in the recipes. The sodium values of each recipe are given at the bottom, *provided that no real salt is added.*

VINEGAR

There are three basic vinegars on the market. Most people buy and use cider vinegar (made from apples), wine vinegar (made from red or white wine), and distilled vinegar. For pickling and meat sauces, use distilled vinegar (sometimes called pickling vinegar). Being colorless, distilled vinegar won't add color to the food being cooked or pickled. Distilled vinegar does not have the sharp bite of cider and wine vinegars, partly because it is lower in acetic acid (4 percent compared with 5 or 6 percent).

You can easily make herb vinegar by adding not more than 2 teaspoons herb per cup vinegar (cider or wine) and allowing it to stand for up to a month or until the flavor suits you. Do not use this herb vinegar in pickle or sauce recipes, as its strength is uncertain and results will be, too.

GELATIN OR AGAR-AGAR

Gelatin is used in many sugarless jams (and other naturally sweetened products) to help keep the liquid from separating from the solids, thus giving a watery consistency. If you want to avoid animal products (gelatin is made from animals), use agar-agar instead. Agar-agar comes from seaweed and is used as a stabilizer (thickener) in some commercial food products.

The easiest form to use is Chinese agar-agar, which comes in sticks (usually two in a package) and can be purchased in health food stores or Oriental food stores. One-half stick can be dissolved in $1/2$-cup liquid, and that liquid must then be accounted for in your recipe. It may be difficult to dissolve, however. Break it into small pieces—using scissors helps. Place the pieces in a small bowl or saucepan and add liquid (you could use some of the fruit juice called for in the recipe); allow the mixture to stand for at least 30 minutes. Then stir and slowly heat to complete dissolving the agar. This will replace 1 tablespoon gelatin (one envelope) in a recipe and will give a firmer jell at warmer temperatures.

SPICES

Some spices enhance the natural sweetness in food. There is a whole category called the "sweet spices" because they have the ability to make food taste sweeter. These include allspice, cardamom, cinnamon, coriander, ginger, mace, and nutmeg. Mixed spice blends such as pumpkin-pie spice, catsup spice, and mixed pickling spice also come under this category. Mint and vanilla flavorings also have the ability to enhance natural sweetness.

If you have a recipe that isn't quite sweet enough for your taste, try adding small amounts of one (or more) of these spices and flavorings and taste—the result will probably be what you wanted.

Pure spices are not supposed to contain additives of any kind. On the other hand, spice mixtures (herb mixes, for example) may contain both salt and sugar in some form. Be sure you buy pure spice and keep it in a dark, cool place in a tightly covered container. Spices are aromatic and will lose their flavor over a period of time. Exposure to light and heat speeds up this process, as well as causing color changes in some of them (my dried parsley turned white after being left for several months where the sun occasionally shone on the jar). Of course, the taste will still be there, but with the color gone, it loses some appeal.

Spices can be frozen if they are packed in an absolutely moisture-proof container. To be sure, I always place the container in a heavy (freeze-type) zip plastic bag to give double protection from moisture.

Don't buy cheap spices. Stick with brand names for top quality, and avoid products on sale, as they may be old and less potent. Buying good spices is an investment, and if you care for them as suggested, they will add enjoyment to your food for several years.

FRUIT PECTIN

Fruit pectin occurs naturally in all fruits, but the amount varies greatly from one fruit to another. Pectin is nature's thickener, and extra pectin is frequently added when making jams or jellies to ensure that the jam or jelly thickens properly. A complete discussion of pectin will be found in the Preserving with Fruit Juice Sweetening chapter (See General Index).

EQUIPMENT YOU'LL NEED

FOR WATER-BATH OR PRESSURE-CANNER CANNING

Large nonaluminum kettle, 8- to 10-quart capacity
Large wooden spoon, long-handled
Slotted spoon, long-handled
Colander or wire basket
Large bowls
Measuring cups (1-, 2-, and 4-cup are handy)
Measuring spoons
Paring knife, slicing knife
Large tongs
Water-bath canner, deep enough for jars on rack, plus 2 inches **or**
Pressure canner (8-quart size) with rack
Teakettle
Canning jars
Canning lids with jar rings
Lettuce/salad spinner (optional)

The USDA (United States Department of Agriculture) *does not recommend using pressure cookers for canning.* If you use one, add 20 minutes at the recommended pressure to ensure a safely sealed product.

There are two types of pressure canners. The weighted-gauge type is guaranteed to give true pressure for the life of the canner. The dial-gauge canners need checking annually before you start your season's canning. Your Cooperative Extension office will recommend a local source that will check the dial gauge for minimal cost.

The U.S.D.A. has no recommended pressure-canner times for high-acid foods (all these recipes). If you do use a pressure canner, you should follow the manufacturer's directions for time and pressure.

Jars must be canning strength and have lids that can seal with processing. According to Jeanne Lesem's book, *The Pleasures of Preserving and Pickling,* Cornell University's College of Human Ecology approves use of peanut butter and pint and quart mayonnaise jars for food requiring water-bath processing. I personally would never recommend the use of jars not designated for home canning. In boiling and pressure processing, noncanning-strength jars may break. Be sure all jars have no chips or cracks, especially around the lips.

I have kept plastic freezing containers for years, using them over and over. If plastic bags are used inside them before adding the vegetable or fruit, they both keep the product from getting freezer burn and prevent the plastic containers from getting stained or picking up flavors. The regular lock-top plastic bags bought in the grocery store work well. They are not cheap, but they contribute to keeping the frozen fruit in A-1 condition.

FOR BLANCHING VEGETABLES

Deep cooker with basket **or** deep-fat fryer with basket (I have an electric deep-fat fryer with a handled basket that I use only for blanching vegetables. Using this gives me control over the temperature of the water and allows a better blanched product.)

ALSO NEEDED FOR MAKING JAM AND JELLY

Jelly jars with sealing lids
Jelly bag (or cheesecloth to make one)

ALSO NEEDED FOR MAKING PICKLES

Food mill, 1-quart size or larger
Meat grinder with various blades
Spice bag (or cloth to improvise one)

FOR FREEZING FRUITS AND VEGETABLES

Freezing containers with tight lids

Plastic-bag liners (optional)

Freezer, preferably with sharp-freeze unit. (Fast freezing gives a more tender result. If no sharp-freeze is available, freeze smaller amounts at a time.)

HOW TO STERILIZE EQUIPMENT

To be sure that home-processed foods stay free from bacteria, jars should be sterilized before use. This isn't hard but takes time so allow for it when you plan your canning and have them ready when needed.

Jars should be clean. Wash them in hot, soapy water and rinse well, or put them in the dishwasher and let it do the work. After cleaning, put them in a deep water bath to boil unless they will be processed again later. Fill the water bath well over half full with hot water. Cover and place over medium heat. (There should be a rack for the jars to sit on so that they don't come in direct contact with the bottom of the water bath.) Using tongs, place jars upright in the bath, tilting as you put them in so that hot water partially fills them and they stand upright without floating. When the bath is full of jars, add boiling water to cover them by at least 1 inch. Replace cover and boil for 20 minutes. Have the jars hot to use when the fruit is ready. Don't take them out and leave them in the open air, or they won't be sterile anymore. You must use sterile tongs and take jars out as needed to keep them sterile.

Be sure to read the manufacturer's instructions before processing your lids. I failed to do so recently and had some foods spoil. The lid manufacturer had introduced new processing techniques without noting the fact on the outside of the lid box. Since I learned to can at home while growing up, I didn't bother to read the instructions—I knew how to do it! Only, with that brand, I found that I didn't. So save yourself some possible failures and take time each year to read the manufacturer's instruction sheet before starting to can. I will from now on. Personally, I prefer using lids that are enameled on the inside (their undersides look whitish).

You still need to have your tongs and jars sterile to avoid any contamination entering your jars. If my jam/jelly/fruit isn't boiling hot when placed in the jar and processed, I use a longer processing time than is recommended by the USDA (at least 5 extra minutes). Just be careful not to overcook, or they will be less eye appealing and tasty.

Even if the manufacturer's instructions recommend inverting jars after processing, *do not do so.* The USDA extension service considers this a dangerous procedure and recommends strongly against it.

SELECTING, CANNING, AND FREEZING VEGETABLES

HOW TO CHOOSE VEGETABLES FOR CANNING AND PICKLING

Home-grown vegetables are always freshest, but some nearly as good can be bought at farmers' stands or country markets during harvest time. Since most vegetables continue to ripen after they are picked, they should be used immediately or kept refrigerated until used. Refrigeration won't completely stop the process of ripening, but it will slow it down. *All vegetables, except tomatoes and pickles, are low-acid foods and therefore must be canned in a pressure canner to reach 240 degrees and thus destroy the botulism spores and assure a safe product.*

SELECTING AND PREPARING VEGETABLES FOR PROCESSING

Asparagus: Asparagus is available late April and early May in most areas. Spears should not have overripened so that they are tough and the stems woody. Snap the stem to be sure it is fresh. It will continue to mature after picking, so process or refrigerate at once. (Three to four days shelf life in refrigerator.)

Asparagus must be blanched and then thoroughly chilled before freezing to get a superior product. I chill in ice water at least eight minutes, then spin in lettuce spinner to quickly remove water before packing as quickly as possible. You may prepare as whole spears or cut into 1-inch pieces. Be sure to process only the tender portion (try snapping to see how much this is).

Beans: Green beans are most available in August, limas in late August. Beans should not be too large, or they become tough. The best just bulge a little from the seeds inside, and green beans should snap easily. Limas should have full, firm pods. Some sizes are deceiving—giant beans may still be very tender even when large. Some don't freeze well. Find out about the varieties and what they are generally used for before you buy them. Your local Extension Agent can supply you with information about what grows best in your area. Stringless varieties may sound superior, but most green beans are stringless if young and tender. Again, process immediately or refrigerate to slow the ripening process.

Remove both ends of bean, sort by size if planning to can whole, or cut them into 1- to 1½-inch pieces. Blanch if planning to freeze them.

Beets: Beets are available all summer long; peak season is in August. Pick beets that are not too large, with fresh, unwilted greens. They should feel firm, and the center stem should not be too thick. Plan to can all beets—they don't freeze well!

To prepare, cut off stems, leaving about 1 inch over top of beet. Place in a deep nonaluminum kettle, cover with water, place cover on pot, and cook until tender. Drain; place a few at a time in a bowl of cold water. Stems and skins will come right off with a little hand help. Cut out any hard spots or pieces of skin that won't come off easily. Slice or dice if desired before processing.

Broccoli: Broccoli is at its peak in August. Buds should be tight— never opened and showing yellow. The stem should not be tough, and leaves should be a good green. Broccoli should never be limp— it is as crisp and "snappy" as green beans when at its best. Refrigerate if not using or processing immediately. It will keep in the refrigerator for three to five days without wilting badly.

Blanch broccoli before freezing. I slice through the stems vertically so that each bud section has a stem section attached. I cut slices about ½-inch thick, but they can be thinner or thicker, according to your taste. For thicker portions, remember to blanch them a longer period of time.

Broccoflower (Green Cauliflower): This cross between broccoli and cauliflower is a delightful new vegetable. It is milder in taste than broccoli and firmer in texture than cauliflower when cooked. Unless you grow your own or know a farmer you can buy from directly, it probably won't be cheap enough to freeze for several years. The batch I tried froze very well. Like its parents, it should be processed as soon as possible or refrigerated until used. Best results come from freezing, not canning! Note directions under broccoli. For freezing, process as for broccoli.

Cabbage: Most cabbage used for pickling and slaw is available in August and early September. Cabbage should look and feel firm, have a good green (or red-purple) color, and feel crisp when you lift an outer leaf. If cabbage has split, it is too ripe. Refrigerate if not using or processing immediately. It will keep in the refrigerator for a week or longer.

In most areas, fresh cabbage is available year-round. It does not freeze or can well, so don't try processing it plain. You can preserve it by pickling or make it into sauerkraut and can it for later use. Sauerkraut can be frozen, but it tends to toughen; it is much superior canned. Recipes for preserving cabbage in various ways (in relish, vegetable salad, etc.) can be found in the Pickle, Relish, and Seasoning Sauces section of both the Fruit Juice and Honey Sweetened recipes (see Recipe Index).

Carrots: Carrots are cheapest in August and September. They should be tender, not woody. When they have been in cold storage for many months, they tend to dry out and will not taste as good as fresh. In winter, picking bulk carrots is best; if you look for medium-sized ones, you will probably avoid those with woody centers. Carrots will store well if kept in a cool, somewhat humid place, like a fruit cellar, and will keep for several weeks in the refrigerator.

To prepare, remove tops, peel, and cut into slices, cubes, or julienne. Blanch before freezing.

Cauliflower: Cauliflower is at its peak in August. It should be creamy white. If yellow, it is probably overripe. Bud segments should be firm and tight; leaves should be green and firm. To keep, remove leaves and refrigerate.

For freezing, process as for broccoli.

Corn: Corn is available from early August through late September in most areas. Be sure you are buying sweet corn (not field corn). The husk should be light green (not yellow) and crisp, with a dark, rather dry tassel. The husk should feel firm. Peel it back and look at the kernels to gauge maturity: Light yellow is sweetest; too pale will be immature; too dark will be overripe.

There are gadgets available to cut corn off the cob. These are really labor and cost saving, as they get more kernels off the cob with less effort. I find that whole-kernel cut corn freezes well with no prior processing.

Cucumbers: Pickling cucumbers are available from mid-August through September. They should be picked when young and green when seeds are still soft. If cucumbers are yellow, they are too ripe and should be thrown away unless used to make ripe cucumber pickles. (Don't try to eat them when they are yellow.) Frozen pickles are not acceptable in texture, so plan to can them. Cucumbers to be used for small, whole, sweet pickles should be from 2 to 4 inches long; for dills, 5 to 6 inches long; and for slicing into bread-and-butter pickles or for relishes, 6 to 8 inches long. Discard any over this size, as the seeds will be tough. Refrigerate until used. Cucumbers should be used within 24 hours of picking for best quality pickle. Grocery store cucumbers are not suitable for pickling because they have a waxy coating that doesn't allow brine to penetrate.

Mushrooms: Mushrooms are available fresh during most of the year. The freshest have closed caps (brown gills do not show). Be sure they are firm, with no soft spots. Just before using, wash gently under cool water. Avoid bruising and do not soak in water longer than necessary to remove dirt. Chop or slice stems and use only in long-cooking dishes. Canned mushrooms contain less moisture than fresh. When using them in a recipe that calls for fresh mushrooms, you may need to add 2 to 3 tablespoons of the liquid per cup. Wild mushrooms may be used as easily as commercially grown (the variations in moisture content are slight and will not make a difference in cooked dishes), but be sure you have expert identification skills. Every year serious illnesses or deaths are caused by people eating wild mushrooms they thought were safe.

Mushrooms are one of the home-canned foods that readily grow the botulin organism, so I recommend that you freeze them to be safe. To prepare, wash in cold water (use a mushroom brush—very soft bristles), trying not to bruise the flesh. Cut off tough ends; halve or quarter if very large, or separate button tops from stems. (You can slice the stems and use them in cooking, and they won't be too tough.) Blanch in boiling water for 3 minutes for slices or up to 5 minutes for thicker pieces. Plunge into cold water, then ice water for 5 minutes to completely chill. Place in lettuce spinner and spin to remove water. Pack in airtight containers leaving $\frac{1}{2}$ inch at top for expansion. Sharp-freeze; move to other part of freezer when hard.

Onions: Onions are available all year long but are most available in late August and September. Among the varieties of onions, there are differences in flavor. Yellow onions are strongest, whereas Bermuda-type (Walla Walla Sweets) are milder and a little softer, as are the sweet red onions. An onion must feel firm. The outer skin should look clean, should show no signs of bruising or mold, and the tops should not be soft, but rather dry with no signs of sprouting. Tiny pickling onions should be white with skins that peel off easily, leaving a firm inside. Red onions will tend to give some red color when cooked with other vegetables. They are recommended primarily for sandwiches and salad use.

Onions that are to be used in cooking can be peeled, chopped, and sharp-frozen in zip-type freezer packages. Be sure all air is exhausted before closing the bags. Onions do not need to be defrosted before using them in any dish that is cooked before serving. Use same amount as fresh.

Peas: Peas are in season from June through mid-July. Pods should be well filled and medium green. They should be firm and not wilted. Different varieties will come in varying lengths, but a 4-inch pod is probably a good size, provided it is filled out properly. Peas should be shelled and processed immediately, or refrigerated unshelled to keep them from overmaturing and losing their tenderness and sweetness. They will stay fresh for two or three days in the refrigerator. Peas with edible pods should barely show the peas they contain. They should be firm, with no signs of wilt. These peas will lose freshness quickly and should be used within a day or two.

Peas can be frozen or canned, depending on your preference. I like them best frozen. I sort by size of the pea so that all the larger ones are together. This gives a better end product, as larger peas require slightly longer blanching time and longer cooking time when thawed. I found that with mixed sizes, some were overcooked and some underdone, so I now sort them.

Blanch smaller peas for $1^1/_2$ minutes and large peas for 2 minutes after water returns to boiling. Plunge into cold water, then ice water for 5 minutes to completely chill. Pack in air-tight containers, leaving $^1/_2$ inch at top for expansion. Drain well. Sharp-freeze; move to other part of freezer when hard.

Peppers: Did you know that green peppers are just immature, sweet, red peppers? They are at their peak late in summer, though you can buy them all year. If you are using a lot of peppers, buy in bulk. They will keep in the refrigerator for several weeks. Peppers should be firm, have no discoloration around the stem, and have a waxy look to the skin. Size is unimportant. They do not toughen as they turn red, so those partly turned are as good as those completely green.

If you plan to use chopped peppers in cooking, you don't have to blanch them. You can freeze them in zip-type freezer bags, being sure that all air is exhausted before closing. These need not be defrosted before using them in any dish that is cooked before serving.

For rings, slices, quarters, or whole peppers, remove stem and seeds, then blanch in boiling water for three minutes after water returns to boiling. Chill in ice water, spin in lettuce spinner to remover water, and pack in air-tight containers, leaving $^1/_2$ inch at top for expansion.

Pumpkins and Winter Squash: Winter squash is available in September and October. Dark green winter squash should not show any really yellow areas; some orange is acceptable. The darker the green the better is the rule for some varieties, whereas others never turn dark green, so you must know what kind you have and what it should look like when mature. Pumpkin should be overall orange. The skin of both winter squash and pumpkin should be tough, not soft. Winter squash should be cut with a 2-inch stem. Let the squash age before you plan to cook it. I usually leave Hubbard-type squash for three weeks to a month to dry before processing for the freezer. Watch to be sure that no water gets on the squash (or pumpkin) because some molds that may form are unhealthy.

Do not can mashed pumpkin. Can pumpkin only in cubes. Always remove skin from pumpkin or squash before canning. I prefer to steam these vegetables (or bake in covered pans with some water in the bottom to prevent sticking) until tender. Then I either put the meat through a Foley-type food mill or process it in a blender to remove any strings. I place it hot in plastic bags within freezing containers, cool in refrigerator, and then sharp-freeze, moving it to another part of the freezer when frozen.

Summer Squash (Zucchini, Crook Neck, Scallop): Summer squash is usually available from mid-July through September. All types should be picked when young and tender. Yellow types should be pale yellow, scallop should be greenish-white, and zucchini should be dark green. Summer squash should feel soft if pressed with a fingernail. Hard rind means overripe squash—discard it. Uncut summer squash will keep for five to seven days in the refrigerator.

Remove ends and slice in $^1/_3$-inch-thick slices. Blanch in boiling water for 2 minutes after water returns to boiling. Chill in ice water, spin in lettuce spinner to remove excess water, and pack in airtight containers, leaving $^1/_2$ inch at top for expansion.

Tomatoes: Peak season for tomatoes varies with climate, but late August into September is usual. The best tomatoes are ripened on the vine. They should feel firm, look ripe (red and juicy), and smell ripe. You can use your nose to tell you about tomatoes as easily as you can about fruit. Unripe tomatoes will ripen eventually, but they won't taste the same as those ripened before picking. If you want to make green-tomato dishes, buy them hard and green. You'll have to store them in the refrigerator, or they will soon be red and ripening. Refrigerate all tomatoes unless using immediately. They will then keep for several days, unless extremely ripe when refrigerated. You can speed ripening in almost ripe tomatoes by placing one or more ripe apples in a container with the tomatoes. Loosely cover the container and let stand overnight. You will be amazed how much riper and tastier they are by morning. Remove those that feel and smell ripe for processing; cover the rest to allow them to ripen longer.

It is essential that tomatoes used in canning be just ripe. Tomatoes become less acidic as they become overly ripe and may be unsafe when canned like fruit in a water-bath canner. Because some tomatoes have been found to be marginally acidic, Pennsylvania State University recommends that citric acid, U.S.P., or lemon juice be added to tomatoes to assure safety in the final product. For every pint, add $1/4$ teaspoon citric acid or 1 tablespoon bottled lemon juice. For every quart, add $1/2$ teaspoon citric acid or 2 tablespoons bottled lemon juice.

If you have lots of freezer room, you can prepare tomatoes as for canning, but instead of bottling them, place them in a large nonaluminum kettle and simmer in their own juice until tender. Pack in clean jars, leaving 1 inch for expansion. Top with clean lids, cool to room temperature, then freeze.

STEWED TOMATOES

Prepare as for plain canned tomatoes. For each 2 cups peeled, cut-up tomatoes, add $1/4$ cup chopped onion, $1/4$ cup chopped green pepper, and $1/4$ cup chopped celery. Simmer on top of stove until added vegetables are tender. Add $1/2$ teaspoon lemon juice for each cup of the mixture before canning. If you wish, you may season with salt and pepper to taste.

BEFORE YOU BEGIN CANNING

Canning vegetables *safely* requires processing to destroy any organisms that could continue to grow and form toxins or poisons. High temperature for sufficient time in air-free containers (jars sealed with lids) will destroy these microorganisms. Canning time is dependent on many factors; use only the tested directions for time and temperature as recommended by the USDA Extension Service!

The acidity level of the vegetable to be processed determines how to safely can it. The bacteria that can cause botulism can survive and grow in low-acid vegetables even when sealed in airless jars! Botulism poisoning from improperly processed vegetables has caused severe illness and death, so there is every reason to be extremely careful to follow directions to prevent this poison from developing in your jars.

Important: You must always use a pressure canner for processing vegetables. Only this will produce temperatures high enough to kill many of the bacteria that may grow in low-acid foods. *You can't taste, smell, or see the changes from the presence of these toxins/-poisons. Don't take a chance on someone's life by cutting corners when processing vegetables!* (It is safe to process fruits with a water-bath canner because these foods are sufficiently acid to prevent these toxins from growing.) *Be sure to read and follow the directions given in the Equipment You'll Need material in the Before You Begin Section, and check the dial gauge on your pressure canner each year before starting to process vegetables.*

Canning most vegetables does not involve adding sugar, except possibly peas and corn. I experimented with juice-sweetened canned corn and peas, but the results were not acceptable. Both these vegetables taste fine canned without added sweetening, so just omit it. I personally prefer both corn and peas frozen, so that is how I process them.

Don't take a chance on botulism poisoning—be sure to discard any canned vegetable product that is at all suspicious. If the lid is not concave in center, or the seal is broken, or there are visible changes such as bubbles, mold, or an "off" odor, do not use the jar or its contents.

Don't taste to check on your judgment—you could get enough of the bacteria to make you very sick! The USDA recommends that you detoxify any suspicious jar by placing the jar with contents and the loose lid in a deep pan; then cover completely with water and boil for 30 minutes. Cool and discard the contents in the garbage or bury it in soil. This will keep any animal from being accidentally poisoned.

PROCESSING VEGETABLES FOR CANNING AND FREEZING

When canning vegetables, I always use water that has been boiled. The water does not have to be salted to successfully preserve vegetables. If the vegetables are packed into the jars so that there is a little space left between pieces, they will taste more like fresh vegetables than if you use a lot of liquid and dilute the flavor.

When freezing vegetables, most need to be blanched to stop enzyme action. To blanch vegetables, prepare as for canning. Blanch in not more than 4-cup portions in a boiling-water bath. Using a deep-fat fryer or an electric cooking pot (crock pot) with temperature control is easiest. Have water actively boiling when you add the basket of vegetables. Start timing from the minute the water returns to boiling. I allow 2–3 minutes for the less dense vegetables and 3 minutes for the thicker pieces. Remove from heat and rinse in cold water; then place in ice water for at least 5 minutes to completely chill. Drain in lettuce spinner to remove any remaining water and package immediately. I place the packages in the refrigerator until I have three or four to take to the freezer; that saves me from constantly opening the freezer door and raising the whole freezer's temperature. Be sure to place the new packages in the sharp-freeze section until hard, then move them to the main part of the freezer for the storage.

I have not been as satisfied with the results when I steam-blanched my vegetables before freezing, so I recommend that you use the tem-

TABLE 1

HOW MUCH FRESH PRODUCE IS NEEDED FOR A QUART?

Vegetable	Pounds Needed
Asparagus	$2^1/_2$–$4^1/_2$
Beans, green, wax, or snap	$1^1/_2$–$2^1/_2$
Beans, lima	3–5
Beets, without tops	2–$3^1/_2$
Carrots, without tops	2–3
Corn, cream-style or whole kernel	3–6
Peas, green	3–6
Pumpkin	$1^1/_2$–3
Spinach and other greens	2–6
Squash, winter	$1^1/_2$–3

Source: Van Hillers, PNW 172, *Canning Vegetables,* A Pacific Northwest Cooperative
Extension Publication, Washington/Oregon/Idaho, 1989

perature-controlled boiling-water bath as described in the Before You Begin Canning section.

When freezing vegetables, I set up an assembly line so that the least possible time is used in packaging the blanched and chilled product. I have freezer cartons and lids freshly washed, dried, and lined up ready to fill before I start blanching, and I keep large bowls with cold water and ice cubes ready to add to promote chilling. I use plastic bags inside the containers so that my products are actually double protected against freezer burn. (For my small family, I pack in pint or $1^1/_2$-pint containers and use sandwich-sized bags.) The bags also keep the inside of the containers from getting stained or holding odor from previous contents. I also fill a kettle with water and heat it to boiling so that I can quickly change the blanching water after every third processing.

If you have questions or feel unsure about what you are doing, contact your local Extension Service for their latest pamphlet on fruit and vegetable processing. This will give you their current recommendations for processing times and any new methods that they feel are safe. Even if you follow these directions for processing your vegetables, the USDA recommends that *if any variation of time or processing method is used,* you *must* boil foods for 10 minutes at altitudes below 1,000 feet and for 1 additional minute for each additional 1,000 feet of elevation before eating.

PROCESSING METHODS FOR CANNING VEGETABLES

There are two methods for canning vegetables: hot pack and raw cold-pack. In the hot-pack method, the vegetable is blanched for 2 to 3 minutes in boiling water or by steaming. Then, while still very hot, it is packed in sterile jars, filled to within $3/_4$ inch of the top with boiling water, topped with sterile lids, and processed in a pressure canner for the recommended number of minutes. Doing this allows you to get more vegetables in the jar (blanching slightly shrinks them), and they will be softer and thus easier to pack. If you use a clean spatula around the inner edges of the jar, you will be able to eliminate air bubbles between the vegetable pieces.

If you choose to use the raw cold-pack method, you just pack the pieces of vegetable in sterile jars, using a spatula around the inner sides of the jar to eliminate air bubbles, cover with boiling water to within 1 inch of the top, cap with sterile lids, and process in a pressure canner as directed in the timetable shown (see Table 2). This method may require a longer processing time, as you will see from reading the table.

CANNING LOW-ACID VEGETABLES

Canning Method. Vegetables must be processed at 240°F. or higher in a pressure canner to prevent botulism poisoning and other spoilage and waste. Operate a weighted-gauge pressure canner at *10* pounds pressure (at sea level) to reach 240°F. The dial-gauge pressure canner is operated at *11* pounds pressure (at sea level) to reach 240°F.

Adjustments for Altitude.
Weighted-gauge pressure canner:
Sea level to 1,000 feet—use 10-pound weight.
Above 1,000 feet—use 15-pound weight.

Dial-gauge pressure canner:
Sea level to 2,000 feet—11 pounds pressure on dial.
2,001-4,000 feet—12 pounds pressure on dial.
4,001-6,000 feet—13 pounds pressure on dial.
6,001-8,000 feet—14 pounds pressure on dial.

Canning Time. The processing time for each food and each jar size is based on the preparation methods described. Processing times are accurate only when all directions are followed exactly.

Headspace. Leave 1 inch headspace in all jars, except as directed for fresh lima beans.

Venting. Air trapped in a pressure canner lowers the temperature in the canner. To be sure foods are safely processed, all types of pressure canners (including those labeled "self-venting") must be vented 10 minutes before the pressure is allowed to rise. To vent a pressure canner, allow steam to escape steadily from the petcock for 10 minutes, then close the petcock or put the weighted gauge on the canner.

FREEZING VEGETABLES

A few vegetables do not freeze well, but most are very easy to freeze. Prepare by blanching in a boiling water bath as directed or steam blanch, adding 1 minute to the recommended times after water has returned to boiling. Blanch not more than 1 pound of vegetable at a time for proper heat penetration of all pieces. Cool in ice water for the same length of time that you blanch, to chill completely. Use lettuce spinner to remove water before packaging the food.

It is recommended that in a 24-hour period you add to your freezer not more than 3 pounds of food per cubic foot of freezer. (For a 21-cubic-foot freezer, this would be 63 pounds.) The containers should be spread out so that each is in contact with the shelf and there is room between for cold air to reach all sides of the package.

Asparagus: Wash; cut stems approximately 5 inches from tip. (You may cut slices from the lower portion down as far as it cuts easily. These can be frozen separately and used as a base for excellent asparagus soup.) Blanch in boiling water for 5 minutes after water returns to boiling. Drain; chill in ice water for 5 minutes. Drain (a lettuce spinner works very well); then pack in plastic freezer bags or boxes. Sharp-freeze. To use, remove from freezer just before cooking. *Do not thaw.* Steaming is recommended.

Beans: String beans should be washed, strings removed, and cut into pieces of the size you prefer. Blanch in boiling-water bath for 2 minutes after water returns to boiling. Drain; chill in ice water for 4–5

TABLE 2
TIMES AND PRESSURES FOR CANNING LOW-ACID VEGETABLES

Process Time (Min.) at 240°F. 10 pounds pressure for weighted gauge; 11 pounds pressure for dial gauge. Adjust for altitude.

VEGETABLE	PREPARATION	Pts	Qts
Asparagus	Wash. Trim off scales, tough ends. Wash again. Cut into 1-inch pieces or leave whole.		
	Hot pack. Cover with boiling water; boil 2–3 min. Loosely pack in jars. Add salt, if desired. Cover with boiling cooking liquid. If liquid is gritty, use freshly boiled water.	30	40
	Raw pack. Pack tightly without crushing. Add salt, if desired; cover with boiling water.	30	40
Beans, green, wax, snap	Wash, trim ends, cut into 1-in. pieces.		
	Hot pack. Cover with boiling water; boil 5 min. Pack loosely; add salt, if desired. Cover with boiling cooking liquid.	20	25
	Raw pack. Pack tightly; add salt, if desired; cover with boiling water.	20	25
Beans, fresh, lima, and similar	Select young, tender beans. Shell and wash.		
	Hot pack. Cover with boiling water; return to boil. Loosely pack, leaving 1 in. headspace. Add salt, if desired. Cover with boiling water.	40	50
	Raw pack. Loosely pack to these headspaces: Small beans: 1 in. for pints; $1\frac{1}{2}$ in. for quarts Large beans: $\frac{3}{4}$ in. for pints; $1\frac{1}{4}$ in. for quarts Do not press down or shake jar. Add salt, if desired, and enough boiling water to cover the beans.	40	50

TABLE 2 (*continued*)

Process Time (Min.) at 240°F. 10 pounds pressure for weighted gauge; 11 pounds pressure for dial gauge. Adjust for altitude.			
VEGETABLE	PREPARATION	Pts	Qts
Beets	Sort for size; cut off tops leaving 1 in. stem and root. Wash. Cover with boiling water; boil 15–25 min. until skins slip. Skin, trim. Leave baby beets whole. Cut medium or large beets in $1/2$-in. cubes or slices. Halve or quarter very large slices. Pack; add salt, if desired, and boiling water.	30	35
Carrots	Wash, peel, and slice or dice.		
	Hot pack: Cover with boiling water, bring to boil. Pack; add salt, if desired, and boiling cooking liquid.	25	30
	Raw pack. Pack tightly. Add salt, if desired, and boiling water.	25	30
Chili peppers*	Wash, remove cores and seeds. Slash two or four slits in each pepper and either blanch in boiling water or blister outer skin with heat (see footnote). Pack loosely; add salt, boiling water. Pack in half-pint or pint jars only. Process time for half-pints is the same as pints. Do not can in quart jars	35	
Corn, cream style	Shuck, silk, and wash ears. Cut kernels from cob at half-kernel depth, then scrape remaining corn from cob with table knife.	85	

*Green chili may be blistered in a hot oven or broiler (400°F.) for 6–8 min. or over a gas or electric burner covered with a heavy wire mesh or on an outdoor charcoal grill (place chilies 5–6 in. above coals). Be sure heat source is very hot. Turn chilies often to prevent scorching and to allow even blistering. Cool before peeling. For easier peeling, place in a pan and cover with a damp towel for a few minutes. Handling chili can burn hands. Wear rubber gloves and keep hands away from eyes.

Table 2 (*continued*)

Process Time (Min.) at 240°F. 10 pounds pressure for weighted gauge; 11 pounds pressure for dial gauge. Adjust for altitude.			
VEGETABLE	**PREPARATION**	**Pts**	**Qts**
	Hot pack. Add 1 pint boiling water for each quart of corn; heat to boiling. Pack in pint jars only (larger jars cannot be used because heat penetrates this thick food very slowly). Add salt, if desired. Do not can in quart jars	85	
	Raw pack. Loosely pack in pint jars only. Add salt; boiling water. Do not can in quart jars.	95	
Corn, whole kernel	Shuck, silk, and wash ears. Cut kernels from cob at two-thirds depth.		
	Hot pack. Add 1 cup hot water for each quart of corn; heat to boiling. Pack, cover with boiling cooking liquid. Add salt, if desired.	55	85
	Raw pack. Pack without shaking or pressing down. Add salt, if desired, and boiling water.	55	85
Mushrooms	Trim stems, discolored spots. Soak in cold water 10 min. to remove clinging soil, then wash in clear water. Leave small mushrooms whole; cut large ones into halves or quarters. Cover with water in saucepan and boil 5 minutes. Pack hot; add salt, if desired. For better color, add $1/8$ t. crystalline ascorbic acid per pint. Cover mushrooms with fresh boiling water. Pack in pint or half-pint jars only. Process time for half-pints is the same as for pints. Caution: Do not can wild mushrooms. Do not can in quart jars	45	

TABLE 2 (*continued*)

Process Time (Min.) at 240°F. 10 pounds pressure for weighted gauge; 11 pounds pressure for dial gauge. Adjust for altitude.			
VEGETABLE	**PREPARATION**	**Pts**	**Qts**
Peas, green	Shell and wash.		
	Hot pack. Cover with boiling water; boil 2 min. Pack loosely. Add salt, if desired, and cooking liquid.	40	40
	Raw pack. Pack without shaking or pressing down. Add salt, if desired, and boiling water.	40	40
Peas, snow, sugar, snap, pod	Not recommended for canning because of poor quality results.		
Pumpkin and winter squash, cubed	Wash, remove seeds, peel. Cut into 1-in. cubes. Add just enough water to cover; boil 2 min.; add salt, if desired, and cooking liquid. Caution: Do not mash or puree before canning.	55	90
Spinach, other greens	Use fresh, tender greens. Wash; remove tough stems, midribs. Place about 1 lb. in blancher basket or cheesecloth bag; steam 3–5 min. or until well wilted. Loosely pack. Add salt, if desired ($1/4$ t. to pints, $1/2$ t. to quarts) and fresh boiling water.	70	90

Source: Van Hillers, PNW 172, *Canning Vegetables,* A Pacific Northwest Cooperative Extension Publication, Washington/Oregon/Idaho, 1989

minutes (longer for thicker pieces). Drain well; pack in plastic freezer bags or boxes. Sharp-freeze. To use, remove from freezer just before cooking. *Do not thaw.* Steaming is recommended.

Lima and shell beans should be shelled, then blanched in boiling-water bath for $1^1/_2$–2 minutes after water returns to boiling. Drain; chill in ice water for 4 minutes. Drain well; pack in freezer bags or boxes. Sharp-freeze. To use, remove from freezer just before cooking. *Do not thaw.* Steaming is recommended.

Note: You may wish to soak broccoflower, broccoli, and cauliflower in salt water to remove any insects that might be present. Rinse well to remove salt if you do this before canning or freezing.

Broccoflower: Process as for cauliflower (see below).

Broccoli: Broccoli can be processed whole by splitting the stems, or chopped into pieces. If using whole broccoli, trim the stems to 5 inches from the top. Split stems so that the pieces are not more than $1/_2$ inch thick. Soak in lightly salted water for 15 minutes to remove any insects. Drain; blanch in boiling-water bath for 3 minutes after water returns to boiling. Drain, chill in ice water for 5 minutes, then drain well. Pack in plastic freezer bags or boxes. Sharp-freeze. To use, remove from freezer just before cooking. *Do not thaw.* Steaming is recommended.

Cauliflower: Remove leaves, cut off bottom stem, and separate into flowerlets. Wash, drain, and blanch in boiling-water bath for 3 minutes after water returns to boiling. Drain; chill in ice water for 4 minutes. Drain well; pack in plastic freezer bags or boxes. Sharp-freeze. To use, remove from freezer just before cooking. *Do not thaw.* Steaming is recommended.

Peas: Both shelled peas and peas with edible pods can be frozen successfully. Shell peas and blanch in boiling-water bath for $1^1/_2$ minutes (longer for larger size vegetables) after water returns to boiling. Drain; chill in ice water for 3 minutes. Drain well; pack in plastic freezer bags or boxes. Sharp-freeze. To use, remove from freezer just before cooking. *Do not thaw.* Steaming is recommended.

Peapods are prepared by removing the stem and blossom end. Wash, drain, and blanch in boiling-water bath for 30 seconds after water returns to boiling. Drain immediately; chill in ice water for 4 minutes. Drain well; pack in plastic freezer bags or boxes. Sharp-freeze. To use, remove from freezer just before cooking. *Do not thaw.* Steaming is recommended.

Peppers: Wash and remove stem and seeds. Blanch in boiling-water bath for 2 minutes after water returns to boiling. Drain; chill in ice water for 5 minutes. Drain well; pack in freezer boxes. Sharp-freeze. To use, remove from freezer just before cooking. *Do not thaw.* Steaming is recommended.

Pumpkin and Winter Squash: These must be cooked and pureed before freezing. Cut up pumpkin or squash, removing stem and seeds. Place in pressure cooker with $3/4$ cup water and cook for 8 to 10 minutes at 15 pounds pressure, or place in deep roasting pan, add $1^1/_2$ cups water, cover, and bake at 325° for $1^1/_2$ hours. Puree cooked vegetable to remove any strings, discarding the outer skin. Pack in plastic freezer bags or boxes; sharp-freeze. To use, remove from freezer just before cooking. *Do not thaw.*

Summer Squash: Use only small, tender squash with small seeds and tender skin (if your fingernail doesn't easily puncture the skin, it's too tough to freeze).

Wash squash, remove both ends, and slice in $1/4$-inch-thick slices. Blanch in boiling water for $2^1/_2$ minutes after water returns to boiling. Immediately plunge into cold water, then ice water, and chill 5 minutes to completely cool. Spin off excess water in a lettuce spinner and pack into airtight freezer containers. Place in the sharp-freeze section of the freezer until hard.

For a savory summer squash mixture, process as directed above, but before freezing, for each cup add and mix in 1 tablespoon chopped, blanched onion, $\frac{1}{2}$ to 1 tablespoon blanched, chopped pepper (for color and taste, use $\frac{1}{2}$ tablespoon hot red pepper and $\frac{1}{2}$ tablespoon chopped green pepper). This makes a delicious vegetable combination.

SELECTING AND PROCESSING FRUIT

HOW TO CHOOSE FRUITS FOR CANNING AND PRESERVING

If this is your first home-canning season, you may be wondering how to find the best varieties of fruit. Of course, the first concern is flavor. *Fruit should be eating-ripe.* Tree-ripened fruit is sweetest and should be first choice. It shouldn't be bruised or overripe (although you can use slightly overripe fruit for part of a jam recipe, overripe fruit won't always give good results).

Eat a piece of fruit from the source you are considering. It should taste delicious! This can't be done until the canning season, but do some reading and asking questions beforehand, so you'll know what variety you want to use. One of the best places to learn about local varieties and their availability is your public library. It will have bulletins put out by your state and federal governments giving information on various regional food crops. Get acquainted with local people and find out what fruits they use for canning and jam. You should ask your local Cooperative Extension Agent (found in county listing in the telephone directory) about available classes and about a "Food Line," which answers questions.

If you have a neighbor or friend who offers to give you fruit (or perhaps you have your own), use it—but you may have to change your idea of what to make with it after eating a piece. Certain apples, for instance, are good for eating, cooking, and freezing; others are good only for eating. Try small batches (see Index for Trial Batch recipes) to see what can best be done with what you have—far better than making a large batch and finding out you don't like the results.

If you plan to buy fruit to process, sort out and use the ripest first, allowing the rest to ripen before cooking. A trick that helps speed fruit ripening is to place a ripe apple or two in with the partially ripe fruit. Cover container loosely and let stand overnight. You can then remove the ripest fruit for processing and leave the rest for a longer time.

Work in small batches as the fruit ripens. Use pint or $^1/_2$-pint jars, unless you have a very large family, and be sure to use any juice or syrup along with the fruit, as between one fourth and one half the water-soluble vitamins and other nutrients are found there.

Fruit processed this way won't taste as sweet as that canned with sugar. It is possible to can, preserve, even make pickles, with fruit juices and honey, but the sweetening you'll add still amounts to much less than the amount the sugar-canned fruits contain. For this reason, people who use lots of sugar may not think your home-canned fruit, jams, jellies, and pickles are sweet enough. Others, with more finely tuned tastes, will applaud!

The following pages offer details to help you decide which fruits to choose. But remember, your area may offer even better choices located with help from your local nursery and library staff or neighbor.

APPLES

Early Crop: Available mid-July to early August. Yellow Transparent and Lodi are among these early apples. They are noted for making good green apple pie and applesauce, but are not as good for eating and keep poorly. These can be allowed to ripen and then frozen in slices (with lemon juice to prevent browning), in unbaked pies, or in applesauce (green or ripe).

Middle Crop: Available mid-August through early September. Gravenstein, Jonathan, McIntosh, Rome and Rome Beauty, Yellow Delicious, and Winesap are good for both eating and canning or freezing. They keep well if left in a cool, well-ventilated place and can be used in all recipes calling for apples.

Late Crop: Available late September through the end of October. King, Granny Smith, Snow, and Wealthy can be cooked or eaten raw equally well and can be stored in a cool, well-ventilated place for use all winter.

Note: Red Delicious apples are not included in this list, as they

TABLE 3

A GUIDE TO APPLE VARIETIES

Variety	Main Season	Flavor & Texture
Cortland	Oct.–Jan.	Mild, tender
Red Delicious	Sept.–June	Sweet, mellow
Golden Delicious	Sept.–May	Sweet, semifirm
Granny Smith	Apr.–July	Tart, crisp
Gravenstein	July–Sept.	Tart, crisp
Jersey Red	Oct.–Apr.	Mild, firm
Jonathan	Sept.–Jan	Tart, tender
McIntosh	Sept.–June	Slightly tart, tender
Newtown Pippin	Sept.–June	Slightly tart, firm
Rome Beauty	Oct.–June	Slightly tart, firm
Stayman	Oct.–Mar.	Tart, semifirm
Winesap	Oct.–June	Slightly tart, firm
Yellow Transparent	July–Aug.	Tart, soft
York Imperial	Oct.–Apr.	Tart, firm

Source: Kyle D. Fulwiler. *The Apple Cookbook,* Seattle: Pacific Search Press, 1980

TABLE 3 (*continued*)

Raw	Baking	Sauce	Freezing
Excel.	Good	V. good	V. good
Excel.	Poor	Fair	Fair
Excel.	V. good	V. good	V. good
V. good	V. good	V. good	V. good
Good	Good	Good	Good
Good	Excel.	V. good	V. good
V. good	Poor	V. good	V. good
Excel.	Fair	Good	Good
V. good	V. good	Excel.	Excel.
Good	Excel.	V. good	V. good
V. good	Good	Good	Good
Excel.	Good	Good	V. good
Poor	Poor	Good	Poor
Fair	Good	V. good	Good

don't cook or can well, although raw they make very good eating. Yellow (Golden) Delicious apples are not the same fruit as Red Delicious and they *are* good cooking and canning apples, although they lack the stronger apple flavor found in Gravenstein, Jonathan, Rome, or Winesap varieties, which are preferable for that reason. To test for ripeness, take a bite. If it doesn't taste delicious, it isn't ripe. Look for color and firmness. If you press the fruit and it doesn't give (feel slightly soft), it will not be a good choice. The background of the apple should show some yellow, too. Fruit picked green will never develop the same flavor as that allowed to fully ripen on the tree.

Table 3 can help you decide which apples to buy.

APRICOTS

Moorpark, Perfection, and Tilton are the best apricot varieties available in Northwest markets. The Tilton is usually smaller and will pack more into a jar than larger types, but for flavor all are good. A few pits left in the jar when canning apricots help give more flavor than when the fruit is canned alone. At their peak in July, apricots must be completely yellow, but not too soft or they are overripe. On the other hand, if apricots are picked too green, they will never reach ideal sweetness. Try to choose fruit that has been allowed to ripen on the tree and has not been held long before you get it. Remember to taste a sample before you buy.

BERRIES

Blackberries: Cascade, Olallie, Himalaya, and Thornless Cory are all in the blackberry class. These have smaller seeds than the loganberry group and therefore make good jam and jelly that tends to be seedy. They do not handle well and may not be available in most stores, but there might be places where you could pick your own (cheaper, too). If you pick wild blackberries, be sure they haven't been sprayed by the highway department. This is especially true of most roadside berries, which are routinely sprayed every year.

Blackberry bushes will also do well in your own garden and take culture similar to that of raspberries. Blackberries should be picked totally ripe and used at once. If they are not completely black and soft, they are not fully ripe. To get the sweetest taste, let them stay on the vine until they are so juicy that when you pick them, your fingers get stained with juice. These are later berries, available into September in most areas.

If you don't like "seedy" jam, but love the flavor of berries, you can remove part of the seeds by mashing and simmering one half the amount of fruit to be used, using some of the liquid called for in the recipe to prevent sticking. When soft, puree or strain through a jelly bag, squeezing the bag until no further materials will come out. Measure and add a little water if too thick. Add this pulp to the remaining fruit in the recipe and proceed as directed. This will give you jam with only one half as many seeds.

Blueberries (and Huckleberries): There are several varieties of domesticated (hybrid) blueberries, and size varies greatly from one to another. Don't let the size of the berry influence you too much— some of the largest, most beautiful blueberries have less flavor than smaller ones. Blueberries must be completely ripe before picking— this means the blue is very dark with no red left. They will be fairly soft. If in doubt, eat one to see if they taste sweet; if they don't, quit picking (or don't buy them). Wild blueberries and huckleberries have more definite flavor, may be sweeter, but are usually seedier than hybrids. Blueberries are generally available late July through August. Check with local farmers or a nursery to see when peak ripening occurs in your area. Huckleberries may not ripen until late August, depending on climate.

Loganberries and Other Thornless Berries: Boysenberries, Loganberries, Olympic berries, and Young berries are among the thornless types. They are sweet, juicy, and when vine-ripened are excellent choices for canning and preserving. Check to learn which varieties grow well in your area. They are not hard to grow but do take a bit more space than raspberries and require the same culture. These berries are ripe when they taste sweet and are very juicy. If picked underripe, they will never achieve the same sweetness as when left on the vine to mature. They are available late August and into early September.

Raspberries: The red raspberry is best for canning, jam, or jelly. The Cuthbert variety has the most typical flavor. Although not as heavy-bearing as some, many people think of it as the ideal raspberry. Cuthbert hybrids may be your best choices. I grow a variety called Meeker, which was developed in western Washington and is larger and has fewer seeds than Cuthbert. Check with your local nursery for what is available and what grows best in your area.

Raspberries are very easy to grow, so you might want to consider raising your own. They are satisfactory shrubs for small areas, but do need water and fertilizer in winter. Otherwise, if you can find a "U-pick" patch, you'll save a lot of money. Ripe raspberries are deep in color, firm to touch, and taste sweet. If too dark, they may be over-ripe and will make poor jam and jelly. Raspberries are available from early to mid-June through July, depending on climate.

Strawberries: Look for local berries to see which you prefer. (In our area I like the Rainiers—they are red and sweet all the way through and have no hard core section to be discarded. These are early berries and may be available late June and into early July.) One of the best ways to tell if strawberries are ripe is to smell them. They have a delicious smell with a sweetish tang when ripe. It is a very strong smell—not like that from less ripe berries. They should also be fully red. Partly green berries will not be as sweet, even if they ripen after picking. Berries should be soft but not mushy—then they are over-ripe. Try to get them directly from the patch; they are so superior to those in grocery stores, you will never be satisfied with anything else again. Strawberries do not keep well when picked fully ripe. Plan to use them within a day or two, or some may mold.

Commercially frozen whole berries are fully ripe when processed.

You can use these for making jams and sauces during the winter with good results.

CHERRIES

Cherries should be dead-ripe before they are picked. They must be juicy and sweet, yet still fairly firm. If they are very soft, they are overripe. Dark varieties should be very dark before they are picked. If they show bright red, they are underripe. Cherries come in three colors and have different ripening times. The sour, red, pie cherries are usually an early crop (June to mid-July), but without sugar it is difficult to get these sweet enough unless you add honey. Don't try canning these in juice-syrup. Pale Royal Anne cherries have a delicious, mild flavor, and are excellent canned alone or used with other fruits, such as in fruit cocktail. Bing and Lambert are dark red, sweet cherries that make good eating and are readily available. Although Royal Anne cherries are on the market in July, most Bings and Lamberts are just appearing in late July and into August. These large, dark fruits are excellent processed in any way: canned, frozen whole (see section on freezing), made into jam or preserves, or added to other fruits in fruit cocktail. Incidentally, these will color pale fruits. You might freeze a few for later use in fruit cocktail; they will give a very attractive pale pink color to the fruit syrup.

GRAPES

Table grapes are available in green and red as well as purple (blue-black), and come seedless and seeded. Ninety percent of the world's grape crop consists of one type: the European grape, now also called the California grape. What you want for eating fresh and what you want for canning may differ. For canning, choose seedless. These include Perlette (green-white, available late May through June), Black Beauty (purple, small, available May and early June), and Thompson (light green, small, available June to October). There are two new, red, seedless varieties: Flame (mid-June through August) and Ruby (mid-August to January). If you are going to cook grapes for juice, seeded varieties are fine. Concord grape varieties include

Exotic and Ribier, the first available in summer from June through August, and the second a winter grape, available July through February. Don't rely on color alone when choosing grapes. When the color seems right, taste one from the end of the bunch—if it is sweet, the grapes are ripe.

If you have a bumper crop of seedless grapes, you can dry them into raisins. Wash, dry, and spread on drying racks. See your dryer's directions for time needed for processing.

NECTARINES

These newer fruits are in our markets in canning lots, but there is usually not much choice in varieties. You must be sure they are sweet and ripe—bite into one before you buy a batch. Many that look and smell good don't taste as good. They should be soft when pressed and should smell sweet. Also, there should be no green around the stem. (Perhaps there are surer tests for ripeness, but I haven't been able to discover them.) Nectarines are available in early August in most areas.

PEACHES

Peaches come in two types: freestone (the fruit comes away from the stone when ripe) and clingstone (the fruit has to be pulled away from the stone when ripe). Most important is that they be grown in a hot, sunny area so that sugar develops and the fruit tastes sweet, and that they are picked almost dead-ripe. Peaches will appear on the market from late July through September. Most people prefer the late August to early September crop for canning and preserving, as they seem sweetest then. Elberta and Hale are still favorites, although your area may have superior varieties. Check with your local nursery or library for information about what grows best locally. Peaches should be checked for color when determining ripeness. The background color should be yellow when they are picked. Some varieties have a pink blush when fully ripe. When you handle a ripe peach, it will feel a little soft. If picked too early, peaches will never get as sweet as they should, and the flesh will be a bit rubbery and not as juicy. Overripe peaches are less sweet, too, so don't pick them either under- or overripe.

PEARS

Pears are easy to grow and easy to process. The Bartletts (Bartlett and Red Bartlett) are ready in August and September and are excellent for both eating and canning. (Don't let them get overripe; they ripen from the core out and can be bad before you realize it.) Late fall pears (Anjou, Bosc, Comice, Nelis, Forgue, and Seckel) are primarily for eating or short-cooking, not for canning and processing. (Check with authorities to find what variety is best locally.) Pears do not freeze well—they turn mushy. This is one fruit that should *not* be allowed to ripen on the tree. Pears should be picked while still firm, or they will develop grittiness and the inside will be spoiled, as mentioned. They should just be turning light yellow-green or red (Red Bartlett, Bosc), and the flesh should be slightly soft. If you plan to keep pears before processing, watch them to be sure they don't overripen and store them in the refrigerator.

PINEAPPLES

When pineapples appear on the market at reasonable prices, you may want to buy them to make jam or to combine with other fruit for canning. To pick a ripe pineapple, look for a gold color overall (no green on the outside), press lightly against the side to see if it is slightly soft (too soft means overripe), and then smell it. Ripe pineapple has a very sweet smell. Last, try to pull out one of the top's inner leaves. If it pulls out easily, the fruit is ripe. Pineapple is usually cheapest in spring.

PRUNES/PLUMS

Have you ever wondered about the difference between a prune and a plum? The technical definition of a prune-plum is one that can be dried whole without removing the pit and without the fruit fermenting. The French plum is used for California dried prunes, but the Italian prune-plum is found most on the market and grown in many backyards. It is a freestone fruit, making it easy to can. Italian prune-plums are good eaten raw, canned, or made into jam or preserves. They are very sweet and juicy and can even be used to help sweeten less sweet fruit. They are available in late August through September in most areas. Santa Rosa and other red plums are much less sweet and need additional sweetening if canned or used for jams and preserves. These are best eaten raw rather than canned for winter use. If you have a tree of these red plums, or know someone who will share with you, can them with apple-pear juice plus a little lemon juice (1 tablespoon per cup of fruit juice) to get them sweet enough. If making jam, use with sweet apples or other sweet fruit to reduce tartness. Don't let color be the deciding factor. Italian prune-plums should be very dark and slightly soft—but taste them to be sure. Taste is also the best test for red plums. The inside of any plum should be yellowish, rather than green, when you cut into it.

CANNING FRUITS

METHODS OF PROCESSING

There are two ways to pack fruit: hot pack or raw cold-pack. There are advantages and disadvantages to both; you may want to try each before settling on one.

In hot-pack canning, place the fruit in a large kettle (non-aluminum is preferred), add sweetening, and cook until tender. Taste the cooked product and add more sweetening, lemon juice, or spices as needed. The hot fruit is then packed into hot, sterile jars, liquid is added to within $1/2$ inch of jar rim, hot, sterile lids are added, and the jar is boiled in a water bath (or pressure canner) for the USDA recommended time to ensure sealing and sterilization. You cannot safely put fruit into sterile jars and omit this final step because air in the jar needs to be sterilized to prevent bacteria or mold growth. Jar tops must be completely covered with boiling water all the time they are processing. In the pressure canner, jars are processed only long enough to ensure sealing.

The raw cold-pack method is simpler, quicker, and saves having a dirty kettle but does not give you a chance to taste the cooked product or make any changes in ingredients, once cooked. In this case, pack peeled (sliced, if desired) fruit directly into hot, sterile jars, add liquid to within 1 inch from top of jar, screw on hot, sterile jar lids, and put into boiling-water bath or pressure canner to process. Liquid must be added to the fruit to help the cooking process. Heat is slow to penetrate solids, and liquid helps spread the heat as well as adding some sweetness to the fruit.

Prepare a small batch of each fruit using the hot-pack method to see how much sweetening or other flavoring is needed. Then go ahead and use the raw cold-pack method for the rest of the batch.

WHAT TO DO FIRST

Choose a fruit combination(s). Using the following Trial Batch Recipe, check to see if the fruits really taste good. If they do but you'd like them sweeter, adjust the sweetening by trying other juices or more concentrated juices (undiluted, possibly). White grape juice gives the sweetest taste; try using that or concentrated apple juice.

Trial Batch Recipe

Chopped fruit   1 cup peeled with blossom and stem ends removed

Selected syrup $1/4$ cup (see directions in this section)

Lemon juice $1/4$ teaspoon

Salt   dash (optional)

Cinnamon, nutmeg, or ginger   dash (optional)

Place fruit in saucepan, add syrup, lemon juice, and salt. Cover and simmer for 8 to 10 minutes or until fruit is soft. Remove from heat; allow to cool before tasting. Add spice(s) if desired. Return to heat for 2 to 3 minutes to allow flavor to partly penetrate the fruit. Cool before tasting. Makes 1 cup.

Once you have tried a batch and are sure it is what you want, proceed with cold-pack canning without worrying about the end product.

PREPARING FRUIT FOR CANNING OR FREEZING

Pick over fruit to select ripe, unbruised pieces. (Set aside bruised pieces for use in preserves or jam.) Wash in cold water to remove dirt or spray. If fruit is to be peeled, prepare a boiling-water bath and a cold-water bath. Do only a few pieces at a time, dropping each into boiling water for about 1 minute, then into cold. This will normally loosen skins so that they can be peeled off quickly. When fruit is peeled, drop into a bowl into which you have added 2 tablespoons lemon juice to cold water (3 tablespoons lemon juice for soft fruit). *Note:* You may substitute for lemon juice by adding $\frac{1}{8}$ teaspoon pure ascorbic acid powder per quart water or pulverize and add $1\frac{1}{2}$ 500-mg vitamin C tablets per quart water. Keep fruit pieces covered with this liquid to prevent browning until ready to use. (You can reuse the liquid by refrigerating and adding more lemon juice the second day. It can then be used as liquid for fruit syrup.)

When processing berries, simply wash in cold water; then pick over to remove leaves, stems, or debris. Dry thoroughly on layers of absorbent towels or in a lettuce spinner, in small batches. If whole strawberries are to be canned or frozen, prick each with a fork so that the liquid (or cold) will penetrate the berry quickly.

CHOOSING AND MAKING THE SYRUP

All these syrups contain fruit juice (or honey), water, and lemon juice. (The recipes in the first section use only fruit juice.) Lemon juice helps preserve color and enhances natural sweetness. No matter which syrup you decide to try, you'll need a large kettle of boiling water, plus a supply of pure lemon juice.

The sweetening required to enhance each fruit varies with each year's crop. Because of this, it is not possible to give exact directions. The suggested juice-fruit combinations are the ones I liked best the year I tried them. Each year, prepare a trial batch for each fruit. Remember, canned fruit tastes less sweet than fresh if no sweetening is added. Using the fruit's natural juice for sweetening will give the truest flavor but may not be sweet enough.

On the following pages you will find suggested dilutions of various juices. *Make only 1 to 2 quarts liquid at one time,* preparing more if needed. This way you won't waste any if you change your mind about what to use. If you have the kettle boiling and your other ingredients handy, it only takes a minute to combine them. How much do you need? In general, between $1/4$ and $1/3$ cup syrup per $1/2$-pint jar, or between and 1 and $1^1/3$ cup for a quart, if you have the fruit really packed in, as already suggested. Roughly measure the amount of fruit to be canned (a quart-sized measuring cup is handy for this), and *prepare about 1 quart liquid for every 3 quarts fruit measured.*

SYRUPS FOR SWEETENING

No-Added-Sweetener Syrup: For each cup boiled water, add 1 to $1^1/2$ teaspoons lemon juice (depending upon how tart the fruit is, use the higher amount for sweet fruit), plus a dash of salt (optional) to help bring out the natural flavor. Leave in (or add) a few fruit pits to add flavor.

Fruit Juice-Sweetened Syrup: Use apple juice (regular or concentrated), white grape juice, pineapple, orange, or any combined juices such as apple-pear, orange-pineapple, etc. To be sure you like the combination you have selected, make only a very small amount of the syrup and try the Trial Batch Recipe. (I cannot emphasize this enough—try before you do a big batch!)

Artificially Sweetened Syrup: Although I don't recommend it, if you wish to use artificial sweetening for canning fruit, I have included guidelines in the chapter Special Information for Diabetics and Hypoglycemics, which will help you choose what to use.

Honey-Sweetened Syrup: Directions for making honey-sweetened syrup are given in the Preserving with Honey chapter.

DIRECTIONS FOR SYRUP MADE WITH NATURAL JUICE

LIGHT SYRUP

$^1/_3$ cup apple juice plus 1 teaspoon lemon juice plus boiled water equals 1 cup syrup

$^1/_4$ cup white grape juice plus 1 teaspoon lemon juice plus boiled water equals 1 cup syrup

$^1/_3$ cup pineapple juice plus 1 teaspoon lemon juice plus boiled water equals 1 cup syrup

$^1/_3$ cup apple-pear juice plus 1 teaspoon lemon juice plus boiled water equals 1 cup syrup

$^1/_2$ cup orange juice plus 1 teaspoon lemon juice plus boiled water equals 1 cup syrup

MEDIUM SYRUP

$^2/_3$ cup apple juice plus 1$^1/_4$ teaspoons lemon juice plus boiled water equals 1 cup syrup

$^1/_2$ cup white grape juice plus 1$^1/_2$ teaspoons lemon juice plus boiled water equals 1 cup syrup

$^2/_3$ cup pineapple juice plus 1 teaspoon lemon juice plus boiled water equals 1 cup syrup

$^2/_3$ cup apple-pear juice plus 1 teaspoon lemon juice plus boiled water equals 1 cup syrup

1 cup orange juice (less 1 teaspoon) plus 1 teaspoon lemon juice equals 1 cup syrup

HEAVY SYRUP

$^1/_2$ cup concentrated apple juice (frozen) plus 1$^1/_2$ teaspoons lemon juice plus boiled water equals 1 cup syrup

1 cup white grape juice (less 2 teaspoons) plus 2 teaspoons lemon juice equals 1 cup syrup

$^1/_2$ cup concentrated pineapple juice (frozen) plus 1$^1/_2$ teaspoons lemon juice plus boiled water equals 1 cup syrup

We do not recommend heavy syrup. The concentrated fruit juice overpowers the natural taste of the fruit. All these syrups are less sweet than those made with sugar.

HOT-PACK CANNING METHOD

Select a large, nonaluminum kettle, with at least two and one-half times the volume you plan to can (stainless steel is good, but watch for sticking). Place peeled, chopped, or otherwise prepared fruit in kettle, measuring volume to know how much syrup to add. For each quart of fruit, add 1 cup syrup. Place over medium heat and, when boiling, turn down to low. Cook 10 to 15 minutes or longer, until fruit is soft. Skim if necessary. While this cooks, prepare jars in boiling water. Place lids and screw caps in separate pan and cover with hot water (keep boiling until ready to use). When fruit is ready, drain jars, using sterile tongs to avoid contaminating jars with your hands.

Pack fruit firmly into jars. Use a sterile spoon-end or knife handle, but don't squash any pieces. Slices pack best and require least syrup. Leave at least 1 inch at top of jar for expansion when cooking. Pour hot fruit liquid over packed fruit, using spoon or knife-end on each side to be sure there are no air pockets in the jar. Cap with sterile lid; screw down firmly. Place in boiling-water bath (or in pressure canner) to process for secure sealing. Jars must be well covered with water for entire boiling time—add more boiling water if necessary during cooking.

Note: Only acid fruits are safe processed in a boiling-water bath. All others must be done in a pressure canner. The following are safe to process in a water bath: apples, apricots, apple-berry mixtures, berries, peaches, pears, nectarines, pineapple, plums, rhubarb, and tomatoes (with lemon juice added to be sure they are acid enough).

Although sugar helps prevent growth of molds and bacteria, there is not enough sugar, even in heavy syrup, to act as a total preservative. If you alter a recipe by removing sugar, be sure to add lemon

Table 4

How Much Fresh Fruit for One Pint Canned?

Fruit	Pounds Needed	Raw Volume Needed*
Apple slices/ sauce	$1\frac{1}{2}$–2	2 cups peeled and quartered
Apricots	$1\frac{1}{2}$–2	2 cups pitted and halved
Berries	$\frac{3}{4}$–1	2 cups washed and drained
Cherries	$1\frac{1}{2}$–2	2 cups stemmed and pitted
Peaches	1–$1\frac{1}{2}$	2 cups, peeled, pitted, and sliced or halved
Pears	$\frac{3}{4}$–1	2 cups, peeled, cored, and sliced or halved
Plums	$\frac{3}{4}$–1	2 cups, pitted and halved

*Approximate amounts given, as fruit pieces will vary in size. Remember that weight measures and volume measures are not the same! A pint equals a pound only with liquid measure such as water.

juice or other acid to help keep down bacterial growth. Vacuum canning actually preserves the fruit, not its sugar content.

All the jam/jelly/relish recipes in this book are high enough in acid that they only require sufficient time in a water bath to ensure sealing. Pressure canning is not recommended for these items as it is not necessary and the extended cooking will give a less attractively colored and poorer textured product.

RAW COLD-PACK CANNING METHOD

This is a time-saving method, once you determine what to use for sweetening. Make a stove-top Trial Batch (see General Index). Each fruit requires different handling, so individual instructions are provided. A boiling-water bath for jars and lids is required for all.

Advantages and Disadvantages of the Raw Cold-Pack Method: It is much quicker to pack raw fruit or vegetables into sterile jars, cover them with boiling syrup, cap with sterile lids, and process in a boiling-water bath than to precook the fruit or vegetable as needed in hot-pack processing. You will note that the same amount of time is used for processing with either method. The reason is that the heat penetrating the contents of the jars determines the length of canning time required to satisfactorily seal the jars while cooking the food at the same time.

The disadvantage of the raw cold-pack method is that you don't get a chance to adjust the sweetening before packing. If you follow my directions and make a test recipe for each fruit, you don't need to hot pack, and you will know how much sweetening the syrup needs to can that specific batch of fruit. If you are processing a good-sized batch of fruit, the time spent in doing the test batch will be more than saved when you can eliminate the precooking time as well as the extra dirty pans.

HOW TO CHECK THE SEAL

You'll be doing at least two types of processing: filling jars or containers with raw or cooked material to be processed in a boiling-water bath or pressure canner. *Fruit must be processed to keep safely.* It is important to check the seal after processing. You should allow the canned fruit to stand until it reaches room temperature before you check the seal. If the seal is a vacuum-type, check it by pressing the center of the lid. If the lid is down and does not move when you press, the jar is sealed.

After food is processed in a water bath or pressure canner, jars should be removed with tongs, then allowed to stand upright until cool. If you hear a popping sound as it cools, a good vacuum is in that jar—just what you want. If the seal has not worked as it should, you either have to keep the food in the refrigerator and use it quickly or reheat it to the boiling point and start over with clean (or sterile) jars and new lids. (Reprocessing means overcooking—less appetizing and attractive.) But if the jars do not have nicks in the edges of the lips and the lids are new, there should not be many that fail to seal when processed properly.

I usually process my fruit (raw cold-pack) longer than the times given in Table 5 to be sure that the interior of the fruit reaches a temperature high enough to kill all bacteria. Being an old-time canner, I'm more comfortable if I process 5 minutes longer than the times shown in Table 5. I have not found my fruit overcooked with this addition.

STORING CANNED FRUIT

Fruit canned without sugar tends to fade, as mentioned before. To help retain the color, keep it in a dark cupboard. (Light speeds up the bleaching process.) Ideal storage would be in a cupboard with doors, or on covered shelves (newspaper works for covering) in a cool basement. Ideal storage temperature is 60 degrees or slightly cooler. Care must be taken that fruit does not freeze, as it will have to be used at once when it thaws or be discarded. You could recan it in new jars and lids, but it won't end up very attractive after double cooking.

If canned fruit smells peculiarly or has mold or other discoloration when you open the jar—discard it. Botulism is not usually found in fruit, but improperly canned fruits could be harmful. Never take chances when it comes to home-canned foods that look suspicious. The botulin toxin thrives in low-acid foods in an airless environment (like an improperly sealed canning jar).

FREEZING YOUR CANNING PRODUCTS

I've already covered the process of freezing raw fruits, but you may also freeze cooked fruits, rather than can them, if you have a large amount of freezer space. Most fruits will freeze well, after cooking, but to maintain the best texture, you should thaw them overnight in the refrigerator.

If you plan to freeze cooked fruit, you don't have to sterilize all the containers and covers, but they must be *clean* and dry. If you use plastic containers (with or without plastic liners), they may be saved and reused year after year. I use plastic-bag liners to both give a double layer of protection and to keep the outer containers clean and unstained (some red and blue fruits tend to stain).

Freezing jams made with regular pectin don't seem to be affected by freezing and thawing, but those made with low-methoxy pectin tend to "water," that is, some liquid separates out from the solid material. This liquid can be mixed back in, and neither flavor nor texture seems to be particularly different, but it is a nuisance to have to remix the jam each time you use it. This tendency to "water" is much greater if you have reheated the jam after adding the calcium solution to make the pectin jell. Always add calcium solution just before packing into containers.

Freezing pickles is not usually a good idea, as the thawed pickle tends to be soft and mushy. On the other hand, you can freeze most sauces and relishes (recipes indicate if a product doesn't freeze well). The only disadvantage here, as in all frozen foods, is that they must be thawed slowly (overnight in the refrigerator is best) to maintain quality.

TABLE 5

CANNING FRUITS

Canning Method. Fruits are acid enough to be safely processed in a water bath canner at 212°F. Begin to count processing time when the water comes back to a rolling boil.

Headspace. Leave $^1/_2$-inch headspace for both the fruit and liquid.

FRUIT	PREPARATION
Apples	Wash, peel, core, slice. To prevent darkening, put into ascorbic acid solution (see page 48). Drain. Boil 5 min. in light syrup or water. Pack, cover with boiling cooking liquid.
Applesauce, other fruit purees	Wash, remove seeds or pits. Cut large fruit into pieces. Simmer until soft. Add a small amount of water or fruit juice to prevent sticking. Put through food strainer or mill. Reheat to simmering (185–210°F) and pack.
Apricots, nectarines, peaches, pears	Wash. Peel if desired (peaches peel best when first dipped in boiling water, then cold water). Halve fruits, remove pits or cores. Slice if desired. To prevent darkening, put into ascorbic acid solution. Drain. ***Hot pack.*** Heat fruit through in hot syrup. If fruit is very juicy, reduce amount of added liquid. Pack fruit and cover with boiling syrup. ***Raw pack.*** Pack fruit, cover with boiling syrup.
Berries	Choose firm berries with no mold. Wash and drain. ***Hot pack.*** Bring berries and syrup ($^1/_2$ c. per quart) to boil in covered saucepan. Shake pan to prevent sticking. Pack hot berries and extracted juice, adding syrup if needed to cover fruit. ***Raw pack.*** Pack berries. Shake jar gently to obtain full pack. Cover with boiling syrup. **Note:** The quality of canned strawberries is poor.

TABLE 5 (*continued*)

Note: In most cases, as much time is required here for hot-pack as for raw cold-pack fruit because it takes just as long for heat to build up inside the jar when fruit is already cooked—much more time than just cooking the fruit takes. The heat is what kills bacteria; the jar must reach a high internal temperature for the process to be effective, thus cooking fruit at the same time.

PROCESS TIME (MIN.) AT VARIOUS ALTITUDES (FT.)

PACK	JAR SIZE	0-1000	1001-3000	3001-6000	OVER 6000
Hot	Pints **or** Quarts	20	25	30	35
Hot	Pints	15	20	20	25
	Quarts	20	25	30	35
Hot	Pints	20	25	30	35
	Quarts	25	30	35	40
Raw	Pints	25	30	35	40
	Quarts	30	35	40	45
Hot	Pints **or** Quarts	15	20	20	25
Raw	Pints	15	20	20	25
	Quarts	20	25	30	35

TABLE 5 (*continued*)

FRUIT	PREPARATION
Cherries, sweet or pie	Wash cherries. Remove pits, if desired. *Hot pack.* Add $1/2$ c. of syrup per quart cherries. Bring to boil in covered saucepan. Pack hot cherries and cover with cooking liquid. *Raw pack.* Pack cherries. Shake jar to obtain full pack. Cover cherries with boiling syrup.
Figs	Select firm, ripe, uncracked figs. Do not can overripe fruit with very soft flesh. Wash thoroughly. Drain. Do not peel or remove stems. *Hot pack.* Cover figs with water and boil 2 min. Drain. Gently boil figs in light syrup for 5 min. Add 2 tablespoons bottled lemon juice per quart or 1 tablespoon per pint to the jars. Fill jars with hot figs and cooking syrup.
Fruit juice (apple, citrus, grape, or pineapple)	Wash fruit; remove pits or seeds, crush fruit. Heat to simmering; stir to prevent sticking. Strain through cloth bag. Reheat to simmering (185–210°F) Pour hot juice into jars; process. (Or use juicer; pour simmering juice into jars; process.)
Plums	Remove stems and wash. To can whole, prick skins on two sides of plums with fork to prevent splitting. Freestone varieties may be halved and pitted. *Hot pack.* Add plums to hot syrup and boil 2 min. Cover saucepan and let stand 20–30 minutes. Fill jars with hot plums, cover with cooking syrup. *Raw pack.* Fill jars with raw plums, packing firmly. Cover with hot syrup.

TABLE 5 (*continued*)

PROCESS TIME (MIN.) AT VARIOUS ALTITUDES (FT.)					
PACK	JAR SIZE	0-1000	1001-3000	3001-6000	OVER 6000
Hot	Pints	15	20	20	25
	Quarts	20	25	30	35
Raw	Pints **or** Quarts	25	30	35	40
Hot	Pints	45	50	55	60
	Quarts	50	55	60	65
Hot	Pints and Quarts	5	10	10	15
	½-Gal.	10	15	15	20
Hot and Raw	Pints	20	25	30	35
	Quarts	25	30	35	40

Source: Van Hillers, *Canning Fruits*, PNW 199, A Pacific Northwest Cooperative Extension Publication, Washington/Oregon/Idaho, 1990

One note of warning: *Don't refreeze any thawed product if you want to be safe: There is too much chance of spoilage and poor quality food!*

PRESERVING WITH FRUIT JUICE SWEETENING

PREPARING AND CANNING FRUITS WITH FRUIT JUICE

The previous chapter includes the USDA table with recommended times for processing the various fruits. I have worked out fruit preparation methods that I find very acceptable and am including them for your information. The processing times I use are those recommended in the previous chapter (Table 5).

Applesauce: This cannot be made cold pack. You must do it hot pack and then process by water bath or freeze to preserve it. For each cup apples (quartered, blossom and stem ends removed), add $1/4$ cup apple juice (use concentrated apple juice if fruit is very tart). Cover; cook very slowly until soft and mushy. You can mash the fruit with a potato masher to break up chunks if you want to hurry the cooking. When very soft, remove from heat and put through food mill or colander to remove skins and other coarse pieces. Season with lemon juice (at least 1 tablespoon per quart applesauce) and spices. First measure pureed sauce, then add lemon juice, mixing well. To this try adding up to $1/4$ teaspoon cinnamon, $1/8$ teaspoon nutmeg, and $1/16$ teaspoon ginger per cup of sauce. Mix well and taste; then reheat. Pack in hot, sterile jars, leaving $1/2$-inch headspace, and top with hot, sterile lids, screwed down firmly. Place in boiling-water bath and cook 15 minutes for pints and 20 minutes for quarts after water has returned to boiling.

Apple Slices: Peel, core, and slice apples, placing in bowl of cold water containing $1 1/2$ tablespoons lemon juice per pint to prevent browning.

When ready to pack, taste to see how sweet they are. If quite sweet, use light syrup; otherwise, medium syrup (apple juice–based syrup is your best choice). Drain into a colander, saving liquid for reuse. Pack into hot, sterile jars, leaving 1 inch at top. Use end of sterile spoon or knife to be sure there are no air pockets between slices. Add hot syrup, leaving $3/4$ inch at top. Cap with hot, sterile lids. Process in boiling-water bath 15 minutes for pints and 20 minutes for quarts after water returns to boiling.

Apricots: These can be processed peeled or unpeeled. To peel, drop (a few at a time) into boiling water for 1 minute, then into cold water. If ripe, the skin should slip off readily. Use light or medium syrup, depending on which is needed. Some apricots are very sweet (Tilton and Moorpark); others are more tart. Always taste before buying a quantity for canning. Diluted apple juice is best for syrup sweetening. Be sure to add lemon juice as directed or the apricots will taste flat. Cut the apricots in half, or in quarters if large. Pack directly into hot, sterile jars, leaving as little space between as you can. Pour in syrup, leaving $3/4$ inch at top. Cap with hot, sterile lids. Process in boiling-water bath 25 minutes for pints or 30 minutes for quarts after water has returned to boiling.

  Note: A pit or two left in each jar will give a mild almond flavor. Add a slice of lemon peel as well for an interesting combination of flavors.

  Combine apricots with sliced apples to make the fruit go further. Use fairly ripe, early Yellow Transparent or Lodi apples. These varieties are so mild that they will not overpower the apricot taste. Prepare slices as directed earlier in this chapter; then combine with quartered apricots in equal amounts (or $1/3$ apples and $2/3$ apricots). Pack and process as for apricots alone.

Berries: Berries vary in sweetness almost more than any other fruit. Pick them fresh and ripe for best results. Pick over berries, removing overripe or bruised fruit. Wash and dry before packing in hot, sterile jars. Do not mash berries, but pack as full as you can without crushing fruit, leaving $3/4$ inch at top for expansion during cooking. If you are canning whole strawberries, prick each with a fork before placing into the jars so that the liquid can penetrate the berry. The following berry-syrup combinations work well together:
Blueberries: White grape juice, medium syrup, extra lemon juice
Boysenberries: White grape juice, medium syrup, extra lemon juice
Huckleberries: White grape juice, medium syrup, extra lemon juice

Loganberries: White grape juice, medium syrup, extra lemon juice
Raspberries: Apple juice, medium syrup
Strawberries: Apple-pear juice, medium syrup
Wild Blackberries: White grape juice, medium syrup, extra lemon juice

You may prefer other combinations—try a sample batch before you pack to save having fruit you don't enjoy eating and to allow adjustment for the change in fruit from year to year. Pack berries in hot, sterile jars, cover with boiling syrup to within $3/4$ inch of the top, and cover with hot, sterile lids. Process in boiling-water bath 15 minutes for pints and 20 minutes for quarts after water returns to boiling.

Note: Berries tend to fade when canned. The presence of refined sugar helps prevent this; if refined sugar isn't used, syrup will be quite colorful, but the berries will fade. To prevent pale fruit (or actually, to cover the fading), you may add $1/4$ teaspoon red food coloring to each cup of syrup, or use beet liquid (see General Index).

Berry Applesauce: Among the most delightful combinations of fruit are apple-berry mixtures: Boysenberry with apple, raspberry with apple, and strawberry with apple are all so good that one of the top commercial canners makes them for the quality restaurant trade. Do try them; they extend the berry flavor with an inexpensive and tasty apple base. To make these combinations, prepare applesauce as directed earlier in this section, but do not add spices. At this point, set aside applesauce until berry puree is ready.

For berry puree, place berries in large saucepan, including $1/4$ cup white grape juice for each 2 cups berries. Cover and cook slowly over low heat until berries are very soft. Place in food mill and sieve to remove most of the seeds. Combine equal amounts pureed applesauce and pureed berries. Taste and add lemon juice and/or lemon rind for flavor. Start with 2 teaspoons per quart of berry-applesauce, adding more if needed. If you decide to use red vegetable food coloring, or beet liquid, start with a few drops and add gradually, mixing well after each addition. Overcolored berry-applesauce is not attractive.

When mixture is ready for packing, pack in hot, sterile jars leaving

$^1/_2$ inch at the top, cap with sterile lids, and process in boiling-water bath for 15 minutes for pints and 20 minutes for quarts, after water returns to boiling. Store in cool, dark place to avoid fading.

Note: This is delicious with chicken, turkey, pork, or veal. Try it for a change on Thanksgiving in place of cranberry jelly.

Cherries: Wash and dry fruit. Remove stems and pits (buy a cherry-pitter at a kitchen supply store). Place pitted fruit in bowl to save juice. (Work over a bowl when pitting, too.) You don't have to use a lemon-water bath to prevent browning with cherries, so when you have enough ready, start packing jars. More colorful and tastier light cherries will result if a few dark ones are included in the jar. Including a few pits will also add to the flavor.

Light cherries: Use medium syrup made from apple or white grape juice. Be sure to use lemon as directed. Pack in hot, sterile jars, leaving 1 inch at top. Cover with boiling syrup leaving $^3/_4$ inch at the top. Cap with sterile lids and process in boiling-water bath for 25 minutes for pints or quarts, after water returns to boiling.

Dark cherries: Use very light syrup unless cherries are not as sweet as usual. White grape juice or apple-based syrup is tasty; try apple-pear as well. Pack in hot, sterile jars leaving $^3/_4$ inch at the top, cap with hot, sterile lids and process as for light cherries. A few pits left in the jar greatly add to the flavor. Plan to save and freeze some choice dark cherries for use in fruit cocktail later in the season.

Grapefruit and/or Orange Sections: If you have a source of freshly picked citrus fruit, you may can for future use. Wash fruit. Pare off rind and separate out sections, using a sharp knife to remove any white skin or seeds. Save any juice that drains off to use for syrup. Pack into hot, sterile jars, leaving $^3/_4$ inch at top for expansion. Cover with drained juice plus enough boiled water to cover the slices (you may use $^1/_4$ volume frozen pure orange or grapefruit juice plus $^3/_4$ volume boiled water if you wish a sweeter product). Cover with hot, sterile lids and process in boiling-water bath for 15 minutes after water returns to boiling.

Grapes: Grapes are so available and tasty year-round that most people don't bother canning them. If you want to try it, here are the directions.

Wash grapes, removing stems. Pack into hot, sterile jars leaving 1 inch at the top. Cover with boiling syrup, leaving $^3/_4$ inch at top. (Medium syrup with white grape juice base is best, being sure to use lemon.) Cap with hot, sterile lids and process in boiling-water bath for 20 minutes for pints and 25 minutes for quarts, after water returns to boiling. When canning large grapes, prick each with fork before you pack them. This will help heat penetrate the grapes and will cook them more evenly.

Nectarines: If you haven't discovered the delicious taste of a ripe nectarine, you have missed some good eating. Nectarines must be soft and ripe to be sweet, and if canned or frozen while hard, they will not be good for anything. Unlike some fruits, they smell good even when not truly ripe. so check each piece to be sure it is ready for processing.

To prepare, dip in boiling water for 1 minute, then in cold water. The skin will slip off easily. Cut into halves or slices, saving a few pits to add for flavor. Cover with syrup quickly to avoid darkening. I like them canned in orange or pineapple juice. Use undiluted orange juice for all the syrup or try a medium syrup and pineapple mixture. Make a trial batch and decide which you prefer. You can pack nectarines in halves, but slices give a sweeter product. Pack fruit into hot, sterile jars as you prepare it, and add syrup to within $^3/_4$ inch from top. Cap with hot, sterile lids and process in boiling-water bath for 25 minutes for pints and 30 minutes for quarts (halves or slices) after water returns to boiling. Nectarines may be included in the fruits used for fruit cocktail. (Use in smaller amounts than peaches or pears; half as much makes a good mixture.)

Peaches: Peaches may all smell good when ripe, but flavor varies greatly from one variety to another. Select those that taste extra good—flavorful and sweet. Save a few peach pits to include in each jar for added flavor. Syrup made with white grape juice or pineapple juice is good; apple juice can also be used, but it does not add as much to the flavor. Most peaches require medium syrup to taste sweet. Peel by dipping in boiling water, then in cold. The skin should slip right off. Pack slices or halves directly into sterile, hot jars, catching juice and adding to jars as you pack. Be sure the fruit is packed firmly without mashing it. Cover with hot syrup, leaving $3/4$ inch at the top. Cap with hot, sterile lids, firmly screwed down. Process in boiling-water bath 25 minutes for pints and 30 minutes for quarts (halves or slices), after water returns to boiling. Peaches can be pickled (see Recipe Index) or spiced. For spiced, drop several whole cloves in each jar and/or break up cinnamon sticks and include at least two pieces in the bottom of each jar. Process as usual. Broken pieces of fruit can be set aside for use in jam. Cover with pineapple juice to prevent browning until you can use them—and, of course, keep them in the refrigerator!

Pears: Pears must be eating-ripe. I like Bartletts for canning, but other varieties are good, too. Pears blend well with most other fruits. Use medium syrup made from apple juice, apple-pear juice, white grape juice, or pineapple juice. For the most natural flavor, use apple-pear juice. Dip pears in boiling water for not more than 30 seconds, then into cold. The skin should peel off easily. (If you leave pears too long in boiling water, some of the skin color may stay on, and the fruit will not look very appetizing.) Remove the core, blossom end, and any fibers. Pack in halves or slice (slices will taste sweeter) directly into hot, sterile jars, using a bowl to catch the juice lost as you work and adding it to the jars along with the fruit. Cover with syrup, leaving $3/4$ inch at top. Cover with hot, sterile lids and process in boiling-water bath 25 minutes for pints and 30 minutes for quarts (halves or slices), after water returns to boiling.

Note: Pears can be prepared for salad or garnish use by adding food coloring and/or spices. Make minted pears by adding green food color and mint extract to syrup just before pouring into jars (3 to 4 drops green color and $1/8$ to $1/4$ teaspoon mint flavor per cup syrup). Do the same thing with red color or beet liquid and cinnamon. Make a small test batch to determine how much flavoring to add.

Pineapples: If you are fortunate enough to have access to plant-ripened pineapples, by all means can your own, but it is not economical to buy at usual retail prices and then can; it is far cheaper to buy already canned in juice. The best syrup is additional pineapple juice—either full strength or diluted half with water—plus 1 teaspoon lemon juice for each cup syrup. Peel the ripe pineapples, removing eyes and cutting out the cores. Cut into chunks.

I have found that hot-pack method makes a better canned pineapple than raw/cold-pack method. Prepare the pineapple as directed. Place in deep nonaluminum pan and cover with medium syrup made with canned pineapple juice. Simmer 5 to 7 minutes until fruit is softened. Drain off liquid and pack fruit into sterile jars; cover with drained hot liquid, leaving $^3/_4$ inch at the top for expansion. Cover with boiling syrup and cover with hot, sterile lids and process in boiling-water bath for 15 minutes for pints and 20 minutes for quarts after water has returned to boiling. You may add a mint leaf to each jar before sealing if you like a faint mint flavor to the fruit.

Small pieces of pineapple can be saved in a jar covered with pineapple juice to keep them fresh. They will last several days in the refrigerator until you can get to making jam or preserves. Pineapple blends well with all types of fruit, and the juice prevents browning by preventing oxidation.

Purple Plums: Plums you plan to can should be sweet and soft. Hard, sour plums will make miserable canned fruit. Both apple juice and white grape juice make good medium syrups for purple plums. Try a small batch to see which you prefer before starting. Do not peel plums, but prick them with a fork if you plan to leave them whole. This will help the canning liquid penetrate the fruit so that it cooks completely. If canning them whole, merely pack washed fruit into hot, sterile jars, filling as full as you can without mashing fruit. If you want a sweeter product, cut into halves or, if large, quarters. Cover with medium-strength hot syrup, leaving $^3/_4$ inch at top. Leave a few pits in each jar for added flavor. Cap with hot, sterile lids and process in boiling-water bath 20 minutes for pints and 25 minutes for quarts, after water returns to boiling.

Mixed Fruit (Fruit Cocktail): The usual fruit cocktail mixture combines peaches, pears, pineapple, and green grapes with maraschino cherries for color. Make this combination when peaches and pears are ripe; if you saved some dark cherries, use them for color. The simplest method is to buy chunk-style pineapple packed in its own juice and use it as the base, adding peeled, sliced peaches, peeled pear slices, seedless green grapes, and dark sweet cherries for color and taste. Use a large can of chunk-style pineapple (16 ounces) to make 2 quarts fruit cocktail. Try adding 2 cups each peach slices, pear slices, and $1/2$ cup sweet cherries. Start with 1 cup green grapes, adding more if desired. Include 1 cup nectarines, if desired. Place in a large bowl and try some to see if the mixture suits you. If not, add more of whatever you think lacking. Try using blueberries (sparingly; they may color the syrup) and orange and grapefruit sections. Other berries may taste fine but won't look as good.

For syrup, use the pineapple juice/water/lemon mixture as given in the section on syrup, or try the white grape juice/water/lemon combination. Whichever you select, use medium syrup, including any juice saved from the fruit as you prepared it. If you have no sweet cherries to add, it won't taste much different but will be less colorful. Red seedless grapes can be substituted, if you can find them; cut the large, red grapes in half if you wish. Mix fruit so that varieties are evenly distributed. Pack into hot, sterile jars; add hot syrup, leaving $3/4$ inch at top. Cap with hot, sterile lids. Process in boiling-water bath 25 minutes for pints and 30 minutes for quarts, after water returns to boiling.

FREEZING FRUITS

Most fruits can be frozen successfully, without sugar, if processed properly. Blanching or steaming (to stop the ripening process) is not needed with soft fruits (apricots, peaches, pears, etc.) as it is with vegetables. Dipping fruit into boiling water is not meant as a cooking procedure but merely helps remove skin without losing any fruit pulp. If fruit is kept at sufficiently low temperatures (0 to 10 degrees F.), enzyme action, which changes the texture and flavor, will be stopped. To prevent discoloration by exposure to oxygen, use a syrup that contains citric acid or ascorbic acid (lemon juice supplies this vitamin C). *Note:* You may substitute for lemon juice by adding $1/8$ teaspoon pure ascorbic acid powder per quart water or pulverize and add $1^1/_2$ 500-mg vitamin C tablets per quart water. There doesn't have to be sugar in the syrup. Directions for making it are in the syrup preparation section (see General Index).

If you wish to use one of the citric/ascorbic mixtures on the market (Fruit-Fresh, etc.) instead of plain lemon juice, use as directed on package, adding before fruit is added to liquid. Add after liquid has been heated (if necessary) and pack fruit directly into it, pouring over fruit as fast as it is packed into containers. It prevents darkening from air exposure but won't remove the dark color once it has developed.

Some fruits do well frozen whole—cherries and berries, for example. They don't need any syrup or other treatment, but they must be well wrapped after freezing to prevent freezer burn and dehydration. They are the easiest to process and taste so good later on. Check the following list to see what the fruit you are planning to use will require.

FRUITS THAT CAN BE FROZEN WITHOUT SYRUP

Blueberries	Pineapples
Boysenberries	Raspberries
Cranberries	Rhubarb
Currants	Sweet Cherries, pitted or with stems
Himalayan Blackberries	left on
Loganberries	Strawberries, sliced or whole (prick
Melons	with fork to allow air release)

Use only tree-ripened fruit, ready to eat. Wash and dry (or use a lettuce spinner to remove surplus water). Place individual pieces on cookie sheet and sharp-freeze until hard. Pack into plastic bags or boxes with tight lids. To protect against freezer burn, place several small bags inside a larger one and secure tightly. Pack only enough for one meal in each container as fruit is best used immediately after thawing.

Blanch blueberries with steam for 1 minute to keep skins tender. Chill before freezing.

FRUITS THAT NEED DIPPING BEFORE FREEZING
Apple slices
Plums, pitted
Pears, peeled and cored

Use only tree-ripened fruit. Wash, dry well, then dip into solution of $1^1/_2$ tablespoons lemon juice (or $^1/_8$ teaspoon ascorbic acid) in 2 cups of cold water. Drain well (or use lettuce spinner); freeze on cookie sheets until hard. Package in tightly covered containers. Freeze in sharp-freeze section of freezer, removing to other storage after 1 hour.

Note: You can freeze these fruits in the syrup you used for dipping. Be sure fruit is under the syrup so that the exposed section doesn't turn dark.

FRUITS BEST FROZEN IN SYRUP/JUICE
Apricots	Nectarines
Grapefruit sections	Orange sections
Grapes	Peaches
Melons	Pears

Use only tree-ripened fruit. Wash, dry well, pack into sturdy containers, and cover with syrup of your choice, leaving 1 inch at top for expansion. Cover tightly and place in sharp-freeze section of freezer until hard. To remove skins before freezing, dip washed fruit into boiling water for 1 minute, then into cold. If the fruit is really ripe, the skin should slip off easily. Cover with syrup and freeze as directed. Use the same juices for freezing as for canning.

TIPS FOR PROCESSING FRUITS FOR CANNING OR FREEZING

I always use boiled water for making syrup for freezing to avoid introducing any water-carried bacteria into the food. I wash my freezing containers in hot, soapy water and rinse with boiled water just before I use them, again to avoid all contamination possible.

My storage freezer is not in my kitchen, so when I have three or four packages ready, I place them in my refrigerator to keep cold until I take the larger number to the freezer at once. This helps keep the freezer colder (less opening of the door) and saves both steps and electricity. If you have a self-defrosting refrigerator, you may find that the freezing unit also partly defrosts on its own. If this happens to your freezer, don't plan on long-term storage of either fruits or vegetables in it. (If you have ice-cube trays in the freezer and the ice cubes evaporate slowly, you may have this type of problem.) Even when carefully wrapped, I have found that vegetables and fruits are affected by this defrosting and become tougher. Use only a nondefrosting freezer for satisfactory long-term food storage!

CHOOSING AND PREPARING FRUIT FOR FREEZING

Freeze fruit in pure juice, adding 2 teaspoons lemon juice per cup to prevent discoloring, or in medium syrup made with fruit juice as described in the syrup preparation section (see General Index). I recommend using medium syrup or pure juice plus lemon juice for best flavor. Don't discard the liquid from frozen fruit—eat it along with the fruit. The same combinations you liked fresh will do well frozen. Try a small batch to see if you like fruit that has been frozen—some people don't. You may prefer apricots, peaches, and pears canned.

Apples: Wash, peel, and core. Cut into $1/8$- to $1/4$-inch slices and drop into lemon water until ready to freeze (3 tablespoons lemon juice per 2 cups water). Pack into rigid containers, leaving 1 inch at top. Cover all fruit with medium apple juice syrup to within $3/4$ inch of top. Place lids on containers. Cover. Freeze immediately. To use, allow to thaw in container or in colander so that liquid can drain into bowl. Use liquid in puddings or other dishes made with the fruit.

Applesauce: Prepare according to your own recipe or see Recipe Index for directions. Pack into rigid containers, leaving $3/4$-inch space at top. Cover tightly; freeze immediately. To use, thaw in container in refrigerator overnight.

Apricots: (I prefer canning these unless the fruit is especially sweet.) Wash and cut in half, removing pits. Pack into rigid containers, covering with medium apple juice or white grape juice syrup to within $3/4$ inch of top. Freeze immediately. To use, thaw overnight in container in refrigerator or in colander so that liquid can drain into bowl.

Blueberries: Discard soft or damaged berries. Wash well and place in lettuce spinner or on paper towels to dry. Spread on cookie sheets and place in sharp-freeze section of freezer. Cover with foil or plastic wrap. When hard, pour frozen fruit into covered plastic containers. To use, thaw overnight in container in refrigerator or use unthawed in fresh fruit cup for texture variety.

Cherries, Sweet and Grapes, Seedless: Discard bruised cherries or grapes. Wash, stem, pit, and dry. Pack in rigid containers and cover with light white grape juice syrup to within $3/4$ inch of top. Cover. Freeze. To use, thaw in container in colander. Use liquid with fruit in making puddings or other desserts.

Orange and/or Grapefruit Sections: To save money on citrus fruit, pack it when the season's peak arrives. Peel and section fruit, removing pits and white membrane. Save juice lost as you are sectioning and add to juice for freezing. Pack into rigid containers, leaving $3/4$ inch at top; cover with undiluted orange or grapefruit juice. Cover. Freeze. To use, thaw in container overnight in refrigerator. Serve in juice.

Peaches and Nectarines: Wash fruit; blanch 1 minute in boiling water, then in cold. Skin should slip off easily. Halve or slice, removing pits. Pack into hot, sterile jars, leaving 1 inch at top; cover with undiluted orange juice. Be sure fruit is covered to prevent browning. Cover. Freeze. To use, thaw overnight in container in refrigerator. Serve in juice.

Pears: (I prefer canning unless fruit is to be used partially frozen.) Wash fruit; drop in boiling water for 1 minute, then in cold water to remove skin. Use dull side of knife to gently scrape off any discolorations. Halve or slice to remove seeds and stem. Heat apple-pear juice syrup (light or medium depending on sweetness of fruit). Drop in pears and poach for about 2 minutes. Drain syrup and allow to cool. Pack into clean containers, leaving $3/4$ inch at top. Pour cooled liquid over fruit to prevent browning. Cover with clean lids. Freeze. To use, thaw overnight in container in refrigerator. Serve in syrup. May be used when still partly frozen as ingredient in fresh fruit cup.

Plums: Plums may be frozen in halves, to be eaten like fresh fruit, without any processing. Wash, pit, and remove stems; then place cut side down on cookie sheets and sharp-freeze. When hard, place in clean containers, cover with clean lids, and store. To use, thaw only enough to soften slightly. Eat while still firm.

Plums may also be frozen in medium syrup (apple or white grape juice) if they are to be cooked when thawed (in puddings, etc.). Place halves in clean container; cover with medium syrup, leaving $3/4$ inch at top; add lid and freeze immediately. To use, thaw in colander, saving liquid for use in puddings or other cooking, or serve as juice.

Raspberries, Boysenberries, Loganberries, etc.: Wash and dry berries (with lettuce spinner or on paper towels). Place on cookie sheet and sharp-freeze. When hard, place in heavy freezing plastic bags or in clean containers with clean lids. To use, thaw in containers. Serve liquid with fruit or save for cooking. Try the berries still partly frozen in fruit cup and other mixed-fruit dishes.

To freeze berries in liquid, use light apple juice syrup. Cover berries completely, leaving $3/4$ inch at top. Cover container and sharp-freeze. Thaw overnight in refrigerator. Serve with liquid.

Rhubarb: Freezing rhubarb is simple. Wash and dry the stalks; cut them into suitable pieces ($1/2$ inch); pack them into firm, covered containers or heavy freezing bags; cover and freeze. To use, thaw in colander or overnight in refrigerator. Add some form of sweetening when cooking rhubarb. This could be concentrated apple juice, applesauce plus juice, or strawberries with white grape juice. It is difficult to get rhubarb sweet enough without combining with another sweeter fruit. Adding lemon juice helps to bring out the natural sweetness of any fruit, and rhubarb is no exception. You may want as much as 1 tablespoon per cup cooked rhubarb—start with less and taste as you add.

Strawberries: Strawberries can be frozen whole (prick with fork) or in halves. When frozen whole, no syrup is needed. Wash berries and dry well (in lettuce spinner or on paper towels). Then place on cookie sheets to sharp-freeze. When frozen, place in heavy plastic bags or clean containers with clean tops. If cut into halves, berries are best frozen in syrup. Place washed, cut, and dried berries in rigid containers, leaving $3/4$ inch at top. Cover with light apple or white grape juice syrup, leaving $1/2$ inch at top. Cover and freeze. Thaw in colander, serving liquid with berries.

Mixed Fruits. Prepare mixed fruit as directed for canning. Put in clean freezing containers, leaving $3/4$ inch at top. Add medium white grape juice syrup, being sure to cover all fruit to prevent browning. Cover with clean lids, and place in the sharp-freeze section of freezer. Move to other section to store. To use, thaw overnight in refrigerator. Serve with juice. A few seedless green grapes are a nice addition to mixed fruit or fruit cocktail. If small, use whole; if large, halve before adding.

JAM AND JELLY

Jam and jelly are usually made by adding pectin to fresh fruit, then adding refined sugar and lemon juice to make the pectin form a jell. Preserves are whole fruits, cooked until thick, with sugar added for flavor and additional thickening. Preserves can be made with-out adding refined sugar. Concentrated fruit juices will serve for both sweetening and liquid; the mixture is then cooked down to the proper consistency. Since gelatin thickens cooled jam, jams containing it do not have to be cooked down as far. (Agar-agar can be used instead of gelatin for this purpose, $1/2$ stick = 1 envelope gelatin.)

Jelly sold in interstate commerce must contain not less than 45 percent fruit and 55 percent sugar, and jam 65 to 68 percent fruit with the rest sugar. Your jam will end up tasting like fresh fruit, not candy, and will be tasty but much less sweet than those containing sugar. Since all jams and jellies in this book are cooked before processing for storage, 5 minutes in a boiling-water bath is sufficient to ensure vacuum sealing. Further processing is not recommended.

If you are going to make spreads without sugar, you also have some decisions to make about what to use for ingredients:

1. Which fruit(s) to use.
2. What form of sweetening to use: Fruit juice? Other sweet fruit? Date sugar? Honey?
3. Whether or not to use pectin. If so, regular (high-methoxy) pectin with glycerine added? Or special (low-methoxy) pectin, which requires only a small amount of calcium to jell? (More about these later.)
4. If not using pectin, which fruits to include to be sure there is enough natural pectin to make a satisfactory jell?

If you plan to use pectin, skip the next few pages and go directly to the recipe sections. This is the easy way—forget about how much pectin nature put into fruit and just use commercial pectin (regular or special) with results you can count on. Nobody will know the difference in the end—and you'll have better results while saving a lot of time and testing.

Where do you start? Let's begin by looking at Table 6 on page 78, which shows how much natural pectin and acid fruits contain.

Notice that tart fruit has more pectin than ripe, sweet fruit. This means that adding a small amount of tart fruit will greatly increase the natural pectin of the mixture. For example, use tart apples with apricots, perhaps only one-fourth to three-fourths volume. Or combine raspberries and strawberries with a very small amount of tart apple for good pectin content.

For fruits low in acid, add lemon juice or combine with one of the high-acid fruits. For example: Strawberries are low in pectin but adequate in acid; combine them with tart apples, which are the reverse, and you get a balanced combination. (Add some lemon juice and use ripe berries for sweetness.)

High heat destroys the natural pectin in fruit. Simmer the fruit—don't keep it boiling or you will not get a satisfactory jell.

How to Check Pectin in Fruit Combinations

First, put together combinations you think you will like, adjusting amounts until they taste good. It's not important if the fruits have enough pectin. You can add that. What is important is that you like the taste and texture of the mixture. Then add your choice of concentrated fruit juice, enough to make it sweet to your taste. Now check to see what amount of pectin is present. Directions for two ways to do this follow:

Method 1: Remove 1 cup mixture and place in separate saucepan. Add $1/2$ tablespoon glycerine. Stir to mix; then return to heat and bring to rolling boil for 1 minute. Remove from heat and pour into dish to cool. (You may hurry the cooling by placing in freezer once the mixture has cooled a little.) Check to see if you have a firm jell. If not, you will need to add some kind of pectin. If you have a partial jell, add half the recommended amount of pectin (see next section). Return this mixture to the original pot, stir, then add pectin, etc. It won't hurt to reheat the glycerine, but it will not jell again. Check the fruit's pectin before you make a batch and are unhappy with the result. If the mix contains at least half apple, that may be enough to jell the whole mixture, but don't count on it—check each batch of fruit.

TABLE 6

CLASSIFICATION OF FRUITS ACCORDING TO PECTIN AND ACID CONTENT

Adequate Pectin and Acid	
Apples, tart	Lemons
Blackberries, sour	Limes
Cherries, sour	Loganberries
Cranberries	Oranges, sour
Currants	Plums, Damson and
Gooseberries	other sour varieties
Grapefruit	Quinces, tart
Grapes, American	Raspberries, red and black
Guavas, sour	
Adequate Pectin, Low Acid	
Bananas, unripe	Melon, ripe
Cherries, sweet	Quinces, ripe
Figs, unripe	
Low Pectin, Adequate Acid	
Apricots	Strawberries, most varieties
Rhubarb	
Low Pectin, Low Acid	
Figs, ripe	Pears, ripe Bartlett
Peaches, ripe	Pomegranates

Source: Ruth M. Griswold. *The Experimental Study of Foods.* Boston: Houghton Mifflin Co., 1962.

Method 2: This is a simpler method, but it involves throwing away your test sample. Stir together equal amounts fruit mixture and methyl alcohol (can be purchased from the drugstore, but you have to sign the poison register, as it is toxic when swallowed). Let this mixture stand for 5 minutes and see what sort of jell you get. If only slightly thickened, add the entire amount of pectin called for in the recipe. If there is a nice thick jell, you don't have to add pectin, but without the alcohol you will have to add glycerine to get it to form a jell unless you are using honey. If there is enough honey in the mixture, it will cause jelling, just like sugar. Remember, *throw away the sample* and be sure to label the alcohol bottle as POISON and store in a safe place.

MORE ABOUT PECTIN

Pectin is a natural carbohydrate found in fruit, but the amount varies greatly among varieties and stages of ripeness (tart fruit is higher in natural pectin than ripe fruit). This natural jelling agent is what thickens jellies and jams. Apples are high-pectin fruits. Commercial pectin is generally made from apple pomace (residue left after juice is extracted) or from the white inner skin of citrus fruits. Apple pectin tends to make a more elastic jelly than that made from citrus fruit; however, most grocery store pectin comes from citrus fruit.

Acid must be added to make pectin jell unless the fruit itself has enough. Most jam and jelly recipes call for lemon juice, but other sources of acid could be vinegar, lime juice, citric acid, or tartaric acid. These give slightly different finished tastes compared to lemon juice. Since lemon juice works well in all recipes, that is what I recommend using unless you want to experiment with the others listed.

Earlier I mentioned that there are two types of pectin: regular (high-methoxy pectin) and special (low-methoxy pectin). Low-methoxy pectin comes from the inner rinds of lime and lemon and is chemically different from grocery store pectin in that it uses a calcium solution, rather than sugar, to make a jell. Regular pectin is usually made to form a jell with sugar, but it also can be jelled using alcohol or glycerine. I recommend glycerine because it has no taste and the resulting texture is good. It is not digestible in the body and is totally harmless in the amount suggested in our jam recipes. (USP grade glycerine [drugstore] is recommended. If no glycerine is used, these sugarless jams will not thicken properly.)

One pectin isn't any better—or worse—than the other; the structures vary and what it takes to make a jell varies accordingly. (If you don't want to add anything processed to your jam, use the preserve recipes. They are made by cooking down fruit and juices only; nothing is added to thicken, but the calorie count will be much higher and you won't get as much volume from the fruit. Since fruit is the most expensive item in your jam, getting less volume will make the cost higher per jar.) An advantage of special low-methoxy pectin is that you can take pure fruit juice, add a little lemon for enhanced flavor, add the pectin solution and enough calcium to make it jell, and the result is beautiful jelly every time. Unfortunately, regular pectin does not make juice into good jelly without sugar.

This special pectin, often labeled "no sugar" pectin, is available in some health food stores and food cooperatives or by mail from Walnut Acres, Penns Creek, PA 17862 (800–433–3398 to order). A package of the calcium needed to form the jell should be included with the pectin so that you don't have to hunt for it (furnished as dicalcium phosphate). It, too, is a naturally occurring substance. One recipe takes very little calcium; the solution can be made up and kept refrigerated for several weeks. This pectin is more economical to use when making large batches of jam or jelly. Depending on shipping charges, the initial cost may be around $15 per pound, but it keeps indefinitely if stored in a dry, airtight place, and compared to 89 cents or more for one package of regular pectin, it's cheap. Using my recipe for making pectin solution, 1 ounce will make at least five batches of jam (4 cups fruit each). At $1.95 per ounce (local CoOp), it's still cheaper than regular pectin. Send for it by the pound if you make jam or jelly each year. It's best to send for it a few weeks early so that you can make the pectin and calcium solutions just before your fruit is ready to process.

The directions that Walnut Acres sends with its pectin suggests using Euell Gibbons's method for making jelly or jam—namely, by dissolving the pectin in boiling water in a blender to completely dissolve it. Using water for the solution only dilutes the sweetness of the fruit; using boiling juice, as I suggest, adds to the sweetness and makes a better product.

Make up the pectin solution and the calcium solution the day before you plan to use it and refrigerate it as soon as cool. This pectin solution will keep up to two weeks if kept refrigerated; after that, the pectin solution tends to mold and must be discarded. If you have all this ready to go, then, when the fruit is ready, all you have to do is gather up your equipment and the fruit and start cooking.

Recipes using this pectin as well as the regular pectin (with glycerine replacing sugar for thickening) are included in this book.

Using white grape juice to dissolve the pectin works wonderfully. It does not dilute the fruit; it flavors and sweetens it. Apple juice is good, too. Bring either to the boiling point, place in blender jar, and add pectin (1 tablespoon per cup of hot juice). Blend for about 1 minute until completely dissolved. Pour into a container and cool; refrigerate until needed. That's all there is to it. The calcium solution is equally simple to make. In a container with a tight lid, place 1 cup water and 1 teaspoon calcium powder. Shake to dissolve partially and place in refrigerator until needed. Shake each time before using as it does not completely dissolve and will have settled out.

Important: Commercial pectin powder lists dextrose as its first ingredient. This is sugar! Use liquid pectin (Certo), which does not contain any sugar. Add 3 ounces liquid pectin (one pouch) to 4 cups fruit or juice. And remember, without sugar, use glycerine to get a jell. Directions are given with individual recipes.

Pectins that are labeled "low sugar pectin" are often regular pectin to which some form of sugar (other than sucrose) has been included in the package. (Dextrose and maltose *are sugars!*) The words "Low-methoxy pectin" should appear on the label, although there may be a brand name as well.

Directions for Preparing

Low-Methoxy Pectin Solution

Heat white grape juice or apple juice to boiling. If you wish to make a large batch of jelly, use 4 cups juice plus $1/2$ cup boiling water; otherwise, use 2 cups juice plus 4 tablespoons boiling water. Place this in the blender jar and add $2^1/2$ tablespoons low-methoxy pectin. Blend first on low and then on high for about 1 minute until all is in solution. Pour this into a wide-mouth jar or other container you can cover tightly. It will be thickening fast, so use a rubber spatula to remove it from the blender jar without wasting any. Work quickly when doing this, and it will be much easier than if it has set up firm. Keep it refrigerated in a tightly covered jar until needed. It will melt in the hot jelly or jam.

You will need to concentrate apple juice slightly to make sugar content equal to that of the grape juice. For each cup juice needed, place $1^1/3$ cups apple juice in saucepan and simmer to reduce volume to 1 cup (about 10 to 15 minutes on low heat).

Calcium Solution

Dissolve 1 teaspoon dicalcium phosphate in 1 cup water. This is best done in a jar, as you won't have to transfer it later. Screw the lid on the jar and put it in the refrigerator. Be sure to shake it well before pouring. It doesn't really dissolve, so much will settle out and have to be remixed each time.

If you have fairly soft water, you will need the amount of calcium suggested in these recipes. If your water is hard, you can use less because there is some calcium in your water—provided water is called for in that recipe. (The way to know if water is hard or soft is by how much soap you have to use to get suds—not much in soft water.)

How to Prepare Juice for Jelly

Juice for jelly is obtained by cooking the fruit until very soft, putting it into a jelly bag (purchase or make from several layers of cheesecloth), and allowing the liquid to drip into a container. This contains more pectin than the fruit juice you buy at the store. (Pectin comes from the skin and pulp, rather than just the juice.)

Fruit should be washed thoroughly to remove dirt or foreign material. Remove stems and blossom ends but leave skin and seeds. Chop into pieces and place in deep nonaluminum kettle, adding $1/4$ cup water per cup of fruit (less if fruit is very juicy). Cover and simmer until fruit is very soft and juice has been extracted. (Using a masher to crush partly cooked fruit will speed up this process.) This will take from 10 minutes to more than half an hour.

Use jelly bag or make bag by folding several layers of wet cheesecloth within colander, being sure they drape over its edge each way so that only juice can get through. Dampen bag or cheesecloth before pouring fruit into it. Suspend bag from hook or place colander over large bowl so that juice can drip without remaining in contact with cooked fruit. Don't squeeze bag, or jelly will be cloudy from suspended fruit particles. It will take several hours for all juice to drip out. (You may check juice for pectin content by mixing with alcohol as described in the section on types of pectin. Add the total amount of pectin recommended if there is little; add half or less if pectin content is high.)

Jelly is usually made in small to medium batches: 4 to 8 cups is best to work with. Glycerine-thickened and low-methoxy pectin jams and jellies form jells after cooling. There is no test that will show the final jell, while still warm, when using these products.

WHAT TO DO IF JAM OR JELLY DOESN'T JELL

Don't give up if your jelly doesn't jell or your jam isn't very thick. As mentioned earlier, there is a lot of difference among fruits—even the same tree from year to year will yield fruit that varies in pectin and acid content. That is why a trial batch should be made each time you start to process fruit. Thin jam or jelly is usually due to pectin that has not jelled because of too much or too little acid, or lack of enough other material that causes jelling (glycerine or calcium solution), or because you have cooked the jam or jelly after adding the calcium solution.

If you continue heating the jam or jelly after you add the calcium, the binding will be weakened and the jam or jelly tends to separate (water), giving a tougher texture. *Never cook mixture after adding the calcium solution!* I discovered this after I had overcooked a batch (reheated after adding calcium) and found that my jam had a watery layer on top that had separated out. This does not happen if you *always* remove the cooked mixture from the heat before adding the calcium.

If your jam or jelly is runny when cooled, it isn't practical to redo the whole process—the fruit will be overcooked and mushy. The easy way is to add gelatin. One to two envelopes of plain gelatin (1 to 2 tablespoons) thickens 4 cups of runny jam or jelly. In regular (not freezing) recipes, use the higher amount when planning to freeze the jelly as it will then have less tendency to weep after thawing. This will not increase the protein content of a serving as it adds such a small amount compared to the total volume of the recipes.

To thicken runny jam, add gelatin and reheat to boiling. Process as originally directed, using $1/2$-pints or pints and processing in a boiling-water bath 5 minutes after water returns to boiling.

To thicken runny jam made with low-methoxy pectin, place 1 cup of the cooked jam in a saucepan. Sprinkle gelatin over the jam and heat slowly until gelatin is dissolved, stirring frequently. Add this to the remaining hot jam. Mix well and process as directed. (This avoids recooking the majority of the jam to which the calcium solution has already been added.)

WHAT TO USE FOR SWEETENING

Concentrated fruit juices or mixed fruit juice concentrates are now available. These can be used for general cooking and/or to sweeten your canning. I have found a great deal of variation in these, some being excellent and others awful! Be sure to make a trial batch with any of these products before using in a recipe.

You can concentrate your own juice by simmering until reduced in volume half or less. Keep the heat very low while simmering to avoid undesirable taste changes. Concentrating volume also concentrates sweetness, making these juice products excellent choices for cooking or canning.

As indicated in Table 7, a huge volume of juice is needed to get much sugar—the most concentrated available contains only approximately $1/3$ cup sugar in 1 cup liquid juice. Naturally sweet fruit can be added to increase sweetness. Dried fruits are sweeter than fresh because the drying process converts some of the sugars to forms that taste sweeter. For example, dried apples will have more sweetening effect than fresh. Dried apples, apricots, dates, pears, prune-plums—all need only to be chopped or ground, then softened in liquid and added to fresh fruit.

Another good sweetening source is applesauce made with very sweet apples. It can be made quite thick (follow directions given in section on canning but reduce liquid to $1/2$ cup per quart chopped fruit) and pureed so that it is very smooth. It can be added to any other fruit without changing the flavor of the other fruit, provided you use $1/3$ total volume applesauce or less ($1/4$ cup of this applesauce equals 6 teaspoons sugar).

Dried dates are another possible source of sweetening; date sugar is ground, dehydrated dates. This is very sweet, almost too sweet, and it has a distinct taste, which can be unpleasant in certain combinations. Use it sparingly to give just a little boost in taste—and add some lemon juice along with it to help mask the date flavor: Start with 1 teaspoon lemon juice for $1/4$ cup date sugar, increasing lemon juice as you taste.

If you don't find date sugar in your area, it can be ordered from either of the following: Hadley Fruit Orchards, P.O. Box 495, Cabazon, CA 92230 (800–854–5655), minimum order $15; or Shields Date Gardens, 80–225 Highway 111, Indio, CA 92201 (619–347–0996). These sources will send you free information with prices.

Table 7

Natural Sugar Content of Fruit Juices

Apple Juice
Regular juice equals 7 teaspoons per cup Concentrated juice equals 28 teaspoons per cup
White Grape Juice*
Regular juice equals 9 teaspoons per cup Concentrated juice equals 18 teaspoons or more per cup   (simmered down to half volume)
Orange Juice
Regular juice equals 6$\frac{1}{2}$ teaspoons per cup Frozen concentrate equals 26 teaspoons per cup
Pineapple Juice
Regular juice equals 8 teaspoons per cup Frozen concentrate equals 32 teaspoons per cup

Note: All sugars are not equally sweet, so these may not taste as sweet as their sugar content might lead you to expect.

*Frozen concentrated white grape juice on the market is sweetened with sugar. Do not use it.

Table 8

My Favorite Fruit Combinations For Jam

Apple and Apricot ($^1/_2$ and $^1/_2$)

Apple and Cranberry ($^1/_2$ and $^1/_2$)

Apple and Purple Grape Pulp ($^1/_3$ and $^2/_3$) (no seeds and skins)

Apple and Quince ($^1/_3$ and $^2/_3$)

Apple and Raspberry ($^1/_3$ and $^2/_3$)

Apple and Strawberry ($^1/_3$ and $^2/_3$)

Orange, Grapefruit, and Green Grapes ($^1/_3$ each)

Peach and Lemon ($^7/_8$ and $^1/_8$) (grind lemon coarsely)

Peach, Pear and Apple ($^1/_3$ each) (plus cinnamon)

Pear and Lemon ($^7/_8$ and $^1/_8$) (grind lemon coarsely)

Plum and Apple ($^3/_4$ and $^1/_4$, or $^1/_2$ and $^1/_2$)

Raspberry and Strawberry ($^1/_3$ and $^2/_3$, or $^1/_2$ and $^1/_2$)

Add lemon juice to all combinations (except those already containing lemon) to help bring out natural sweetness. Don't be afraid to try other mixtures. Some of my best jams came from odds and ends I threw together and then couldn't duplicate because I hadn't kept track of what went into the pot. (They surely were good while they lasted!)

Table 8 is a list of combinations I have tried and liked well enough to remake. If you don't want to experiment, go right to the recipes that follow and you won't have to make any decisions about what to use or which to combine—it's all been done for you. But don't be afraid to try other combinations, too.

Nutritional values: The figures given under the heading "Nutritional value" at the end of each recipe show the grams of protein, fat, and carbohydrate per serving and are calculated using first ingredient listed, rather than alternates. The food calorie is the kilocalorie (1,000 calories) and is written with a capital "C" in this book.

Trial Batch

You cannot be sure, from year to year, that fruit will be sweet enough to suit you. Thus, it is important that you make a trial batch after deciding what combination(s) of fruit to try, which pectins to use (none for preserves), and what juice to use for sweetening. (This recipe does not use pectin and will not thicken; however, it does give you a chance to experiment before committing yourself to a whole batch.)

You can convert honey-sweetened recipes to fruit juice-sweetened by using Table 9 (see page 234). If you then want to find the calories in the converted recipe, you will find easy to follow directions in Table 11 (page 238) . Once you have converted a recipe, be sure to make a copy so you can repeat it at will.

Trial Batch Recipe for Jam Sweetness

Fruit $2^1/_2$ cups peeled, pitted, and chopped
Concentrated Fruit·juice $^1/_4$ cup
Lemon juice   2 teaspoons

Combine ingredients in small saucepan. Cover and simmer 5 to 8 minutes until fruit is soft (add a small amount of water if necessary).

Remove from heat. Cool, taste, and adjust sweetening. Makes about 2 cups.

Note: This recipe represents the equivalent of light syrup. If not sweet enough, add date sugar or more concentrated fruit juice. Doubling the juice will make the equivalent of medium syrup.

MAKING JAM, JELLY, AND PRESERVES

This section includes recipes using regular pectin and special low-methoxy pectin and is followed by a section on preserves using no added pectin. Low-methoxy pectin is easy to use. With it you can correct any batch of jam or jelly that is too soft or too firm; it makes good clear jellies without sugar and never fails to jell! Send for some and try it yourself. If any jar fails to seal, refrigerate and use within ten days.

JAM

Basic Jam Recipe with Fruit Juice

Fruit   10 cups chopped, stems and pits removed
Lemon juice   3 to 5 tablespoons (the higher amount for
      sweeter fruit)
Concentrated fruit juice (white grape, apple, or orange)
      ³/₄ cup
Salt   dash (optional)
Regular or low-methoxy pectin

Wash, dry, and chop or grind fruit. (Large pieces are not used in jam, so be sure pieces are small.) Place fruit in large nonaluminum kettle; add juices and salt. Cook over low heat, stirring frequently to prevent sticking. As foam forms, skim off and discard. When fruit is soft, remove from heat. You are now ready to add pectin.

For regular pectin, add:

Liquid pectin   3 to 6 ounces ($^1/_2$ to 1 package) (depending on the natural pectin in fruit)
Glycerine   5 to 7 tablespoons
Unflavored gelatin   1 to 2 tablespoons (1 to 2 envelopes) (optional)

Stir in pectin and glycerine, return to heat, and bring to rolling boil. Boil for exactly 1 minute. Remove from heat. Sprinkle gelatin over hot mixture, stirring to completely dissolve. Pack in hot, sterile $^1/_2$-pint or pint jars, leaving $^1/_2$ inch at top. Top with hot, sterile lids. Process in boiling-water bath 5 minutes after water returns to boiling. Makes 11 cups.

For special, low-methoxy pectin, add:

Low-methoxy pectin solution   2 cups
Dicalcium phosphate solution   3 to 4 tablespoons (1 teaspoon per cup fruit)

Stir in pectin solution; then add calcium solution. Mix well. Pack in hot, sterile $^1/_2$-pint or pint jars leaving $^1/_2$ inch at the top. Top with hot, sterile lids, and process in boiling-water bath for 5 minutes after water returns to boiling.

Note: The jell sets up as it cools, so don't try to estimate firmness when it is hot. To check the firmness, put a small amount of the jam or jelly in a sauce dish and chill it in the freezer until cool. If it remains runny, add gelatin as directed on page 84. Makes 12 cups using low-methoxy pectin.

Freezing Directions: Pack in clean freezer containers or jars, leaving $^1/_2$ inch at top for expansion. Cover with clean lids and cool to room temperature before placing in sharp-freeze section of freezer. When frozen, remove to other section of freezer for storage. Thaw overnight in refrigerator before using.

Nutritional value: Depending on fruit used, 1 tablespoon contains 4 to 12 Calories (P0,F0,C1–3). From 5 to 15 tablespoons = 1 diabetic fruit exchange. If salt is omitted, 1 tablespoon contains less than 1 milligram sodium. Recipe contains 0 cholesterol.

JAM RECIPES USING REGULAR PECTIN
Apple-Berry Jam

Apples (pick sweet, soft apples like Yellow Transparents)
    5 cups peeled, cored, and sliced
Strawberries, raspberries, or boysenberries 5 cups mashed
    or chopped
Concentrated apple juice 1 cup
White grape juice 1 cup
Liquid pectin (regular)* 3 to 6 ounces ($^1/_2$ to 1 package)
Glycerine 6 tablespoons
Salt dash (optional)
Lemon juice 4 to 6 tablespoons (depending on sweetness
    of apples)

Wash, dry, and prepare fruit. Place in large nonaluminum kettle. In separate pan, combine apple and grape juices. Simmer to reduce volume to about 1 cup. Add to fruit, bring to boil, and simmer until fruit is soft, not more than 12 to 15 minutes. Remove from heat and mash to blend berries with apple pulp. Add pectin, glycerine, salt, and lemon juice. Return to heat after stirring to dissolve pectin. Bring to rolling boil. Boil exactly 1 minute. Remove from heat, pack in hot, sterile pint jars, leaving $^1/_2$ inch at top; cap with hot, sterile lids. Process in boiling-water bath for 5 minutes after water

---

*Note: Unless you have checked the mixture's natural pectin content and know it is high, use the whole package (6 ounces) pectin.

returns to boiling. If any jars fail to seal, refrigerate and use within ten days *or* freeze for later use. Store in cool, dark place to prevent color fading.

If you prefer to freeze, pack in clean freezer containers or jars, leaving $1/2$ inch at top for expansion. Cover with clean lids and cool to room temperature before placing in sharp-freeze section of freezer. When frozen, remove to other section of freezer for storage. To use, thaw overnight in refrigerator. Makes 12 cups.

Nutritional value: 1 tablespoon contains 12 Calories (P0,F0,C3). 2 tablespoons = $1/3$ diabetic fruit exchange. If salt is omitted, 2 table-spoons contain less than 1 milligram sodium. Recipe contains 0 cholesterol; 1 teaspoon can be used without diabetic replacement.

Apple-Lemon Jam (a little bit tangy!)

Soft, sweet apples   5 cups peeled, cored, and chopped
Concentrated apple juice   1 cup
Lemon juice, fresh or frozen $1/3$ to $1/2$ cup
Lemon rind, freshly grated $1/2$ to 1 tablespoon
Liquid pectin   3 ounces
Glycerine   3 tablespoons
Salt   dash (optional)
Cinnamon stick $1/3$ to $1/2$ (optional but very good)
Yellow food coloring $1/4$ teaspoon (optional)

Combine apples, apple juice, lemon juice and rind (and optional cinnamon stick) in deep nonaluminum pan. Simmer, stirring occasionally to prevent sticking. Cook until fruit is soft (mash with potato masher, if desired). Taste, adding more apple juice, lemon rind, or juice if you wish. Stir in pectin, glycerine, and salt. Return to heat after stirring to dissolve pectin. Bring to a rolling boil and boil exactly 1 minute.

Remove from heat and add food coloring. Pack in hot, sterile $1/2$-pint or pint jars, leaving $1/2$ inch at top for expansion. Top with hot, sterile lids and process in boiling-water bath for 5 minutes after water returns to boiling. If any jars fail to seal, refrigerate and use within ten days or freeze for later use. When cooled, store in cool, dark place to help preserve fruit color.

To freeze, pack in clean freezer containers or jars, leaving $1/2$ inch at top. Cover with clean lids and cool to room temperature before placing in sharp-freeze section of freezer. When frozen, remove to other section of freezer for storage. To use, thaw over-night in refrigerator. Makes 6 cups.

Nutritional value: 1 tablespoon contains 13 Calories (P0,F0,C3). $1^{1}/_{2}$ tablespoons = $1/3$ diabetic fruit exchange. If salt is omitted, 3 tablespoons contain less than 1 milligram sodium. Recipe contains 0 cholesterol; 1 teaspoon can be used without diabetic replacement.

Apricot-Lemon Jam

Fresh apricots   9 cups quartered and pitted
Large lemon $1/2$ sliced paper-thin
Lemon juice   4 tablespoons
Concentrated white grape juice   1 cup (simmered down
      from 2 *cups)*
Glycerine   6 tablespoons
Liquid pectin (regular)   6 ounces (1 package)
Salt   dash (optional)
Almond extract $1/4$ to $1/2$ teaspoon
Unflavored gelatin   1 to 2 tablespoons (1 to 2 envelopes)

Pit and quarter apricots (leave a few pits in for flavor); slice lemon, removing seeds. Place fruit in large nonaluminum kettle, adding lemon juice and about half the concentrated grape juice. Cook until tender, about 20 minutes. Remove from heat; add glycerine, pectin, and salt. Return to heat and boil for exactly 1 minute. Remove from heat; add almond extract plus gelatin dissolved in the remaining fruit juice (heated if necessary). Stir well. Pour into hot, sterile pint jars, leaving $1/2$ inch at top. Cap with hot, sterile lids. Process in boiling-water bath for 5 minutes after water returns to boiling. If any jar fails to seal, refrigerate and use within ten days, or freeze for later use. Store in cool, dark place. Makes $10^1/_2$ cups.

To freeze, pack in clean freezer containers or jars, leaving $1/2$ inch at top for expansion. Cover with clean lids and cool to room temperature before placing in sharp-freeze section of freezer. When frozen, remove to other section of freezer for storage. To use, thaw overnight in refrigerator. Makes $10^1/_2$ cups.

Variation: This can be made with dried apricots. Soak 24 ounces dried apricots in the 2 cups white grape juice. Allow to stand overnight to soften fruit. Drain liquid and simmer down to 1 cup. Follow recipe as directed.

Nutritional value: 1 tablespoon contains 5 Calories (P0,F0,C1$1/_4$). 4 tablespoons = $1/_3$ diabetic fruit exchange. If salt is omitted, 1 tablespoon contains less than 1 milligram sodium. Recipe contains 0 cholesterol; 2 teaspoons can be used without diabetic replacement.

Apricot Marmalade

Fresh apricots   4 pounds *or Dried apricots* 1 pound,
        chopped and soaked in the juice for 2 hours
Oranges   2, very thinly sliced
Lemon $1/_2$, very thinly sliced
White grape juice $3/_4$ cup (simmered down from 1$1/_2$ cups)
Concentrated orange juice   1 cup
Lemon juice   2 tablespoons
Liquid pectin (regular)   6 ounces (1 package)
Glycerine   6 tablespoons
Salt   dash (optional)
Unflavored gelatin   1 to 2 tablespoons (1 to 2 envelopes)

Remove pits from apricots and chop into $1/4$-inch pieces. Slice oranges and lemons and remove seeds. Place fruit in large nonaluminum kettle. Add grape juice and orange juice concentrate. Bring to a boil; then turn down heat and simmer, covered, for about 15 minutes until fruit is soft. Remove from heat. Sprinkle gelatin over hot mixture. Add lemon juice, pectin, glycerine, and salt. Stir. Return to heat and bring to a boil, boiling for exactly 1 minute. Remove from heat. Place in hot, sterile pint jars, leaving $1/2$ inch at top. Cap with hot, sterile lids. Process in boiling-water bath for 5 minutes after water returns to boiling. If any jars fail to seal, refrigerate and use within ten days, or freeze for later use. Store in cool, dark place.

To freeze, pack in clean freezer containers or jars, leaving $1/2$ inch at top. Cover with clean lids and cool to room temperature before placing in sharp-freeze section of freezer. When frozen, remove to other section of freezer for storage. To use, thaw overnight in refrigerator. Makes 10 cups.

Nutritional value: 1 tablespoon contains 14 Calories (P0,F0,C3$1/2$). $1 1/2$ tablespoons = $1/3$ diabetic fruit exchange. If salt is omitted, 1 tablespoon contains 1 milligram sodium. Recipe contains 0 cholesterol; 1 teaspoon can be used without diabetic replacement.

Apricot Marmalade Preserves

This recipe can be made into preserves by omitting the pectin, glycerine, and gelatin. Do not include these three ingredients during preparation; continue to simmer over low heat until thick, stirring frequently. Process as directed above.

Nutritional value: 2 teaspoons contain 14 Calories (P0,F0,C3$1/2$). 2 teaspoons = $1/3$ diabetic fruit exchange. If salt is omitted, 2 teaspoons contain less than 1 milligram sodium. Recipe contains 0 cholesterol. $1/2$ teaspoon can be used without diabetic replacement.

Blueberry Jam

Blueberries   10 cups washed, stems removed
Concentrated apple juice $^1/_2$ cup *or*
>   **Concentrated white grape juice** $^2/_3$ cup (simmered down
>   from 1$^1/_3$ cups) *or*
>   **Concentrated orange juice** $^2/_3$ cup (frozen, undiluted)

Lemon juice   4 tablespoons
Lemon rind $^1/_2$ teaspoon grated
Salt $^1/_2$ teaspoon (optional)
Nutmeg $^1/_2$ teaspoon (optional)
Liquid pectin (regular)   6 ounces (1 package)
Glycerine   6 tablespoons
Unflavored gelatin   2 tablespoons (2 envelopes)

Place fruit, juices, lemon rind, and salt in deep saucepan. Bring to a hard boil for 1 minute. Remove from heat and add nutmeg, pectin, and glycerine. Return to heat and bring to a rolling boil for 1 minute. Stir in gelatin by sprinkling over top of hot liquid and stirring well to dissolve. Pour into hot, sterile pint jars, leaving $^1/_2$ inch at top for expansion. Top with hot sterile lids. Process in boiling-water bath for 5 minutes after water returns to boiling. If any jars fail to seal, refrigerate and use within ten days, or freeze for later use. Store in cool, dark place.

To freeze, place jam in clean freezer containers or jars, leaving $^1/_2$ inch at top, cover with clean lids and cool to room temperature before placing in sharp-freeze section of freezer. When frozen, remove to other section of freezer for storage. To use, thaw overnight in refrigerator. Makes 10$^1/_2$ cups.

Nutritional value: 1 tablespoon contains 8 Calories (P0,F0,C2). 3$^3/_4$ tablespoons = $^1/_2$ diabetic fruit exchange. If salt is omitted, 7$^1/_2$ tablespoons contain 1 milligram sodium. Recipe contains 0 cholesterol. 1$^1/_2$ teaspoons can be used without diabetic replacement.

Blueberry Preserves

This recipe can be made into preserves by omitting the pectin, glycerine, and gelatin. Do not include these ingredients during preparation; continue to simmer over low heat until thick, stirring frequently. Process as directed.

Nutritional value: 2 teaspoons contain 8 Calories (P0,F0,C2). $2\frac{1}{2}$ tablespoons = $\frac{1}{2}$ diabetic fruit exchange. If salt is omitted, $2\frac{1}{2}$ tablespoons contain less than 1 milligram sodium. Recipe contains 0 cholesterol. 1 teaspoon can be used without diabetic replacement.

Boysenberry Jam*

Boysenberries   10 cups washed and hulled
Lemon juice   3 tablespoons
Lemon rind   2 teaspoons grated
Liquid pectin (regular)   6 ounces (1 package)
Glycerine   5 tablespoons
Salt   dash (optional)
Concentrated apple juice   1 cup and
White grape juice $\frac{1}{2}$ cup (simmered down to 1 cup total)
Unflavored gelatin   1 tablespoon (1 envelope)
Cold water $\frac{1}{2}$ cup

Mash or crush half of the boysenberries and place in nonaluminum kettle; add lemon juice, rind, pectin, glycerine, fruit juices, and salt. Bring to a full rolling boil for exactly 1 minute, stirring constantly. Remove from heat; add remainder of berries (whole or

---

*This boysenberry recipe can be made with a mixture of berries (some wild if desired). If you love the taste of wild berries but don't like all the seeds, mash and puree half the berries before cooking, using only the pulp. You may wish to increase the lemon juice with wild berries. Taste and add the lemon juice (if desired) before you pack them for canning or freezing.

crushed, as you prefer). Add gelatin to $1/2$ cup cold water; allow to stand about 5 minutes, then warm to dissolve completely; add to berry mixture. Pour into hot, sterile pint jars, leaving $1/2$ inch at top for expansion. Top with hot, sterile lids. Process in boiling-water bath for 5 minutes after water returns to boiling. If any jars fail to seal, refrigerate and use within ten days, or freeze for later use. Store in cool, dark place.

To freeze, pack in clean freezer containers or jars, leaving $1/2$ inch at top. Cover with clean lids and cool to room temperature. Place in sharp-freeze section of freezer. When frozen, remove to other section of freezer for storage. To use, thaw overnight in refrigerator. Makes $10^{1}/_2$ cups.

Nutritional value: 1 tablespoon contains 6 Calories (P0,F0,C1$1/2$). $3^{1}/_2$ tablespoons = $1/3$ diabetic fruit exchange. If salt is omitted, $3^{1}/_2$ tablespoons contain less than 1 milligram sodium. Recipe contains 0 cholesterol. $1^{1}/_2$ teaspoons can be used without diabetic replacement.

Boysenberry Preserves

This recipe can be made into preserves by omitting the pectin, glycerine, and gelatin. Do not include these ingredients during preparation; continue to simmer over low heat until thick, stirring frequently. Process as directed above.

Nutritional value: 2 teaspoons contain 6 Calories (P0,F0,C1$1/2$). $2^{1}/_4$ tablespoons = $1/3$ diabetic fruit exchange. If salt is omitted, $2^{1}/_2$ tablespoons contain less than 1 milligram sodium. Recipe contains 0 cholesterol. 1 teaspoon can be used without diabetic replacement.

Mixed Soft Fruit Jam

Apricots, peaches, pears, nectarines, etc.   10 cups sliced, finely chopped, or ground
Concentrated apple juice $1/2$ cup ***or Concentrated white grape juice*** $2/3$ cup (simmered down from $1^{1}/_3$ cups)

Lemon juice   6 tablespoons
Whole cloves   1 tablespoon (optional)
Liquid pectin (regular)   6 ounces (1 package)
Glycerine   6 tablespoons
Salt   dash (optional)
Unflavored gelatin   1 tablespoon (1 envelope)

Peel and prepare fruit (leave a few pits in for almond flavor). Save juice and put it and fruit in a deep nonaluminum kettle. Add fruit juice and cloves and cook over low heat, stirring often. After fruit has come to a boil, cover and cook until soft, 15 to 20 minutes at most. Remove from heat. Sprinkle gelatin over hot mixture. Add pectin, glycerine, and salt. Stir well. Return to heat, bring to rolling boil, and cook for exactly 1 minute. Remove from heat, pack in hot, sterile pint jars, leaving $1/2$ inch at top. Cap with hot, sterile lids. Process in boiling-water bath for 5 minutes after water returns to boiling. If any jars fail to seal, refrigerate and use within ten days, or freeze for later use. Store in cool, dark place.

To freeze, pack in clean freezer containers or jars, leaving $1/2$ inch at top for expansion. Cover and cool to room temperature before placing in sharp-freeze section of freezer. When frozen, remove to other section of freezer for storage. To use, thaw overnight in refrigerator. Makes 11 cups.

Nutritional value: 1 tablespoon contains 10 Calories (P0,F0,C2$1/2$). 2 tablespoons = $1/3$ diabetic fruit exchange. If salt is omitted, 2 tablespoons contain less than 2 milligrams sodium. Recipe contains 0 cholesterol. 1 teaspoon can be used without diabetic replacement.

Preserves

This recipe can be made into preserves by omitting the pectin, glycerine, and gelatin. Do not include these ingredients during preparation; continue to simmer over low heat until thick, stirring frequently. Process as directed above.

Nutritional value: 2 teaspoons contain 10 Calories (P0,F0,C2$\frac{1}{2}$). 4 teaspoons = $\frac{1}{3}$ diabetic fruit exchange. If salt is omitted, 4 teaspoons contain less than 2 milligrams sodium. Recipe contains 0 cholesterol. 1 teaspoon can be used without diabetic replacement.

Plum Jam

Ripe sweet plums   10 cups stemmed, pitted, and quartered
Concentrated white grape juice   1 cup (simmered down
    from 2 cups)
Lemon juice   6 tablespoons
Lemon rind   1$\frac{1}{2}$ tablespoons coarsely grated
Date sugar   6 tablespoons (optional; use if plums are
    less sweet)
Liquid pectin (regular)   6 ounces (1 package)
Glycerine   6 tablespoons
Salt   dash (optional)
Unflavored gelatin   1 tablespoon (1 envelope) (optional)

Prepare fruit and place in large nonaluminum kettle. Add juices and rind. Bring to a boil and simmer, covered, over low heat until fruit is soft—about 12 to 15 minutes. Taste, add date sugar if desired, and stir well. Remove from heat. Sprinkle gelatin over hot mixture. Add pectin, glycerine, and salt, stirring to mix. Return to heat, bring to a rolling boil, and boil exactly 1 minute. Remove from heat. Place in hot, sterile pint jars, leaving $\frac{1}{2}$ inch at top. Cap with hot, sterile lids. Process in boiling-water bath for 5 minutes after water returns to boiling. If any jars fail to seal, refrigerate and use within ten days, or freeze for later use. Store in cool, dark place.

To freeze, pack in clean freezer containers or jars, leaving $\frac{1}{2}$ inch at top. Cover with clean lids and cool to room temperature before placing in sharp-freeze section of freezer. When frozen, remove to another section of freezer for storage. To use, thaw overnight in refrigerator. Makes 11 cups.

Nutritional value: $2^1/_2$ tablespoons contains 28 Calories (P0,F0,C7). $2^1/_2$ tablespoons = $^1/_2$ diabetic fruit exchange. If salt is omitted, $2^1/_2$ tablespoons contain less than 2 milligrams sodium. Recipe contains 0 cholesterol. 1 teaspoon can be used without diabetic replacement.

Plum Preserves

This recipe can be made into preserves by omitting the pectin, glycerine, and gelatin. Do not include these ingredients during preparation; continue to simmer over low heat until thick, stirring frequently. Process as directed.

Nutritional value: $1^2/_3$ tablespoons contain 28 Calories (P0,F0,C7). $1^2/_3$ tablespoons = $^1/_2$ diabetic fruit exchange. If salt is omitted, $1^2/_3$ tablespoons contain less than 2 milligrams sodium. Recipe contains 0 cholesterol. $^2/_3$ teaspoon can be used without diabetic replacement.

Raspberry Jam

Raspberries, red or black   3 cups
Concentrated apple juice   1 cup
Lemon juice, fresh or frozen   1 tablespoon
Liquid pectin   2 ounces ($^1/_3$ package)
Glycerine $1^2/_3$ tablespoons
Salt   dash (optional)
Unflavored gelatin $^1/_2$ tablespoon ($^1/_2$ envelope) (optional)

Pick over berries, discarding any that are not totally ripe. Place first five (or six) ingredients in a deep nonaluminum kettle. Mash fruit. Bring to a full rolling boil for 1 minute, stirring constantly. If you wish a thicker jam, sprinkle gelatin over jam, stirring well to be sure it is all dissolved. Remove from heat and pack in hot, sterile $^1/_2$-pint jars, leaving $^1/_2$ inch at top for expansion. Cover with hot, sterile lids and process in boiling-water bath for 5 minutes after water returns to boiling. If any jars fail to seal, refrigerate and use within ten days, or freeze for later use. When cooled, store in cool, dark place.

To freeze, pack in clean freezer containers or jars, leaving $1/2$ inch at top. Cover with clean lids and cool to room temperature before placing in sharp-freeze section of freezer. When frozen, remove to another section of freezer for storage. To use, thaw overnight in refrigerator. Makes $4^1/2$ cups.

Nutritional value: 1 tablespoon contains 10 Calories (P0,F0,C2). $3^1/2$ tablespoons = $1/2$ diabetic fruit exchange. If salt is omitted, 2 tablespoons contain 1 milligram sodium. Recipe contains 0 cholesterol; 1 teaspoon can be used without diabetic replacement.

Raspberry Preserves

This recipe can be made into preserves by omitting the pectin, glycerine, and gelatin. Do not include these ingredients during preparation; continue to simmer over low heat until thick, stirring frequently. Process as directed above.

Note: This raspberry recipe can be made with wild blackberries. If you love the taste but don't like all the seeds, mash and puree half the amount of berries before cooking. You may wish to increase the lemon juice when using wild berries. Taste before you pack them for canning or freezing and then add the lemon juice if desired.

Nutritional value: 2 teaspoons contain 10 Calories (P0,F0,C2$1/2$). $2^1/4$ tablespoons = $1/2$ diabetic fruit exchange. If salt is omitted, $1^1/2$ tablespoons contain 1 milligram sodium. Recipe contains 0 cholesterol. 1 teaspoon can be used without diabetic replacement.

Strawberry Jam

Strawberries   10 cups washed and hulled
Lemon juice   2 tablespoons
Liquid pectin (regular)   6 ounces (1 package)
Glycerine   5 tablespoons
Salt   dash (optional)

Concentrated white grape juice 1 cup (simmered down
  from 3 cups)
Unflavored gelatin 2 tablespoons (2 envelopes)
Cold water $1/2$ cup

Mash half the amount of berries after cleaning and culling any
that are overripe or green; place in nonaluminum kettle with lemon
juice, pectin, glycerine, salt, and grape juice. Bring to a full rolling
boil for 1 minute, stirring constantly. Remove from heat. Add remainder of berries (diced, sliced, or whole). Combine gelatin with water;
allow to stand 5 minutes; then heat gently to dissolve. Add to berries;
stir well to mix. Pour into hot, sterile pint jars, leaving $1/2$ inch at top
for expansion. Top with hot, sterile lids and process in boiling-water
bath for 5 minutes after water returns to boiling. If any jars fail to
seal, refrigerate and use within ten days, or freeze for later use.

To freeze, pour into clean freezer containers or jars, leaving $1/2$
inch at top. Cover with clean lids and allow to cool to room temperature. Place in sharp-freeze section of freezer until frozen. Move to
other section of freezer for storage. To use, thaw overnight in refrigerator. Makes $10 1/2$ cups.

Nutritional value: 1 tablespoon contains 6 Calories (P0,F0,C1$1/2$) 3$1/2$
tablespoons = $1/3$ diabetic fruit exchange. If salt is omitted, 3$1/2$ tablespoons contain less than 1 milligram sodium. Recipe contains 0
cholesterol. 1 tablespoon can be used without diabetic exchange.

Strawberry Preserves
This recipe can be made into preserves by omitting pectin, glycerine, and gelatin. Do not include these ingredients during preparation;
continue to simmer over low heat until thick, stirring frequently.
Process as directed above.

Nutritional value: 2 teaspoons contain 6 Calories (P0,F0,C 1$1/2$).
2$1/4$ tablespoons = $1/3$ diabetic fruit exchange. If salt is omitted, 2$1/2$

tablespoons contain less than 1 milligram sodium. Recipe contains 0 cholesterol. 1 teaspoon can be used without diabetic replacement.

Jam Recipes Using Low-Methoxy Pectin

Don't forget that you can make any of the jams listed in the previous section (Jam Recipes Using Regular Pectin) with low-methoxy pectin, and vice versa. Use the proportions given in the Basic Jam Recipe on page 89 to make replacements. Nutritional values will be unchanged.

Any Berry Jam

Berries (strawberries, raspberries, boysenberries)   4 cups washed and halved
Concentrated white grape juice   1 cup (simmered down from 2 cups)
Lemon juice   4 tablespoons
Lemon rind $^1/_4$ teaspoon grated (optional)
Salt   dash (optional)
Low-methoxy pectin solution $^3/_4$ cup
Unflavored gelatin   1 to 2 tablespoons (1 to 2 envelopes)
Calcium solution   scant 4 teaspoons

Place berries, juices, rind, and salt in deep saucepan. Bring to a boil. Stir in pectin solution and gelatin. Reheat to boiling. Remove from heat, add calcium solution, and mix well. Pour into hot, sterile pint jars and top with hot, sterile lids, leaving $^1/_2$ inch at top for expansion. Process in boiling-water bath for 5 minutes after water returns to boiling. If any jars fail to seal, refrigerate and use within 10 days or freeze for later use.

To freeze, pour into clean freezer containers or jars; cover with clean lids and allow to cool to room temperature. Place in sharp-freeze section of freezer until frozen. Move to other section of freezer for storage. To use, thaw overnight in refrigerator. Makes $5^1/_2$ cups.

Berry/Apple Jam Variation

This can be made with $1/3$ apples. Peel, core, and chop sweet apples into $1/2$-inch cubes. Reduce volume of berries by $1/3$ ($1^1/4$ cups). You may want to add 1 or more teaspoons lemon juice to this recipe if you make it with part apple. Taste before adding pectin and add lemon juice then, if desired. Nutritional value will not be significantly changed with this substitution.

Nutritional value: 2 tablespoons contain 12 Calories (P0,F0,C3). 5 tablespoons = $1/2$ diabetic fruit exchange. If salt is omitted, 5 tablespoons contain less than 1 milligram sodium. Recipe contains 0 cholesterol. 2 teaspoons can be used without diabetic replacement.

Any Berry Preserves

This recipe can be made into preserves by omitting the pectin, glycerine, and gelatin. Do not include these ingredients during preparation; continue to simmer over low heat until thick, stirring frequently. Process as directed.

Nutritional value: $1^1/3$ tablespoons contain 12 Calories (P0,F0,C3). 3 $1/3$ tablespoons = $1/2$ diabetic fruit exchange. If salt is omitted, $3^1/3$ tablespoons contain less than 1 milligram sodium. Recipe contains 0 cholesterol. 1 teaspoon can be used without diabetic replacement.

Apricot-Pineapple Jam

Dried apricots   12-ounce package
Crushed pineapple $1^1/4$ cups (in own juice)
Water $1^1/2$ cups (approximate)
Lemon juice   2 tablespoons
Concentrated orange juice (frozen, undiluted)   3 tablespoons
Lemon rind $1^1/2$ teaspoons grated
Salt   dash (optional)

Low-methoxy pectin solution $^1/_2$ cup
Calcium solution $2^1/_2$ teaspoons

Place apricots and pineapple in deep saucepan. Add enough water to completely cover fruit (about $1^1/_2$ cups). Heat to boiling, cover, and set aside for 1 hour or longer to allow apricots to soften. Add lemon juice, orange juice, lemon rind, and salt, and reheat to boiling point. Add pectin solution, stir, return to heat, and return to boil. Remove from heat, add calcium solution, and mix well. Pour into hot, sterile pint jars, leaving $^1/_2$ inch at top. Cap with hot, sterile lids. Place in boiling-water bath for 5 minutes after water returns to boiling. If any jars fail to seal, refrigerate and use within ten days.

To freeze, pack in clean freezer containers or jars, leaving $^1/_2$ inch at top for expansion. Cover and cool to room temperature before placing in sharp-freeze section of freezer. When frozen, move to other section of freezer for storage. To use, thaw overnight in refrigerator. Makes 6 cups.

Nutritional value: 1 tablespoon contains 12 Calories (P0,F0,C3). $2^1/_2$ tablespoons = $^1/_2$ diabetic fruit exchange. If salt is omitted, 1 tablespoon contains 1 milligram sodium. Recipe contains 0 cholesterol. 1 teaspoon can be used without diabetic replacement.

Apricot-Pineapple Preserves

This recipe can be made into preserves by omitting the pectin and calcium solutions. Do not include these ingredients during preparation, continue to simmer over low heat until thick, stirring frequently. Process as directed above.

Nutritional value: 2 teaspoons contain 12 Calories (P0,F0,C3). $1^2/_3$ tablespoons = $^1/_2$ diabetic fruit exchange. If salt is omitted, 2 teaspoons contain 1 milligram sodium. Recipe contains 0 cholesterol. $^2/_3$ teaspoon can be used without diabetic replacement.

Blueberry-Orange Jam

Blueberries   4 cups washed, stems removed
Concentrated orange juice $1/2$ cup
Lemon juice   4 tablespoons
Lemon rind $1/4$ to $1/2$ teaspoon (optional)
Water $1/2$ cup
Low-methoxy pectin solution $3/4$ cup
Unflavored gelatin   1 to 2 tablespoons
       (1 to 2 envelopes)
Calcium solution   scant 4 teaspoons
Nutmeg $1/4$ teaspoon (optional)
Salt   dash (optional)

Place fruit in deep nonaluminum kettle. Add juices, rind, and water and simmer until fruit is very soft. Stir in pectin and gelatin (and spice). Return to boiling, add calcium solution, skim and pour into $1/2$-pint hot, sterile jars, leaving $1/2$ inch at top. Cap with hot, sterile lids. Process in boiling-water bath for 5 minutes after water returns to boiling. If any jars fail to seal, refrigerate and use within ten days or freeze for later use.

To freeze, pour into clean freezer containers or jars, leaving $1/2$ inch at top. Cover with clean lids and allow to cool to room temperature. Place in sharp-freeze section of freezer until frozen. Move to other section of freezer for storage. To use, thaw overnight in refrigerator. Makes $5^1/2$ cups.

Nutritional value: 1 tablespoon contains 8 Calories (P0,F0,C2). $3^1/2$ tablespoons = $1/2$ diabetic fruit exchange. If salt is omitted, 2 tablespoons contain less than 1 milligram sodium. Recipe contains 0 cholesterol. $1^1/2$ teaspoons can be used without diabetic replacement.

Blueberry-Orange Preserves

This recipe can be made into preserves by omitting the pectin and calcium solutions. Do not include these ingredients during preparation; continue to simmer over low heat until thick, stirring frequently. Process as directed.

Nutritional value: 2 teaspoons contain 8 Calories (P0,F0,C2). $2^1/_3$ tablespoons = $^1/_2$ diabetic fruit exchange. If salt is omitted, $2^1/_3$ tablespoons contain less than 1 milligram sodium. Recipe contains 0 cholesterol. 1 teaspoon can be used without diabetic replacement.

Extra Good Plum Jam

Sweet plums   5 cups pitted, chopped
Raisins, seedless $1^1/_2$ cups
Orange   1 large seeded
Lemon   1 medium seeded
Orange juice, concentrated $^1/_2$ cup
Water $^1/_2$ cup
Salt   dash (optional)
Walnut pieces   1 cup
Low-methoxy pectin solution   1 cup
Calcium solution   4 tablespoons

Grind plums, raisins, orange, and lemon medium coarse. Place in deep nonaluminum kettle along with juice, water (and salt). Mix well and simmer over low heat until fruit is very soft ($^1/_2$ hour or longer), stirring frequently. Stir in nuts, then pectin solution. Remove from heat; add calcium solution. Mix well. Pour into hot, sterile pint jars leaving $^1/_2$ inch at top for expansion. Cap with hot, sterile lids and process in boiling-water bath for 5 minutes after water returns to boiling. If any jars fail to seal, refrigerate and use within ten days or freeze for later use.

To freeze, pour into clean freezing containers or jars, leaving $^1/_2$ inch at top. Cover with clean lids and allow to cool to room temperature before placing in sharp-freeze section of the freezer. When frozen, move to other section for storage. To use, thaw overnight in refrigerator. Makes 9 to $9^1/_2$ cups.

Nutritional value: 1 tablespoon contains 17 Calories (P0,F1,C3). $2^1/_2$ tablespoons = $^1/_2$ diabetic fruit exchange + $^1/_2$ diabetic fat exchange. If salt is omitted, $1^1/_2$ tablespoons contain 1 milligram sodium. Recipe contains 0 cholesterol. 1 teaspoon can be used without diabetic replacement.

Extra Good Plum Preserves

This recipe can be made into preserves by omitting the pectin and calcium solutions. Do not include these ingredients during preparation; continue to simmer over low heat until thick, stirring frequently. Process as directed.

Nutritional value: 2 teaspoons contain 17 Calories (P0,F1,C3). $1^1/_2$ tablespoons = $^1/_2$ diabetic fruit exchange and $^1/_2$ diabetic fat exchange. If salt is omitted, 1 tablespoon contains 1 milligram sodium. Recipe contains 0 cholesterol. $^2/_3$ teaspoon can be used without diabetic replacement.

Mixed Soft Fruit Jam

Apricots, peaches, pears, nectarines, etc.   10 cups sliced, finely chopped, or ground
Concentrated apple juice $^1/_2$ cup *or Concentrated white grape juice* $^2/_3$ cup (simmered down from $1^1/_3$ cups)
Lemon juice   6 tablespoons
Cinnamon stick, quartered $^1/_2$ stick
Low-methoxy pectin solution   2 cups
Calcium solution   3 to 4 tablespoons*
Salt   dash (optional)

Peel and prepare fruit (leave in a few pits for almond flavor). Save juice and put it along with the fruit into a deep non-aluminum kettle.

---

*Use higher amount for thicker jam.

Add fruit juice and cloves; cook until soft, 15 to 20 minutes at most. Remove from heat. Sprinkle gelatin over hot mixture, mixing well. Add pectin and calcium solutions (and salt). Stir well again. Pack into hot, sterile $1/2$-pint or pint jars, leaving $1/2$ inch at top. Top with hot, sterile lids and process in boiling-water bath for 5 minutes after water returns to boiling. If any jars fail to seal, refrigerate and use within ten days or freeze for later use.

To freeze, pour into clean freezing containers or jars, leaving $1/2$ inch at top. Cover with clean lids and allow to cool to room temperature before placing in sharp-freeze section of the freezer. When frozen, remove to other section for storage. To use, thaw overnight in refrigerator. Makes 11 cups.

Nutritional value: 1 tablespoon contains 10 Calories (P0,F0,C2$1/2$). 3 tablespoons = $1/2$ diabetic fruit exchange. If salt is omitted, 3 tablespoons contain less than 2 milligrams sodium. Recipe contains 0 cholesterol. 1 teaspoon can be used without diabetic replacement.

Mixed Soft Fruit Preserves

This recipe can be made into preserves by omitting the pectin and calcium solutions. Do not include these ingredients during preparation; continue to simmer over low heat until thick, stirring frequently. Process as directed above.

Nutritional value: 2 teaspoons contain 10 Calories (P0,F0,C2$1/2$). 2 tablespoons = $1/2$ diabetic fruit exchange. If salt is omitted, 2 tablespoons contain less than 2 milligrams sodium. Recipe contains 0 cholesterol. $2/3$ teaspoon can be used without diabetic replacement.

Red Raspberry Jam

Raspberries   4 cups, washed, stems removed
White grape juice $1/2$ cup (simmered down from 2 cups)
Lemon juice   4 tablespoons

Lemon rind $^1/_4$ teaspoon grated (optional)
Low-methoxy pectin solution $^3/_4$ cup
Unflavored gelatin 1 to 2 tablespoons (1 to 2 envelopes)
Calcium solution scant 4 teaspoons
Salt dash (optional)

Place fruit in deep nonaluminum kettle. Add juices and rind, cover, and place over low heat. Simmer until fruit is soft, about 8 minutes. Stir in pectin and gelatin. Return to heat, bringing to a boil. Remove from heat; add calcium solution and salt. Mix well. Skim and pour immediately into hot, sterile pint jars, leaving $^1/_2$ inch at top for expansion. Cover with hot, sterile lids. Process in boiling-water bath for 5 minutes after water returns to boiling. If any jars fail to seal, refrigerate and use within ten days or freeze for later use.

To freeze, pour into clean freezer containers or jars, leaving $^1/_2$ inch at top. Cover with clean lids and allow to cool to room temperature. Place in sharp-freeze section of freezer until frozen. Move to other section of freezer for storage. To use, thaw overnight in refrigerator. Makes $5^1/_2$ cups.

Nutritional value: 1 tablespoon contains 8 Calories (P0,F0,C2). $2^1/_2$ tablespoons = $^1/_3$ diabetic fruit exchange. If salt is omitted, 2 tablespoons contain less than 1 milligram sodium. Recipe contains 0 cholesterol. 1 teaspoon can be used without diabetic replacement.

Red Raspberry Preserves

This recipe can be made into preserves by omitting the pectin and calcium solutions. Do not include these ingredients during preparation; continue to simmer over low heat until thick, stirring frequently. Process as directed above.

Nutritional value: 2 teaspoons contain 8 Calories (P0,F0,C2). $3^1/_2$ tablespoons = $^1/_2$ diabetic fruit exchange. If salt is omitted, $3^1/_2$ tablespoons contain less than 1 milligram sodium. Recipe contains 0 cholesterol. 1 teaspoon can be used without diabetic replacement.

Spicy Blueberry-Plum Jam

Italian prunes   5 cups halved and pitted
Blueberries (may be frozen)   6 cups
Lemon   1 large with skin, seeded
Pear or peach, ripe   1 medium stemmed, cored or pitted
Concentrated apple juice $1^1/_2$ cups
Lemon juice   2 tablespoons
Ground cinnamon $^1/_2$ to $^2/_3$ teaspoon
Salt $^1/_2$ to 1 teaspoon (optional)
Low-methoxy pectin solution   1 cup
Calcium solution   2 tablespoons

Grind or finely chop prunes, lemon, and peach or pear. Place in deep nonaluminum kettle. Add blueberries and apple juice. Simmer over low heat for $^1/_2$ hour, stirring often. Add cinnamon and salt. Continue simmering until slightly thickened. Stir in pectin solution; then remove from heat and add calcium solution. Mix very well. Pour into hot, sterile jars, leaving $^1/_2$ inch at top for expansion. Top with hot, sterile lids and process in boiling-water bath for 5 minutes after water returns to boiling. If any jars fail to seal, refrigerate and use within ten days or freeze for later use.

To freeze, pour into clean freezing containers or jars, leaving $^1/_2$ inch at top. Cover with clean lids and allow to cool to room temperature before placing in sharp-freeze section of freezer. When frozen, move to other section of freezer for storage. To use, thaw overnight in refrigerator. Makes $12^1/_2$ cups.

Nutritional value: 1 tablespoon contains 9 Calories (P0,F0,C2). $2^1/_2$ tablespoons = $^1/_3$ diabetic fruit exchange. If salt is omitted, 2 tablespoons contain 1 milligram sodium. Recipe contains 0 cholesterol. $^1/_2$ tablespoon can be used without diabetic replacement.

Spicy Blueberry-Plum Preserves

This recipe can be made into preserves by omitting the pectin and calcium solutions. Do not include these ingredients during preparation; continue to simmer over low heat until thick, stirring frequently. Process as directed.

Nutritional value: 2 teaspoons contain 9 Calories (P0,F0,C2). $2^1/_2$ tablespoons = $^1/_2$ diabetic fruit exchange. If salt is omitted, $2^1/_2$ tablespoons contain less than 1 milligram sodium. Recipe contains 0 cholesterol. 1 teaspoon can be used without diabetic replacement.

Jelly

I have not been able to make good jelly using regular pectin but have made excellent jelly with low-methoxy pectin. You can substitute any fruit juice in the Basic Jelly recipe given, but you will have to adjust the added ingredients (lemon juice, spice) to what you prefer with that fruit juice. I have made some suggestions for you to try, but be sure to make a trial batch before you make a whole recipe to avoid disappointment.

Basic Jelly Recipe

Concentrated fruit juice   2 cups (apple, orange, grape—
        simmered down from 5 cups)
Water   1 cup
Lemon juice   1 to 2 tablespoons
Low-methoxy pectin solution $^3/_4$ cup
Calcium solution   scant 4 teaspoons
Orange or lemon rind $^1/_2$ to 1 teaspoon grated (optional)
Salt   dash (optional)
Unflavored gelatin   1 tablespoon (1 envelope)
Spices (see list below) $^1/_4$ teaspoon ground (optional)

Place juices and water in saucepan, add pectin solution, and bring to boil. Sprinkle gelatin over hot mixture, stirring well to dissolve. Stir in calcium solution and pour into hot, sterile $^1/_2$-pint or pint jars, leaving $^1/_2$ inch at top. Cap with hot, sterile lids. Process in boiling-water bath for 5 minutes after water returns to boiling. If any jars fail to seal, refrigerate and use within ten days, or freeze for later use.

To freeze, pour into clean freezing containers or jars, leaving $^1/_2$ inch at top. Cover with clean lids and allow to cool to room temperature before placing in sharp-freeze section of freezer. When frozen, move to other section of freezer for storage. To use, thaw overnight in refrigerator. Makes 4 cups.

Here are some spice combinations that I like:

Apple with ginger or cinnamon
Orange with ginger or lemon or orange rind
Grape with nutmeg or very small amount allspice

Nutritional value: 1 tablespoon contains 8 to 10 Calories (P0,F0,C2–3). 5 to $7^1/_2$ tablespoons = 1 diabetic fruit exchange. If salt is omitted, 5 tablespoons contain less than 1 milligram sodium. Recipe contains 0 cholesterol.

Note: Be sure that all juice you buy is labeled "Pure Juice." Federal law allows juice to be sweetened, but it must show on the label. Pure fruit juice has *no* added sweetening.

Apple Jelly

Concentrated apple juice (frozen, undiluted) $2^1/_2$ cups
Water $1^1/_2$ cups
Lemon juice   1 $^1/_2$ tablespoons
Low-methoxy pectin solution   1 cup
Calcium solution   5 teaspoons
Salt   dash (optional)

Place juices and water in deep saucepan. Heat to boiling. Add pectin solution and reheat until completely dissolved; bring to full boil. Remove from heat; add calcium solution and salt. Stir well. Pour into hot, sterile $1/2$-pint or pint jars; top with hot, sterile lids. Process in boiling-water bath for 5 minutes after water returns to boiling. If any jars fail to seal, refrigerate and use within ten days or freeze for later use.

To freeze, pour into clean freezing containers or jars, leaving $1/2$ inch at top. Cover with clean lids and allow to cool to room temperature before placing in sharp-freeze section of freezer. When frozen, move to other section of freezer for storage. To use, thaw overnight in refrigerator. Makes 5 cups.

Nutritional value: 1 tablespoon contains 12 Calories (P0,F0,C3). $2^1/_2$ tablespoons = $1/_2$ diabetic fruit exchange. If salt is omitted, $2^1/_2$ tablespoons contain less than 1 milligram sodium. Recipe contains 0 cholesterol. 1 teaspoon can be used without diabetic replacement.

Note: Use this base for flavored jellies such as geranium, mint, and herb mixtures. Steep geranium or other leaves with hot apple juice, having first crushed them to release volatile odors and flavor. Strain out leaves/herbs and continue with recipe as directed. Add $1/_4$ teaspoon coloring if desired (red for geranium, green for mint, etc.). The nutritional value given will not be changed by the addition of any of these flavorings or herbs.

Grape Jelly

Concentrated frozen grape juice   2 cups
Water   1 cup
Lemon juice   1 to $1^1/_2$ tablespoons
Low-methoxy pectin solution   1 cup
Calcium solution   4 tablespoons
Salt   sprinkle (optional)

Combine juices in nonaluminum kettle. Simmer until hot. Stir in pectin solution; remove from heat. Mix in calcium solution (and salt). Pour into hot, sterile jars, leaving $1/_2$ inch at top. Cover with hot, sterile lids and process in boiling-water bath for 5 minutes after water returns to boiling. If any jars fail to seal, refrigerate and use within ten days or freeze for later use.

To freeze, pour into clean freezing containers or jars, leaving $1/2$ inch at top. Cover with clean lids and allow to cool to room temperature before placing in sharp-freeze section of freezer. When frozen, move to other section of freezer for storage. To use, thaw overnight in refrigerator. Makes 4 cups.

Nutritional value: 1 tablespoon contains 7 Calories (P0,F0,C2). $2^{1}/_{2}$ tablespoons = $1/_{3}$ diabetic fruit exchange. If salt is omitted, $2^{1}/_{2}$ tablespoons contain 1 milligram sodium. Recipe contains 0 cholesterol. $1^{1}/_{2}$ teaspoons can be used without diabetic replacement.

Note: Frozen concentrated white grape juice is available in my market only in a sweetened form. To avoid sugar, be sure the juice is labeled "Pure Juice," or use the purple variety to be positive (check label).

Orange Juice Jelly

Concentrated orange juice (frozen, undiluted)   1 cup
Water (or white grape juice for sweeter jelly)   1 cup
Orange rind   1 teaspoon grated
Lemon juice   1 tablespoon
Low-methoxy pectin solution $1/_{2}$ cup
Salt   dash (optional)
Calcium solution   2 to $2^{1}/_{2}$ teaspoons

Mix juices and rind in deep saucepan. Heat to boiling; add pectin solution. Mix in calcium solution (and salt). Pour into hot, sterile $1/_{2}$-pint or pint jars, leaving $1/_{2}$ inch at top. Cap with hot, sterile lids. Process in boiling-water bath 5 minutes after water returns to boiling. If any jars fail to seal, refrigerate and use within ten days or freeze for later use.

To freeze, pour into clean freezing containers or jars, leaving $^1/_2$ inch at top. Cover with clean lids and allow to cool to room temperature before placing in sharp-freeze section of freezer. When frozen, move to other section of freezer for storage. To use, thaw overnight in refrigerator. Makes $2^1/_2$ cups.

Variation: Substitute another concentrated juice in place of orange: Try frozen concentrated pineapple juice and substitute lemon rind for orange.

Nutritional value: When made with orange juice, 1 tablespoon contains 12 Calories (P0,F0,C3). $2^1/_2$ tablespoons = $^1/_2$ diabetic fruit exchange. When made with pineapple juice, 1 tablespoon contains 16 Calories (P0,F0,C4). $3^1/_2$ tablespoons = 1 diabetic fruit exchange. If salt is omitted, $3^1/_2$ tablespoons (either recipe) contain less than 1 milligram sodium. Recipe contains 0 cholesterol. When made with orange juice, 1 teaspoon can be used without diabetic replacement; when made with pineapple juice, $^2/_3$ teaspoon can be used without diabetic replacement.

Tangy Orange-Grapefruit Jelly

Concentrated frozen orange juice   1 cup
Concentrated frozen grapefruit juice $^3/_4$ cup
Water $2^1/_4$ cups
Lemon juice   1 tablespoon
Salt   sprinkle (optional)
Grated orange rind $^1/_2$ teaspoon (optional)
Low-methoxy pectin solution   1 cup
Calcium solution $4^1/_2$ tablespoons

Mix juices and water (salt and rind) in deep nonaluminum kettle. Heat to boiling; then stir in pectin solution. Remove from heat; mix in calcium solution. Pour into hot, sterile pint canning jars, leaving $^1/_2$ inch at top for expansion. Cover with hot, sterile lids and process in boiling-water bath for 5 minutes after water returns to boiling. If any jars fail to seal, refrigerate and use within ten days.

To freeze, pour into clean freezing containers or jars, leaving $1/2$ inch at top. Cover with clean lids and allow to cool to room temperature before placing in sharp-freeze section of freezer. When frozen, move to other section of freezer for storage. To use, thaw overnight in refrigerator. Makes $5^1/2$ cups.

Nutritional value: 1 tablespoon contains 8 Calories (P0,F0,C2). $3^1/2$ tablespoons = $1/2$ diabetic fruit exchange. If salt is omitted, 5 tablespoons contain 1 milligram sodium. Recipe contains 0 cholesterol. $1^1/2$ teaspoons can be used without diabetic replacement.

Pineapple-Grapefruit Jelly

Substitute 1 cup concentrated frozen pineapple juice for the orange juice in the recipe above. Increase lemon juice to $1^1/2$ tablespoons. Omit orange rind. Follow directions as given above.

Nutritional value: 1 tablespoon contains 9 Calories (P0,F0,C2). $3^1/2$ tablespoons = $1/2$ diabetic exchange. If salt is omitted, 5 tablespoons contain 1 milligram sodium. Recipe contains 0 cholesterol. $1^1/2$ teaspoons can be used without diabetic replacement.

Preserves

Most fruits can be used to make preserves, but expensive fruits will go further with some apple included. Up to one third of the total volume can be apple and the preserve will still taste and look undiluted. Unless the fruit is very sweet, or dried fruit is added, you will probably want to add sweetening. Concentrated fruit juices work well, with date sugar added to give needed zip in a few combinations. (Add date last, if at all.)

You may want to make fruit go further by thickening with gelatin or agar-agar and not cooking down as much. (Use one envelope gelatin as directed in jam recipes or dissolve $1/2$ stick of agar-agar in $1/2$ cup water, breaking into small pieces and allowing to soak. When almost dissolved, heat to finish melting. This mixture will remain firm at room temperature, whereas gelatin has to be kept chilled to stay thick.)

Preserves freeze beautifully and will not "water" when thawed. To freeze, simply allow to cool to room temperature after packed, then place in sharp-freeze section of freezer. To use, thaw overnight in refrigerator.

Suggested Combinations for Preserves

Apricot and apple with lemon
Apple, lemon, and date
Plum, apple, and orange
Orange, grapefruit, and apple (use small amounts of orange rind, concentrated orange juice, and lemon)
Raspberry and apple
Strawberry and apple
Strawberry and raspberry with apple

This only begins to suggest fruits you can combine. Most fruits blend together, and if you make a trial batch as suggested, you can adjust the amounts of each to find which you like best.

PRESERVES MADE WITHOUT PECTIN

Basic Preserve Recipe

Fruit or berries $7^1/_2$ cups washed, pitted, chopped
Apples $2^1/_2$ cups peeled, cored, sliced
Concentrated apple juice   1 cup *or White grape juice*   1 cup (simmered down from 2 cups)
Lemon juice $^1/_4$ cup plus 2 teaspoons
Finely ground rind from $^1/_4$ medium lemon

Salt   dash (optional)
Unflavored gelatin   1 to 2 tablespoons (1 to 2 envelopes)
   (optional) *or Agar-agar* $^1/_2$ stick, dissolved in $^1/_2$ cup hot
   water (optional)
Spices (ground cinnamon, nutmeg, cloves, etc.)   1 teaspoon

Prepare fruit and place in large nonaluminum kettle. Stir in juices
and rind. Simmer slowly over low heat until thickened, stirring frequently. (Fruit may be mashed for more uniform preserves.) Depending on fruits selected, it may take 2 hours or more to thicken.
Cooking should be interrupted when it is almost thick enough and
salt, gelatin or agar-agar, and spices added. If gelatin or agar-agar is
used, preserve must be stirred well and returned to boiling to ensure
complete dissolving. Remove from heat and skim if necessary. Pour
into hot, sterile pint jars, leaving $^1/_2$ inch at top. Top with hot, sterile
lids. Process in boiling-water bath for 5 minutes after water has
returned to boiling. If any jars fail to seal, refrigerate and use within
ten days or freeze for later use.

To freeze, pour into clean freezing containers or jars, leaving $^1/_2$
inch at top. Cover with clean lids and allow to cool to room temperature before placing in sharp-freeze section of freezer. When frozen,
move to other section of freezer for storage. To use, thaw overnight in
refrigerator. Makes $7^1/_2$ cups.

Nutritional value: 2 tablespoons contain 40 Calories (P0,F0,C10).
$1^1/_2$ tablespoons = $^1/_2$ diabetic fruit exchange. If salt is omitted, $1^1/_2$
tablespoons contain less than 1 milligram sodium. Recipe contains 0
cholesterol. $^2/_3$ teaspoon can be used without diabetic replacement.

Apple Butter

Apples   6 cups peeled, diced
Concentrated apple juice   1 $^1/_2$ cups
Apple cider   4 $^1/_2$ cups
Lemon juice   7 tablespoons

Cinnamon   1 tablespoon
Nutmeg   1 teaspoon
Cloves $3/4$ to 1 teaspoon
Salt $1/8$ teaspoon (optional)

Peel and core apples and remove stem and blossom ends. Place in large nonaluminum kettle; add apple juice, cider, and lemon juice. Cook over low heat until volume is reduced to about half (the consistency of applesauce). Stir frequently to avoid sticking. Add spices and salt and mix well. Heat 1–2 minutes to blend spice flavors with fruit. Remove from heat. Pack in hot, sterile pint jars, leaving $1/2$ inch at top. Cap with hot, sterile lids. Process in boiling-water bath 5 minutes after water returns to boiling. If any jars fail to seal, refrigerate and use within ten days or freeze for later use.

To freeze, pour into clean freezing containers or jars, leaving $1/2$ inch at top. Cover with clean lids and allow to cool to room temperature before placing in sharp-freeze section of freezer. When frozen, move to other section of freezer for storage. To use, thaw overnight in refrigerator. Makes $5^1/2$ cups.

Nutritional value: 1 tablespoon contains 16 Calories (P0,F0,C4). Scant 2 tablespoons = $1/2$ diabetic fruit exchange. If salt is omitted, $1^1/2$ tablespoons contain less than 1 milligram sodium. Recipe contains 0 cholesterol. $2/3$ teaspoon can be used without diabetic replacement.

Cherry Conserve

Dark, sweet cherries   3 cups pitted and chopped
Concentrated apple juice   2 cups
Large orange   1 finely chopped, including $1/2$ rind and juice
Lemon juice   2 tablespoons
Lemon rind $1/2$ to 1 teaspoon
Walnuts or pecans $1/2$ cup coarsely chopped
Salt   dash (optional)

Cook cherries with apple juice until slightly thickened. Add remaining ingredients. Cook until thickened, stirring often to prevent sticking. Pour into hot, sterile pint jars, leaving $^1/_2$ inch at top. Cap with hot, sterile lids. Process in boiling-water bath for 5 minutes after water returns to boiling. If any jars fail to seal, refrigerate and use within ten days or freeze for later use.

To freeze, pour into clean freezing containers or jars, leaving $^1/_2$ inch at top. Cover with clean lids and allow to cool to room temperature before placing in sharp-freeze section of freezer. When frozen, move to other section of freezer for storage. To use, thaw overnight in refrigerator. Makes $5^1/_2$ cups.

Nutritional value: 1 tablespoon contains 16 Calories (P0,F0,C4). Scant 2 tablespoons = $^1/_2$ diabetic fruit exchange. If salt is omitted, 2 tablespoons contain less than 1 milligram sodium. Recipe contains 0 cholesterol. $^2/_3$ teaspoon can be used without diabetic replacement.

Peach Butter

Very ripe peaches   2 quarts peeled, pitted, chopped
Apple cider   3 cups
Concentrated white grape juice   1 cup (simmered down
      from 2 cups)
Lemon juice   2 tablespoons
Lemon rind $^1/_4$ to $^1/_2$ teaspoon grated (to taste)
Salt   dash (optional)
Almond extract $^1/_2$ teaspoon (optional)

Place all ingredients (except almond extract) in large nonaluminum kettle. Cook over low heat until thick, stirring frequently and skimming if necessary. When suitably thick, taste. Add extract if desired. Pour into hot, sterile pint jars, leaving $^1/_2$ inch at top. Cap with hot, sterile lids. Process in boiling-water bath for 5 minutes after water returns to boiling. If any jars fail to seal, refrigerate and use within ten days or freeze for later use.

To freeze, pour into clean freezing containers or jars, leaving $\frac{1}{2}$ inch at top. Cover with clean lids and allow to cool to room temperature before placing in sharp-freeze section of freezer. When frozen, move to other section of freezer for storage. Thaw in refrigerator overnight before using. Makes 6–7 cups.

Nutritional value: 2 tablespoons contains 20 Calories (P0,F0,C5). 3 tablespoons = $\frac{1}{2}$ diabetic fruit exchange. If salt is omitted, 3 tablespoons contain less than 1 milligram sodium. Recipe contains 0 cholesterol. 1 teaspoon can be used without diabetic replacement.

Plum Marmalade

Purple plums, ripe   6 cups, pitted and ground
Sweet apples (medium sized)   2 cups, cored and ground
Seedless raisins   1 cup ground
Orange   1 large, seeded and ground
Lemon $\frac{1}{2}$ medium, seeded and ground
Orange juice concentrate (frozen, undiluted)   1 cup
White grape juice   1 cup
Water   1 cup
Salt   dash (optional)

Combine all ingredients in a deep nonaluminum kettle. Simmer over low heat until thickened, stirring frequently to avoid sticking. When thickened, taste and add more lemon juice or fruit juice if desired. Pour into hot, sterile pint jars, leaving $\frac{1}{2}$ inch at top. Cap with hot, sterile lids and process in a boiling-water bath for 5 minutes after water returns to boiling. If any jars fail to seal, refrigerate and use within 10 days or freeze for later use.

To freeze, pour into clean freezing containers or jars, leaving $\frac{1}{2}$ inch at top. Cover with clean lids and allow to cool to room temperature before placing in sharp-freeze section of freezer. When frozen hard, move to other section of freezer for storage. Thaw in refrigerator overnight before using. Makes $9\frac{1}{2}$ cups.

Nutritional value: 1 tablespoon contains 13 Calories (P0,F0,C3). $2^1/_3$ tablespoons = $^1/_2$ diabetic fruit exchange. If salt is omitted, 3 tablespoons contain 1 milligram sodium. Recipe contains 0 cholesterol. 1 teaspoon can be used without diabetic replacement.

Strawberry Date Nut Preserves

*Fresh or frozen whole strawberries** 2 cups halved
Dates $^1/_2$ cup chopped medium-fine
White grape juice 1 cup (simmered down from 2 cups)
Lemon rind 1 teaspoon grated
Lemon juice $1^1/_2$ tablespoons
Salt dash (optional)
Walnuts or pecans $^1/_2$ cup chopped

Combine all ingredients except nuts in a deep saucepan. Simmer over low heat until fairly thick. Stir in nuts. Return to heat and continue to cook until thick, stirring frequently to prevent sticking. Remove from heat. Pour into hot, sterile $^1/_2$-pint jars, leaving $^1/_2$ inch at top. Cap with hot, sterile lids. Process in boiling-water bath for 5 minutes after water returns to boiling. If any jars fail to seal, refrigerate and use within ten days or freeze for later use.

To freeze, pour into clean freezing containers or jars, leaving $^1/_2$ inch at top. Cover with clean lids and allow to cool to room temperature before placing in sharp-freeze section of freezer. When frozen, move to other section of freezer for storage. Thaw in refrigerator overnight before using. Makes $2^1/_2$ cups.

Nutritional value: 1 tablespoon contains 27 Calories (P0,F0,C4$^1/_2$). $1^3/_4$ tablespoons = $^1/_2$ diabetic fruit exchange. If salt is omitted, $1^1/_2$ tablespoons contain less than 1 milligram sodium. Recipe contains 0 cholesterol. $^1/_2$ teaspoon can be used without diabetic replacement.

*These preserves can be made with other berries, but strawberries are best.

FROZEN JAM RECIPES USING GELATIN OR AGAR-AGAR FOR THICKENING

Basic Jam Recipe with Gelatin or Agar-Agar
(Lazy Person's Jam)

Fresh fruit 4 cups washed and chopped
Concentrated white grape juice 1 cup (simmered down
    from 2 cups) *or Concentrated apple juice* $^2/_3$ cup
Lemon $^1/_4$, chopped with juice *or Lemon juice* $2^1/_4$
    tablespoons
Unflavored gelatin 2 tablespoons (2 envelopes) *or*
    Agar-agar 1 stick
Salt dash (optional)

Place chopped fruit, juice, and chopped lemon into a deep saucepan. Cover and simmer for 8 minutes until fruit is barely cooked. Remove from heat and sprinkle gelatin over hot mixture, stirring well to dissolve evenly. Add spices (see Variations) and salt, taste, and add more lemon or fruit juice, if desired. Pour into clean, hot jars, leaving $^1/_2$ inch at the top. Cover with clean, hot lids and set aside to cool to room temperature. Freeze in sharp-freeze section of freezer; then move to other shelf for storage. To use, thaw overnight in refrigerator or refrigerate and use within ten days maximum or freeze for later use. Makes $4^1/_2$ to 5 cups.

If using agar-agar, break into small pieces and soak in $^1/_2$ cup warm water for approximately 1 hour. Gently heat to dissolve any solid pieces. Add as directed for gelatin.

Variations:
With apple: Add $^1/_2$ teaspoon cinnamon + $^1/_4$ teaspoon nutmeg +
    $^1/_8$ teaspoon ginger (or more of each if you like it spicy).
With berries: Add 1 tablespoon extra lemon juice.

With plums: Add $^1/_4$ to $^1/_2$ teaspoon ground nutmeg or cloves.
With sour apples: Add $^1/_4$ cup chopped raisins (soak in hot juice before using juice with fruit).

Nutritional value: 1 tablespoon contains 4 to 8 Calories (P0,F0,C1–2), depending on fruit used. $3^1/_2$ to $7^1/_2$ tablespoons = $^1/_2$ diabetic fruit exchange. If salt is omitted, 5 tablespoons contain 1 milligram sodium. Recipe contains 0 cholesterol. 1 teaspoon (any variety) may be used without diabetic replacement.

Lazy Person's Berry Jam

Strawberries (or other fresh berries)   4 cups halved
Concentrated white grape juice $^1/_2$ cup (simmered down from $1^1/_2$ cups)
Lemon juice $2^1/_2$ tablespoons
Lemon rind $^1/_4$ teaspoon grated
Unflavored gelatin   2 tablespoons (2 envelopes)
Salt   dash (optional)

Place berries, juices, rind, and salt in saucepan. Mash berries to release juice. Heat to boiling. Sprinkle gelatin over hot mixture, stirring well to dissolve. Remove from heat, skim, and pack immediately into hot, sterile pint jars, leaving $^1/_2$ inch at top, and top with hot, sterile lids. Process in boiling-water bath for 5 minutes after water returns to boiling. If any fail to seal, refrigerate and use within ten days or freeze for later use in sharp-freeze section of freezer; move to main section for storage. To use, thaw overnight in refrigerator. Makes $4^1/_2$ cups.

Nutritional value: 1 tablespoon contains 6 Calories (P0,F0,C1$^1/_2$). 5 tablespoons = $^1/_2$ diabetic fruit exchange. If salt is omitted, 1 tablespoon contains less than 1 milligram sodium. Recipe contains 0 cholesterol. $^1/_2$ tablespoon can be used without diabetic replacement.

Lazy Person's Peach Jam

Peaches 4 cups peeled, pitted and chopped
Lemon rind $^1/_4$ teaspoon grated
Lemon juice $2^1/_2$ tablespoons
Concentrated white grape juice 1 cup (simmered down
   from 2 cups)
Unflavored gelatin $1^1/_2$ tablespoons
   ($1^1/_2$ envelopes)
Cinnamon $^1/_2$ teaspoon
Salt dash (optional)
Nutmeg $^1/_4$ teaspoon (optional)
Ginger $^1/_4$ teaspoon (optional)

Place chopped fruit, rind, and juices into a deep saucepan. Cover and simmer for 8 minutes until fruit is barely cooked. Remove from heat and sprinkle gelatin over hot mixture, stirring well to dissolve. Add spices (and salt), taste, and more lemon juice, fruit juice, or spice, if desired. Pour into hot, sterile pint jars, cover with hot, sterile lids, leaving $^1/_2$ inch at top, and process in boiling-water bath for 5 minutes after water returns to boiling. If any jars fail to seal, refrigerate and use within ten days or freeze for later use.

If you wish to freeze jam, pour hot jam into clean containers or jars, cover with clean lids and cool covered jars to room temperature. Freeze in sharp-freeze section of freezer, then move to main section for storage. To use, thaw overnight in refrigerator. Makes 5 cups.

Nutritional value: 1 tablespoon contains 8 Calories (P0,F0,C2). $3^1/_2$ tablespoons = $^1/_2$ diabetic fruit exchange. If salt is omitted, 1 tablespoon contains less than 1 milligram sodium. Recipe contains 0 cholesterol. $1^1/_2$ teaspoons can be used without diabetic replacement.

Lazy Person's Plum Jam

Dried prunes* 4 cups pitted, soaked before measuring
Prune juice $^{1}/_{2}$ cup
Lemon juice 3 tablespoons
Concentrated white grape juice $^{1}/_{2}$ cup (simmered down
    from 1 cup)
Water $^{1}/_{2}$ cup
Lemon rind $^{1}/_{2}$ teaspoon grated
Nutmeg $^{1}/_{2}$ teaspoon **or Cloves** $^{1}/_{4}$ teaspoon
Salt dash (optional)
Unflavored gelatin 2 tablespoons (2 envelopes)

Soak prunes in juices and water overnight to soften. Place in deep nonaluminum saucepan and simmer until soft. Mash to break up pieces and return to heat. Add rind, spices, and salt and sprinkle gelatin over hot mixture, stirring well. Pour into hot, sterile, pint jars, leaving $^{1}/_{2}$ inch at top for expansion. Cover with hot, sterile lids and process in boiling-water bath for 5 minutes after water returns to boiling. If any fail to seal, refrigerate and use within ten days or freeze for later use.

If you wish to freeze jam, cool to room temperature. Freeze in sharp-freeze section of freezer, removing to other section for storage.

To use, thaw overnight in refrigerator. Makes 5 cups.

Nutritional value: 1 tablespoon contains 10 Calories (P0,F0,C2$^{1}/_{2}$). 3 tablespoons = $^{1}/_{2}$ diabetic fruit exchange. If salt is omitted, 1 tablespoon contains less than 1 milligram sodium. Recipe contains 0 cholesterol. 1 teaspoon can be used without diabetic replacement.

---

*Depending on size of prunes, it will take from 2 to 2$^{1}/_{2}$ cups dried to make 4 cups after soaking.

Lazy Person's Soft Fruit Jam

Mixed soft fruit   6 cups peeled, pitted and chopped
Concentrated apple juice $1^1/_2$ cups
Lemon juice $^1/_4$ cup
Lemon rind $^1/_3$ teaspoon grated
      (optional but good!)
Salt   dash (optional)
Allspice or Cinnamon $^1/_3$ teaspoon ground
Unflavored gelatin   2 tablespoons (2 envelopes)
      or Agar-agar   1 stick (dissolved in $^1/_2$ cup water)

Combine fruit, juices, and rind in deep nonaluminum kettle. Cover and simmer for 8 to 10 minutes until fruit is soft but not mushy. Remove from heat and sprinkle gelatin (or dissolved agar-agar) over jam. Mix well, returning to heat if necessary to completely dissolve the gelatin. Add spice (and salt). Stir well; then taste to determine if you wish to add more lemon juice, lemon rind, or spice. Pour into hot, sterile pint jars, leaving $^1/_2$ inch at top. Cover with hot, sterile lids and process in boiling-water bath for 5 minutes after water returns to boiling. If any jars fail to seal, refrigerate and use within ten days or freeze for later use.

If you plan to freeze jam, pour hot jam into clean containers or jars. Cover with clean lids and allow capped jars to cool to room temperature. Place in sharp-freeze section of freezer, moving to other section for storage when frozen. Makes 7 cups.

Nutritional value: For $^1/_3$ each apricots, peaches, and pears, 1 tablespoon contains 11 Calories (P0,F0,C3). $2^1/_3$ tablespoons = $^1/_2$ diabetic fruit exchange. If salt is omitted, 2 tablespoons contain 1 milligram sodium. (If made with agar-agar, same sodium content.) Recipe contains 0 cholesterol. 1 teaspoon can be used without diabetic replacement.

JELLY RECIPES USING GELATIN OR AGAR-AGAR FOR THICKENING

Jellies made with gelatin for thickening must be kept refrigerated to stay firm. They also must be used within ten days to avoid spoiling. They may be canned or frozen but tend to water when thawed. *These are best made in small amounts and used within the specified time.*

Basic Jelly Recipe with Agar-Agar or Gelatin

Concentrated fruit juice (frozen, undiluted)   1 cup
Water   1 cup
Lemon juice   2 to 3 teaspoons
Salt   dash (optional)
Agar-agar $^1/_4$ to $^1/_2$ stick broken into small pieces **or**
Gelatin, unflavored $^1/_2$ to 1 tablespoon ($^1/_2$–1 envelope)
Ground ginger, nutmeg, grated orange or lemon rind $^1/_8$
      to $^1/_4$ teaspoon (optional)

Combine juices in nonaluminum kettle. Taste and add more water, and/or lemon juice, then spice/rind as desired. Dissolve gelatin or agar-agar in $^1/_2$ cup water, heating if necessary to dissolve completely. Add to juices and heat to boiling. Pour into clean $^1/_2$-pint jars, leaving $^1/_2$ inch at top. Cover with clean lids and refrigerate when cooled. Use within ten days to avoid spoiling. **Or** pour into hot, sterile pint jars, leaving $^1/_2$ inch at top. Cap with hot, sterile lids and process in boiling-water bath for 5 minutes after water returns to boiling. If any jars fail to seal, refrigerate and use within ten days. *Does not freeze well.* Makes $2^1/_2$ cups.

Note: This jelly must be kept refrigerated after opening. The extra heating during canning may weaken the jell, so it could water (liquid might separate out) when thawed. If this happens, just mix the liquid back into the solids and use. I prefer jelly made with agar-agar as it has a better texture (less like Jell-O).

Nutritional value: 1 tablespoon contains 12 Calories (P0,F0,C3). 1 2/3 tablespoons = $^1/3$ diabetic fruit exchange. If salt is omitted, 2 tablespoons contain less than 1 milligram sodium. Recipe contains 0 cholesterol. 1 teaspoon can be used without diabetic replacement.

Apple Juice Jelly

Concentrated apple juice (frozen, undiluted)   1 cup
Water   1 cup
Lemon juice   2 teaspoons
Salt   dash (optional)
Agar-agar $^1/4$ stick broken into small pieces **or**
Gelatin, unflavored   1 tablespoon (1 envelope)
Ginger $^1/8$ teaspoon ground (optional)
Lemon rind $^1/8$ to $^1/4$ teaspoon grated (optional)

Place juices and $^1/2$ cup water in nonaluminum kettle. Dissolve agar-agar or gelatin in remaining $^1/2$ cup water, heating to completely dissolve if necessary. Add to juices. Taste; add salt, spice, and/or rind if desired. Heat to boiling. Pour into clean jars and cap with clean lids. Cool to room temperature before refrigerating. Use within ten days. Or pack into hot, sterile $^1/2$-pint jars, leaving $^1/2$ inch at top. Cap with hot, sterile lids and process in boiling-water bath for 5 minutes after water returns to boiling. If any jars fail to seal, refrigerate and use within ten days. *Does not freeze well.* Makes 2 cups.

Note: See suggestions for modifications beneath recipe for Apple Juice Jelly with Low-Methoxy Pectin (see Recipe Index). These substitutions can also be used with this recipe.

Nutritional value: 1 tablespoon contains 16 Calories (P0,F0,C4). 1$^2/3$ tablespoons = $^1/2$ diabetic fruit exchange. If salt is omitted, 2 teaspoons contain less than 1 milligram sodium. Recipe contains 0 cholesterol. 1 teaspoon jelly can be used without diabetic replacement.

Grape Juice Jelly

Concentrated purple Concord grape juice   1 cup (simmered
   down from 2 cups)
White grape juice   1 cup
Lemon juice   1^1/$_2$ tablespoons
Salt   dash (optional)
Lemon rind ^{1}/$_4$ teaspoon grated (optional)
Nutmeg ^{1}/$_{16}$ teaspoon ground (optional)
Agar-agar ^{1}/$_4$ stick **or**
Gelatin, unflavored ^{1}/$_2$ tablespoon
Water ^{1}/$_2$ cup

Break agar-agar into small pieces and dissolve in ^{1}/$_2$ cup water or
sprinkle gelatin over ^{1}/$_2$ cup water. Allow to stand for 15 minutes or
longer, then slowly heat to completely dissolve. Place juices in deep
nonaluminum kettle and heat to boiling. Then add agar-agar or
gelatin solution. Taste and add salt, rind, and/or spice to taste. Mix
well. Pour into clean jars, top with clean lids, and refrigerate until
used (within ten days to avoid spoiling). Or pour into hot, sterile ^{1}/$_2$-
pint jars, leaving ^{1}/$_2$ inch at top for expansion. Top with hot, sterile
lids and process for 5 minutes in boiling-water bath after water
returns to boiling. If any jars fail to seal, refrigerate and use within ten
days. *Does not freeze well.* Makes about 2^1/$_2$ cups.
   Note: Store in dark, cool place to slow color fading.

Nutritional value: 1 tablespoon contains 16 Calories (P0,F0,C4). 1^2/$_3$
tablespoons = ^{1}/$_2$ diabetic fruit serving. If salt is omitted, 1 tablespoon
contains 1 milligram sodium. Recipe contains 0 cholesterol. 1 teaspoon can be used without diabetic replacement.

Orange Juice Jelly

Concentrated orange juice (frozen, undiluted)   1 cup
Water (or half white grape juice half water for sweeter jelly)
   $^3/_4$ cup
Lemon juice $1^1/_2$ teaspoons
Orange rind $^1/_4$ to $^1/_2$ teaspoon grated
Salt   dash (optional)
Agar-agar $^1/_3$ stick broken into small pieces **or**
Gelatin, unflavored $^1/_2$ teaspoon ($^1/_2$ envelope)
Water $^1/_2$ cup

Mix juices, water, and rind in nonaluminum kettle. Dissolve agar-agar or gelatin in $^1/_2$ cup water, heating to completely dissolve. Add to juices and heat to boiling. Pour into clean jars. Cover and refrigerate when cooled. Use within ten days to avoid spoilage. Or pour into hot, sterile $^1/_2$-pint jars, leaving $^1/_2$ inch at top. Cover with hot, sterile lids and process in boiling-water bath for 5 minutes after water returns to boiling. If any jars fail to seal, refrigerate and use within ten days. *Does not freeze well.* Makes 2 cups.

Nutritional value: 1 tablespoon contains 8 Calories (P0,F0,C2). $2^1/_2$ tablespoons = $^1/_3$ diabetic fruit exchange. If salt is omitted, 1 tablespoon contains less than 1 milligram sodium. Recipe contains 0 cholesterol. 2 teaspoons can be used without diabetic replacement.
   Note: Fruit juice mixtures such as orange-grapefruit or pineapple-grapefruit or orange-grapefruit may be substituted for the orange juice in this recipe.

Nutritional value: If made with pineapple-grapefruit juice, Calories and exchanges are the same as given for original recipe. 1 tablespoon contains 2 milligrams sodium. Recipe contains 0 cholesterol. 2 teaspoons can be used without diabetic replacement.

Fruit Syrups

Fruit Sauces and Syrups

Elegant and easy fruit syrups can be made from fruit and concentrated fruit juices, or by using less pectin in fruit jams. Low-methoxy pectin works so perfectly in making syrups; do try some. These all make excellent replacements for pancake and waffle syrups that contain sugar. They can be made without honey, making them usable for diabetics and hypoglycemics (see end of recipe).

Basic Fruit Juice Syrups

Concentrated fruit juice   1 cup
Water   1 cup, boiling
Lemon rind $\frac{1}{4}$ teaspoon grated (optional)
Lemon juice   1 tablespoon (optional)
Low-methoxy pectin solution $\frac{1}{4}$ cup
Calcium solution $1\frac{1}{4}$ teaspoons
Salt   Dash (optional)

Combine fruit juice, water, lemon rind, and lemon juice in saucepan. Add pectin solution and bring to a boil. Taste and add more lemon if desired. Add calcium solution after removing from heat. Pour into hot, sterile $\frac{1}{2}$-pint jars, leaving $\frac{1}{2}$ inch at top. Cap with hot, sterile lids and process in boiling-water bath for 5 minutes after water returns to boiling. If any jars fail to seal, refrigerate and use within ten days or freeze for later use.

To freeze, cool lidded jars to room temperature, then place in sharp-freeze section of freezer. Store in regular section. To use, thaw overnight in refrigerator.

To make with grape sauce, simmer 3 cups juice down to $1\frac{1}{2}$ cups and reduce water to $\frac{1}{2}$ cup. Makes $2\frac{1}{4}$ cups.

Apple juice syrup: $\frac{1}{4}$ cup contains 54 Calories (P0,F0,C13). $4\frac{1}{2}$

tablespoons = 1 diabetic fruit exchange. 1 tablespoon contains less than 1 milligram sodium. Recipe contains 0 cholesterol. 1 teaspoon can be used without diabetic replacement.

Grape juice syrup: $^1/_4$ cup contains 57 Calories (P0,F0,C14). $^1/_4$ cup = 1 diabetic fruit exchange. 1 tablespoon contains less than 1 milligram sodium. Recipe contains 0 cholesterol. 1 teaspoon can be used without diabetic replacement.

Orange juice syrup: $^1/_4$ cup contains 51 Calories (P0,F0,C12). Scant $^1/_3$ cup = 1 diabetic fruit exchange. 1 tablespoon contains less than 1 milligram sodium. Recipe contains 0 cholesterol. 1 teaspoon can be used without diabetic replacement.

Follow recipes in section using low-methoxy pectin: Apricot-Pineapple, Pineapple, or Strawberry Jam recipes will make good syrups (see Recipe Index). Reduce both pectin and calcium solution to $^1/_2$ amount required. Omit gelatin. Nutritional values will be unchanged from those given. Be sure to freeze or process canned sauces in boiling-water bath or pressure canner so that they will not spoil.

Superb Blueberry-Orange Syrup

Blueberries   4 cups washed, stems removed
Concentrated orange juice $^1/_2$ cup
Lemon juice   4 tablespoons
Lemon rind $^1/_4$ to $^1/_2$ teaspoon (optional)
Water $^1/_2$ cup
Low-methoxy pectin solution $^3/_8$ cup (6 tablespoons)
Calcium solution   scant 2 teaspoons
Nutmeg $^1/_4$ teaspoon (optional)
Salt   dash (optional)

Place fruit in deep nonaluminum kettle. Add juices, rind, and water and simmer until fruit is very soft. Stir in pectin (salt and spice). Return to boiling. Remove from heat and add calcium solution; skim. Pour into hot, sterile $^1/_2$-pint jars, leaving $^1/_2$ inch at top. Cap with hot, sterile lids. Process in boiling-water bath for 5 minutes after water returns to boiling. If any jars fail to seal, refrigerate and use within ten days or freeze for later use.

To freeze, pour into clean freezer containers or jars, leaving $1/2$ inch at top. Cover and cool to room temperature before placing in sharp-freeze section of freezer. Move to regular section of freezer for storage. Makes $5\frac{1}{2}$ cups.

Nutritional value: 1 tablespoon contains 8 Calories (P0,F0,C2). $7\frac{1}{2}$ tablespoons = 1 diabetic fruit exchange. If salt is omitted, 2 tablespoons contain less than 1 milligram sodium. Recipe contains 0 cholesterol. $1/2$ tablespoon may be used without diabetic replacement.

PICKLES, RELISHES, AND SEASONING SAUCES

Although pickles are traditionally thought of as sour, sweet pickles (and some not-so-sweet)—bread-and-butter pickles, sweet relish, catsup, chili, cocktail sauce, and many others—are all loaded with sugar, but they don't have to be; they can be made without any sugar at all if you don't mind a slightly less "sweet" pickle.

Grandmother probably packed her hot pickles into sterile jars, put on hot lids, and that was that. Today we think it wiser to process them in a boiling-water bath or pressure canner to make sure they are bacteria-free and can be stored indefinitely.

Pickles don't freeze well; they get soft and mushy. If canned, they stay firm and crisp. Relishes and sauces can be frozen, if freezer space is available and time is short, but they taste better to me when they've been processed.

I love pickles! Among the hardest things to give up when eliminating sugar from my diet were the family pickles. It took a while, but I have learned how to make them without sugar, and they are just as good. Some of these recipes are adapted from my family's recipes, and others have been given to me by friends.

Important: The time required to process pickles increases with altitude. The times given on the charts (and in the recipes) are for areas less than 1,000 feet high. For areas from 1,000 to 3,000 feet, add 5 minutes to recommended processing time. For areas at 3,000 to 6,000 feet, add 5 more minutes for quart-sized jars (no increase for smaller size); over 6,000 feet, add an additional 5 minutes for all sizes. If jar size is given, **don't use larger size without increasing processing time.** Example: If recipe calls for 5 minutes processing time, at 3,000 to 6,000 feet use 10 minutes processing time.

Important Things to Remember

1) Be sure to always use vinegar with at least 5 percent acidity. Cider vinegar has a milder taste than distilled white vinegar and is a better choice for all except light-colored pickles (such as onions).

2) Don't use zinc, copper, brass, galvanized metal, iron, or aluminum pans for pickling. These metals may react with acids (vinegar and lemon juice) and/or salt and affect the quality and safety of home-canned pickles. (This leaves stainless steel and porcelain-lined kettles as best choices.)

As with all home canned products, look for spoilage before using. If in doubt—throw it out!

Bread-and-Butter Pickles

Cucumbers   9 large or 12 medium
Onions   2 small or 8 pickling size
Coarse pickling salt $1/4$ cup
White grape juice   3 cups (simmered down from 6 cups)
Vinegar (pickling strength) $1 1/3$ cups
Whole mustard seed $2/3$ teaspoon
Celery seed $1/2$ teaspoon
Black pepper   1 teaspoon
Turmeric powder   scant $1/2$ teaspoon

Score cucumbers lengthwise with tines of fork. Cut into medium-thick slices (5 per inch or less); discard hard ends. Slice onions a bit thinner. Put both in bowl and cover with pickling salt. Mix so that all slices are covered and allow to stand for at least 30 minutes. Combine cucumbers, onions, fruit juice, and seasonings in large nonaluminum kettle. (Discard liquid that comes off cucumbers and onions as you transfer them to the kettle.) Heat to boiling and boil for about 8 minutes, until slices look slightly transparent. Pack immediately in hot, sterile pint jars, leaving $^{1}/_{2}$ inch at top. Seal with hot, sterile lids. Process in boiling-water bath for 15 minutes after water returns to boiling. (Refer to page 137 for times to use at altitudes higher than 1,000 feet.) If any jars fail to seal, refrigerate and use within ten days. *Do not freeze!* Makes 4 pints.

Variations: Cauliflower, celery stalks, carrot strips or slices, and green pepper slices all make good pickles. Prepare as above.

Nutritional value: $^{1}/_{4}$ cup contains 32 Calories (P0,F0,C8). $2^{1}/_{2}$ tablespoons = 20 calories (P0,F0,C5). $2^{1}/_{2}$ tablespoons = 1 diabetic vegetable exchange. This recipe cannot be made without salt and should not be used on a low-salt diet. Recipe contains 0 cholesterol.

Dilled Mushroom and Zucchini Pickles

Hot peppers or chili peppers (red or green)   3 to 6
White vinegar   1 quart
Water   1 cup
Noniodized pickling salt or salt substitute $^{1}/_{2}$ cup
Dill   3 teaspoons
Mushrooms   3 cups, in $^{1}/_{4}$-inch slices
Zucchini   3 cups, in $^{1}/_{8}$-inch slices
Small garlic cloves   6

Remove stems and seeds from peppers; cut in half if using 3. Combine vinegar, water, and salt in saucepan; bring to boil and keep hot. Place $^{1}/_{4}$ teaspoon dill in bottom of each of 6 sterilized pint jars.

Pack mushroom and zucchini slices into jars and add 1 garlic clove and $\frac{1}{2}$ to 1 hot pepper per jar. Pour hot vinegar liquid over vegetables, leaving at least $\frac{1}{2}$ inch at the top; add remaining $\frac{1}{4}$ teaspoon dill per jar and top with hot, sterile lids. Process in hot-water bath for 20 minutes after water returns to boiling. (Refer to page 137 for times to use at altitudes higher than 1,000 feet.) If any jars fail to seal, refrigerate and use within ten days. *Do not freeze!* Allow to age several weeks before opening. Serve chilled as relish, garnish, or finger food. Makes 6 pints.

Nutritional value: $\frac{1}{2}$ cup contains 28 Calories (P2,F0,C5). $\frac{1}{2}$ cup = 1 diabetic vegetable exchange. If made with salt substitute, $\frac{1}{2}$ cup will contain 3 milligrams sodium. Recipe contains 0 cholesterol.

Mustard Pickles

Cucumbers (tiny, 2 inches or less)   2 quarts
Pearl onions (tiny, white, peeled)   2 quarts
Green beans   2 quarts, trimmed, cut into thirds
Green tomatoes   2 quarts, quartered
Cauliflower   2 heads, cut into 1-inch buds
White cabbage   1 small head, coarsely chopped (optional)
Green peppers   6 small, coarsely chopped
Pickling salt $\frac{1}{4}$ cup
Turmeric powder   3 tablespoons (1 ounce)
Concentrated apple juice   2 cups (4 cups simmered down)
Cider vinegar   2 cups (more as needed)
Whole mustard seed   2 tablespoons
Celery seed   2 tablespoons
Whole cloves $\frac{1}{2}$ tablespoon
Whole allspice   1 tablespoon
Dry mustard $\frac{2}{3}$ cup
Whole wheat flour $\frac{3}{4}$ cup
Lemon juice $\frac{1}{4}$ cup (plus water if needed to dissolve flour)
Date sugar $\frac{1}{4}$ cup (optional)

Place cut vegetables in deep bowl, cover with salt, and mix so that pickling salt is evenly distributed. Place a weighted plate over vegetables so that they will stay down in bowl; let stand 24 hours. Drain, discarding liquid. Place apple juice and vinegar in large non-aluminum kettle and simmer to reduce volume even further—to about 3 cups total. Pour over drained vegetables and add spices and enough vinegar to completely cover. Place over heat and bring to a boil. Boil for 5 minutes or until vegetables are slightly soft but not mushy. Drain liquid and save. Make a thick paste with flour, lemon juice, and water. Add to liquid and cook until slightly thickened. Add vegetables (and sweetening, if desired) and heat through. Pack into hot, sterile pint jars, leaving $1/2$ inch at top. Cap with hot, sterile lids. Process for 20 minutes in boiling-water bath after water returns to boiling. (Refer to page 137 for times to use at altitudes higher than 1,000 feet.) If any jars fail to seal, refrigerate and use within ten days. *Do not freeze.* Makes about 16 pints, depending on the size you cut the vegetables.

Variations: Almost any vegetable can be pickled in this mixture. Try broccoli buds, zucchini slices, or chunks of yellow summer squash. It is also good made with wax beans and small pickling onions.

Nutritional value: $1/4$ cup contains 28 Calories (P2,F0,C5). $1/4$ cup = 1 diabetic vegetable exchange. This recipe cannot be made without salt and should not be used on a low-salt diet. Recipe contains no cholesterol.

Pickled Onions

Small white onions   5 cups
Salt or salt substitute   6 tablespoons
Hot water   1 quart
Pickling vinegar (distilled)   1 quart
Concentrated apple juice $1/4$ cup
Lemon juice   1 tablespoon

Whole black peppercorns $1^1/_2$ teaspoons
Whole cloves $1^1/_2$ teaspoons
Whole allspice $1^1/_2$ teaspoons

Place onions in boiling hot water for 10 minutes; drain and discard water. Remove outer skins of onions, add salt and onions to quart of boiling water. Bring to a boil; then remove from heat and allow to stand in the water for 12 hours. One hour before the standing time is up, combine vinegar, juices, and spices; simmer for $^3/_4$ hour. Drain onions, discarding liquid. Place onions in hot, sterile pint jars, leaving $^1/_2$ inch at top. Cover onions with boiling liquid, cap with hot, sterile lids, and process in boiling-water bath for 15 minutes. (Refer to page 137 for times to use at altitudes higher than 1,000 feet.) If any jars fail to seal, refrigerate and use within ten days. *Do not freeze!* Makes 3 pints.

Nutritional value: $^1/_3$ cup contains 20 Calories (P0,F0,C5). $^1/_3$ cup = 1 diabetic vegetable exchange. If salt is omitted, $^1/_3$ cup contains 4 milligrams sodium. Recipe contains 0 cholesterol.

Pickled Peaches

Small peaches, eating-ripe 8
White vinegar (distilled) 1 cup
Concentrated white grape juice 2 cups (simmered down from 4 cups)
Lemon juice 2 tablespoons
Cinnamon sticks 2, broken into pieces
Whole cloves 1 teaspoon

Drop fruit into boiling water for 1 minute, then into cold. Skins should peel off easily. Cut into halves and remove pits, saving 2 for each jar of peaches. Place remaining ingredients in nonaluminum kettle and bring to a boil. Reduce heat and gently drop in peaches, a few at a time. Simmer over low heat until fruit is tender, about 10 minutes. Drain, pack peach halves in hot, sterile pint jars (add a couple of pits to each for flavor), and cover with hot liquid, leaving $1/2$ inch at top. Seal with hot, sterile lids and process in boiling-water bath for 15 minutes after water has returned to boiling. (Refer to page 137 for times to use at altitudes higher than 1,000 feet.) If any jars fail to seal, refrigerate and use within ten days or freeze for later use. Makes 2 pints.

Variation: For brandied pickled peaches, add $1/2$ cup brandy when finished cooking.

Nutritional value: $3/4$ small peach + $1 1/2$ tablespoons liquid contain 60 Calories (P0,F0,C16). $3/4$ small peach ($1 1/2$ halves) + $1 1/2$ tablespoons juice = 1 diabetic fruit exchange. $3/4$ peach + $1 1/2$ tablespoons juice contain 3 milligrams sodium. Recipe contains 0 cholesterol.

Note: Medium-sized, ripe nectarines may also be pickled using the same recipe. Use only $1/2$ nectarine for same nutritional value as whole peach.

Fancy Spiced Pears

Pears, small, not overripe   4 pounds (10 to 12 or more)
Concentrated apple juice   1 cup
Concentrated white grape juice   1 cup (simmered down from 2 cups)
Cinnamon sticks   4 (broken into pieces)
Whole cloves   2 tablespoons
Peel from $1/2$ large lemon   cut into strips
Ginger root $1/2$ inch, sliced (optional)
Pickling vinegar $1 1/4$ cups
Red or green vegetable food coloring $1/2$ teaspoon (optional)

Peel, core, and halve pears. Place in deep saucepan and add juices; cover and simmer for 10 to 15 minutes until fruit is getting soft but not mushy. Place spices in small cloth bag and add to pears along with vinegar. Simmer for 5 minutes. Remove spice bag and add coloring if desired. Immediately pack into hot, sterile pint jars, cover with hot syrup leaving $1/2$ inch at top. Cover with hot, sterile lids and process in boiling-water bath for 15 minutes after water returns to boiling. (Refer to page 137 for times to use at altitudes higher than 1,000 feet.) If any jars fail to seal, refrigerate and use within ten days. *Do not freeze.* Makes 4 pints.

Nutritional value: $1/2$ small pear without syrup contains 60 Calories (P0,F0,C15), $1/2$ pear with juice (1 tablespoon) contains 64 Calories (P0,F0,C16). $1/2$ pear with 1 tablespoon juice = 1 diabetic fruit exchange. If salt is omitted, $1/2$ pear with 1 tablespoon juice contains 3 milligrams sodium. Recipe contains 0 cholesterol.

Celery Chutney

Celery   3 cups finely diced
Ripe tomatoes   6 cups chopped (or canned and omit 2
    teaspoons salt)
Green pepper $1/4$ cup finely diced
Medium onion   1, diced
Medium garlic clove   *1, minced*
Cider vinegar $1/2$ cup
Concentrated apple juice $1/2$ cup
Lemon juice   2 tablespoons
Salt or salt substitute   1 tablespoon (use 1 teaspoon if using
    canned tomatoes)
Black pepper $1/2$ teaspoon
Whole celery seed   1 teaspoon
Mustard seed $1/2$ teaspoon (optional)
Turmeric or mace $1/4$ teaspoon (optional)

Combine all ingredients in large nonaluminum kettle and simmer until thick, stirring often. Skim and pack immediately in hot, sterile pint jars, leaving $1/2$ inch at top. Cap with hot, sterile lids. Process in boiling-water bath for 15 minutes after water returns to boiling. (Refer to page 137 for times to use at altitudes higher than 1,000 feet.) If any jars fail to seal, refrigerate and use within ten days or freeze for later use. Makes 8 cups.

Nutritional value: 1 tablespoon contains 12 Calories (P0,F0,C3). $1^{1}/_{2}$ tablespoons = 1 diabetic vegetable exchange or $^{1}/_{3}$ bread exchange. If salt is omitted and fresh or salt-free canned tomatoes are used, 1 tablespoon contains 5 milligrams sodium. Recipe contains 0 cholesterol. 1 teaspoon can be used without diabetic replacement.

Chow Chow Relish

Green tomatoes   *4 cups chopped*
Large onions   2, chopped
Large green peppers   2, seeded and chopped
Hot red pepper   1, seeded and chopped
Salt or salt substitute   2 teaspoons
Whole cloves   6
Bay leaf   1, broken into pieces
Cinnamon   1 teaspoon
Allspice   1 teaspoon
Dry mustard   2 teaspoons
Pickling vinegar   1 cup
Concentrated apple juice   1 cup
Horseradish   2 tablespoons (optional)

Place tomatoes, onions, and peppers in large bowl. Sprinkle with salt and leave overnight. In the morning, drain liquid and discard. Place drained vegetables in deep nonaluminum kettle. Place cloves and bay leaf in small cloth bag. Add spice bag, other spices, vinegar, and apple juice to vegetables and simmer for 20 to 30 minutes until vegetables are tender and mixture has thickened. Add horseradish if desired and stir well. Remove spice bag and pack into hot, sterile pint jars, leaving $^{1}/_{2}$ inch at top for expansion. Cap with hot, sterile lids. Process in boiling-water bath for 15 minutes after water has returned to boiling. (Refer to page 137 for times to use at altitudes higher than 1,000 feet.) If any jars fail to seal, refrigerate and use within ten days or freeze for later use. Makes 8 cups

Nutritional value: 1 tablespoon contains 12 Calories (P1,F0,C2). $2^1/_2$ tablespoons = 1 diabetic vegetable exchange. If salt and horseradish are omitted, 1 tablespoon contains 9 milligrams sodium. Recipe contains 0 cholesterol. 1 teaspoon can be used without diabetic replacement.

Cucumber Catsup

Medium-large cucumbers   2
Large, tart apples   2 (including skin), cored and seeded
Medium onion   1
White grape juice $^1/_4$ cup
Horseradish   1 to 2 tablespoons grated
Concentrated apple juice $^1/_4$ cup
Lemon juice   2 teaspoons
Cider vinegar   1 cup
Salt or salt substitute $1^1/_2$ teaspoons
Black pepper $^1/_2$ teaspoon
Paprika $^1/_2$ teaspoon (optional)

Grind cucumbers, apples, and onion in meat grinder using coarse blade. (A food processor makes it too fine.) Place all in deep nonaluminum kettle. Add remaining ingredients and place over heat. Bring to a boil, then turn down and cook for 8 to 10 minutes until tender. Taste and adjust seasonings if desired. Pour into hot, sterile pint jars, leaving $^1/_2$ inch at top. Cap with hot, sterile lids and process in boiling-water bath for 15 minutes after water returns to boiling. (Refer to page 137 for times to use at altitudes higher than 1,000 feet.) If any jars fail to seal, refrigerate and use within ten days or freeze for later use. Makes 7 cups.

Nutritional value: 1 tablespoon contains 5 Calories (P0,F0,C1^1/4). ^{1}/4 cup = 1 diabetic vegetable exchange. If salt is omitted and horseradish used, ^{1}/4 cup contains less than 1 milligram sodium. Recipe contains 0 cholesterol. 2 teaspoons can be used without diabetic replacement.

Piccalilli

Tomatoes (green or slightly underripe)   8 cups ground
Red sweet peppers   3 large
Green peppers   2 large
Onions   5 medium
Apple   1 medium, peeled and cored
Celery   2 cups finely chopped or ground
Salt or salt substitute   1 tablespoon
Pickling vinegar   1^1/8 cups
Concentrated apple juice   1 cup
Concentrated white grape juice ^{1}/2 cup (simmered down
      from 1 cup)
Mustard seed ^{1}/2 teaspoon
Celery seed ^{3}/4 teaspoon
Allspice ^{1}/2 teaspoon
White pepper ^{1}/2 teaspoon
Garlic powder ^{1}/4 to ^{1}/2 teaspoon (optional)

Grind tomatoes, peppers, onions, apple, and celery in meat grinder using coarse blade. Place in large bowl, add salt, mix well, and allow to stand overnight. In the morning, drain and discard liquid. Place in large nonaluminum kettle and add remaining ingredients. Bring to a boil; then cook slowly for 1 hour, stirring frequently. If not thick enough, continue cooking up to 30 minutes longer. Pour into hot, sterile pint jars, leaving ^{1}/2 inch at top. Cap with hot, sterile lids and process in boiling-water bath for 15 minutes after water returns to boiling. (Refer to page 137 for times to use at altitudes higher than 1,000 feet.) If any jars fail to seal, refrigerate and use within ten days or freeze for later use. Makes 15 cups.

Nutritional value: 1 tablespoon contains 4 Calories (P0,F0,C1). 5 tablespoons = 1 diabetic vegetable exchange. If salt is omitted, 1 tablespoon contains 2 milligrams sodium. Recipe contains 0 cholesterol. 1 tablespoon can be used without diabetic replacement.

Salsa for Nachos (Mild or Hot)

Trial recipe:

Green pepper   1 cup seeded and chopped fine
Tomato (raw)   1 large, cored and chopped fine
Jalapeño or green chili peppers $1^1/_2$ cored, seeded

and chopped fine
Onion $^1/_4$ cup, chopped fine
Cider vinegar $1^1/_2$ tablespoons
Apple juice $^1/_2$ to 1 tablespoon
Salt $^1/_2$ teaspoon (optional)
Black pepper $^1/_4$ teaspoon ground
Chili powder $^1/_2$ teaspoon

For hot salsa, add:
Cayenne pepper $^1/_4$ to $^1/_2$ teaspoon, ground
Tabasco sauce $^1/_8$ to $^1/_4$ teaspoon

Combine ingredients (using lesser amounts where there is a choice) and mix well. Cover and refrigerate for 1–2 hours before tasting. If desired, add more of any of the seasonings, apple juice, or additional chopped onion to taste. Makes about 2 cups.

When you have modified the recipe to suit your taste, make a record of your final recipe for future use. Multiply ingredients by six to eight times to make a large batch for processing. Place ingredients in a deep nonaluminum kettle. Bring to a boil. Then pour into hot, sterile jars, leaving $1/2$ inch at top. Cover with hot, sterile lids and process for 15 minutes after water returns to boiling. (Refer to page 137 for times to use at altitudes higher than 1,000 feet.) If any fail to seal, refrigerate and use within ten days or freeze for later use.

Nutritional value: $1/3$ cup contains 17 Calories (P0,F0,C4). $1/3$ cup = 1 diabetic vegetable exchange. If salt is omitted, $1/3$ cup contains 5 milligrams sodium. Recipe contains 0 cholesterol. $1^1/3$ tablespoons can be used without diabetic replacement.

Spanish Barbecue Sauce

Tomatoes   4 cups chopped or ground
Green pepper $1/4$ cup seeded, chopped, or ground
Onion $1/2$ cup peeled, chopped, or ground
Dry mustard $1/2$ teaspoon
Salt or salt substitute   1 teaspoon
White grape juice $3/4$ cup
Lemon juice 2 tablespoons
Tabasco sauce $1/8$ teaspoon
Cayenne pepper   several sprinkles

Grind or chop vegetables as directed. Place in deep nonaluminum kettle; add remaining ingredients. Simmer for 20 minutes or until mixture is thick. (Put through food mill to remove seeds, if desired. Reheat before packing.) Pack into hot, sterile $1/2$-pint jars, leaving $1/2$ inch at top. Cap with hot, sterile lids. Process in boiling-water bath for 15 minutes after water has returned to boiling. (Refer to page 137 for times to use at altitudes higher than 1,000 feet.) If any jars fail to seal, refrigerate and use within ten days or freeze for later use. Makes 3 cups.

To freeze, set aside to cool and freeze in sharp-freeze area of freezer until hard.

Nutritional value: 1 tablespoon contains 6 Calories (P0,F0,C1$\frac{1}{2}$). 4 tablespoons = 1 diabetic vegetable exchange or $\frac{1}{3}$ bread exchange. If salt is omitted, 1 tablespoon contains 4 milligrams sodium. Recipe contains 0 cholesterol. 2 teaspoons can be used without diabetic replacement.

Tomato Catsup

Large, ripe tomatoes   12, peeled and cored
Large onions   2, peeled, finely chopped
Large green peppers   4, seeded, finely chopped
Pickling vinegar   4 cups
Concentrated apple juice   1 cup
Lemon juice   1$\frac{1}{2}$ tablespoons
Salt or salt substitute   2 tablespoons
Ginger   1 tablespoon
Cinnamon   1 tablespoon
Mustard   1 tablespoon
Nutmeg   1 teaspoon
Black pepper $\frac{1}{2}$ teaspoon

Place all ingredients in deep nonaluminum kettle. Bring to a boil and simmer until thick (about 3 hours), stirring often. Skim and pack immediately in hot, sterile pint jars, leaving $\frac{1}{2}$ inch at top. Cap with hot, sterile lids. Process for 15 minutes in boiling-water bath after water has returned to boiling. (Refer to page 137 for times to use at altitudes higher than 1,000 feet.) If any jars fail to seal, refrigerate and use within ten days or freeze for later use. Makes 8 cups.

Nutritional value: 1 tablespoon contains 8 Calories (P0,F0,C2). 2$\frac{1}{2}$ tablespoons = 1 diabetic vegetable exchange or $\frac{1}{3}$ bread exchange. If salt is omitted, 1 tablespoon contains 2 milligrams sodium. Recipe contains 0 cholesterol. 1$\frac{1}{2}$ teaspoons can be used without diabetic replacement.

Tomato Jam
(an old Australian recipe)

Ripe tomatoes   4 pounds
Large lemons   3
Concentrated apple juice   4 cups
Allspice $^1/_4$ teaspoon or Ginger and mace $^1/_4$ teaspoon each
Salt or salt substitute   1 teaspoon (optional)

Peel and chop tomatoes. Place in deep nonaluminum kettle. Peel lemons as thinly as possible; cut peel into shreds. Squeeze lemons; add juice and shredded peel to tomatoes. Add juice, spice, and salt and simmer until thick. Pack into hot, sterile pint jars leaving $^1/_2$ inch at top. Cover with hot, sterile lids and process in boiling-water bath for 15 minutes after the water returns to boiling. (Refer to page 137 for times to use at altitudes higher than 1,000 feet.) If any jars fail to seal, refrigerate and use within ten days or freeze for later use. Makes 10 cups.

Variations: You may use green instead of ripe tomatoes and oranges can be substituted for 2 of the lemons (use 2 oranges plus 1 lemon). The flavor is different, but the nutritional value is approximately the same.

Nutritional value: 1 tablespoon contains 4 Calories (P0,F0,C1). 5 tablespoons = 1 diabetic vegetable exchange or $^1/_3$ diabetic fruit exchange. If salt is omitted, 5 tablespoons contain less than 2 milligrams sodium. Recipe contains 0 cholesterol. 1 tablespoon can be used without diabetic replacement.

Tomato Sauce for Tacos

Ripe tomatoes   6 cups peeled, cored, and finely chopped
Garlic clove   1 large, minced
Onion $2^1/_2$ cups, finely chopped
Jalapeño pepper   1 to $1^1/_2$, seeded and finely chopped*

Green chiles   1 long, finely chopped
Cider vinegar   1 cup
Concentrated apple juice   1 tablespoon
Lemon juice $1/2$ teaspoon (optional)
Salt $1/4$ to $1/2$ teaspoon (optional)
Black pepper $1/4$ teaspoon ground
Oregano (dried)   1 tablespoon
Cumin   pinch (optional)

Combine all ingredients (using smaller amounts of seasonings where there is an option) in a deep nonaluminum kettle. Mix well and bring to a boil. Reduce heat and simmer until thick, stirring often. Taste; add remaining seasonings, if desired. Reheat to boiling if additions are made. Pour into hot, sterile pint jars leaving $1/2$ inch at top. Cap with hot, sterile lids. Process in boiling-water bath for 15 minutes after water returns to boiling. (Refer to page 137 for times to use at altitudes higher than 1,000 feet.) If any jars fail to seal, refrigerate and use within ten days or freeze for later use. Makes about 8 cups.

Nutritional value: 2 tablespoons contain 6 Calories (P0,F0,C1$1/2$). 3$1/2$ tablespoons = 1 diabetic vegetable exchange. If salt is omitted, 2 tablespoons contain 2 milligrams sodium. Recipe contains 0 cholesterol. 1$1/2$ tablespoons can be used without diabetic replacement.

MEATLESS MINCEMEAT

An early 1800s cookbook refers to the ingredients for mincemeat as "a good piece of lean beef, boiled the day before it is needed. Half a pound of raw suet, chopped fine may be added . . . mix with twice the quantity of fine juicy apples . . . then put in the fruit, next the

*For mild sauce, use 1 pepper; for medium sauce, use 1$1/4$ peppers; and for fairly hot sauce, increase to 1$1/2$. For really hot sauce, use 2 and add $1/2$ teaspoon Tabasco sauce.

sugar and spice and lastly the liquor (brandy)." Other early recipes call for suet only, omitting lean beef. These recipes go one step further and omit the suet as well—creating vegetarian mincemeat!

Commercial mincemeat is very high in sugar. Make your own without added sweetening or use modest amounts of honey (see recipe index); the results will be very good. You'll need a meat grinder (a food processor does not make the right size pieces), patience, and the time to put it all together. Mincemeat can be frozen without processing. Put it into a tightly covered container and sharp-freeze, moving to another area in the freezer when hard. Thaw overnight in refrigerator before use. If you prefer to can your mincemeat (limited freezer space?), follow directions given, adding time for altitudes over 1,000 feet.

Basic Sugarless Vegetarian Mincemeat

Apple pulp   3 cups coarsely ground (including some skins)
Large lemon $1/2$, coarsely ground, including peel
Medium orange   1, coarsely ground, including peel
Seedless raisins   1 cup coarsely ground
Whole seedless raisins   1 cup
Currants   1 cup
Cinnamon   2 teaspoons
Nutmeg $3/4$ teaspoon
Cloves $3/4$ teaspoon
Allspice $3/4$ teaspoon (optional)
Salt $1/2$ teaspoon (optional)
Flour   2 tablespoons *or Arrowroot flour*   1 tablespoon
Date sugar $1/4$ cup (optional)
Brandy $1/3$ cup *or Rum flavoring* $1 1/2$ teaspoons (optional)

Quarter and core apples, but do not peel. Grind in old-fashioned meat grinder (food processor makes them too fine), using medium-coarse blade. Remove seeds from lemon and orange, grind, and add to apples. Grind 1 cup raisins. Mix all ingredients (except brandy or rum flavoring) in large bowl, stirring in spices and flour, then date sugar if desired. Add brandy or rum flavoring and mix again. Place in covered bowl or other container with tight lid; refrigerate at least one week before using.

If you wish to make this some time ahead, allow to stand for the recommended week before pouring into hot, sterile pint or quart jars, leaving $1/2$ inch at top. Cap with hot, sterile lids and process in boiling-water bath 20 minutes for pints (25 for quarts) after water returns to boiling. (Refer to page 137 for times to use at altitudes higher than 1,000 feet.) If any jars fail to seal, freeze for later use.

To freeze after refrigerating for the recommended week, place in clean freezing containers or jars, leaving $1/2$ inch at top. Cover with clean lids and place in sharp-freeze section of freezer until frozen. Move to another area of the freezer for storage. Thaw overnight in the refrigerator before using. Makes 1 quart, enough for 2 8-inch pies.

Note: This recipe is both vegetarian and sugarless. Most of the alcohol in brandy and rum flavoring evaporates during baking, so you do not have to allow for those calories; however, you may omit them entirely.

Nutritional value: $1/4$ cup contains 116 Calories (P1,F0,C28). $1/4$ cup equals 2 diabetic fruit exchanges. If salt is omitted, $1/4$ cup contains 7 milligrams sodium. Recipe contains 0 cholesterol.

Green Tomato Mincemeat

Green tomatoes   4 cups, peeled and chopped or coarsely ground
Apples   4 cups, cored, seeded, and chopped (half unpeeled)
Seedless raisins   4 cups (2 cups coarsely ground)
Currants   2 cups
Date sugar   8 tablespoons
Medium lemon $1/2$, including peel, coarsely ground
Cinnamon   1 tablespoon
Nutmeg $1 1/2$ teaspoons
Cloves $3/4$ teaspoon

Allspice $^1/_2$ teaspoon (optional)
Salt   1 teaspoon
Flour   3 tablespoons
Brandy $^1/_2$ cup *or Rum flavoring*   2 teaspoons
Lemon juice   2 tablespoons

Grind ingredients as directed for Basic Mincemeat, combining in large bowl. Stir to mix evenly. Add remaining ingredients, mixing after each addition. Place in covered container and refrigerate at least overnight or several days if not needed immediately. This may be canned or frozen for future use but *is better fresh.*

To process, pour into hot, sterile pint or quart jars, leaving $^1/_2$ inch at top. Cover with hot, sterile lids and process in boiling-water bath for 20 minutes for pints (25 minutes for quarts) after water returns to boiling. (Refer to page 137 for times to use at altitudes higher than 1,000 feet.) If any jars fail to seal, refrigerate and use within ten days or freeze for later use.

To freeze, pour into clean freezing containers or jars, leaving $^1/_2$ inch at top. Cover with clean lids and allow to cool to room temperature before placing in the sharp-freeze section of the freezer. When hard, move to other section for storage. Thaw overnight in the refrigerator before using. Makes 15 cups.

Nutritional value: $^1/_4$ cup contains 62 Calories (P1$^1/_2$,F0,C15). $^1/_4$ cup = 1 diabetic fruit exchange. If salt is omitted, $^1/_4$ cup contains 5 milligrams sodium. Recipe contains 0 cholesterol.

WINTER RECIPES

Canning and preserving don't have to be limited to summer months. Foods are available all year long that can be used to make good jams, jellies, and pickles. Citrus fruits (their peak season is during winter, not summer), winter pears, winter grapes, late fall apples, cabbage, cucumbers, celery, green peppers, and onions are in the market year-round. So you see there are a number of foods that can be used, plus the frozen fruits and vegetables that we can buy all year. They will be more expensive than if purchased in season, but they will still taste good.

I have called these "Winter" recipes, but they are really "Year-Round" treats, and can be made any time with what is normally in the grocery store.

Berry Applesauce

Berry Puree (see below)   8 cups
Applesauce   5 cups (unsweetened, plain)
Lemon juice $2^{1}/_{2}$ to 3 tablespoons
Lemon rind $^{1}/_{2}$ to $^{1}/_{3}$ teaspoon grated
Salt   dash
Red food color $^{1}/_{2}$ teaspoon (optional)

Puree: Cook together 8 cups frozen berries, 1 cup concentrated apple juice, and 1 cup water. Simmer until soft, mashing berries to be sure there are no large pieces left. When fruit is very soft, puree in food mill to remove some of the seeds **or** place in jelly bag and squeeze to get all the pulp and juice from the fruit (this will make a smaller amount of puree).

Combine all ingredients except food color and heat to boiling. Taste and add more lemon juice, lemon rind, or if not sweet enough, add a small amount of concentrated apple juice. Mix well, add coloring, and pour into hot, sterile pint jars, leaving $^{1}/_{2}$ inch at top. Cap with hot, sterile lids and process in boiling-water bath for 20 minutes after water returns to boiling. (Refer to page 137 for times to use at altitudes higher than 1,000 feet.) If any jars fail to seal, refrigerate and use within 10 days or freeze for later use.

To freeze, pour into clean freezing containers or jars, leaving $^{1}/_{2}$ inch at top. Cover with clean lids and cool to room temperature before placing in sharp-freeze section of freezer. When frozen, move to another part of the refrigerator for storage. Thaw overnight before using. Makes $12\frac{1}{2}$–13 cups.

Nutritional value: $\frac{1}{2}$-cup serving contains 56 Calories (P0,F0,C14). $\frac{1}{2}$ cup = 1 diabetic fruit exchange. If salt is omitted, $\frac{1}{2}$ cup contains 3 milligrams sodium. Recipe contains 0 cholesterol.

Applesauce Apple Butter

White grape juice   2 cups
Unsweetened applesauce   4 cups
Concentrated apple juice $1\frac{1}{4}$ to $1\frac{1}{2}$ cups (use larger
    amount for sweeter butter)
Cinnamon   2 teaspoons, ground
Cloves $\frac{1}{3}$ teaspoon, ground
Allspice $\frac{1}{3}$ teaspoon, ground
Lemon rind   1 teaspoon, grated fresh
Lemon juice $1\frac{1}{2}$ to 2 tablespoons

Simmer grape juice over low heat in deep nonaluminum kettle until reduced to half volume. Add next two ingredients, stirring to mix. Return to heat and bring to a boil; then turn down heat and simmer until slightly thickened, stirring frequently. Remove from heat, stir in remaining ingredients, and continue to simmer, stirring often. After 5 minutes, taste and add additional apple juice and/or lemon juice if desired. Continue to cook until butter reaches the desired thickness, stirring frequently. Pour into hot, sterile pint jars, leaving $\frac{1}{2}$ inch at top. Cap with hot, sterile lids. Process in boiling-water bath for 20 minutes after water returns to boiling. (Refer to page 137 for times to use at altitudes higher than 1,000 feet.) If any jars fail to seal, refrigerate and use within ten days or freeze for later use. Makes $5\frac{1}{2}$ cups.

Nutritional value: 1 tablespoon contains 15 Calories (P0,F0,C4). 2 tablespoons = $\frac{1}{2}$ diabetic fruit exchange. 1 tablespoon contains 1 milligram sodium. Recipe contains 0 cholesterol. $^2/_3$ teaspoon can be used without diabetic substitution.

Christmastime Marmalade

Medium grapefruit   1, seeded, with juice
Whole orange   1, seeded, with juice
Oranges   3 (pulp only), seeded, with juice
Tangerine   1, seeded, with juice
Lemon $^1/_2$, seeded, with juice
Concentrated apple juice   1$^1/_2$ cups
White grape juice $^1/_2$ cup
Lemon juice   3 tablespoons
Unflavored gelatin   1 tablespoon (1 envelope)
Low-methoxy pectin solution   1 cup
Calcium solution   5 teaspoons
Salt   dash (optional)

Slice all fruit very thin, including rinds, except from 3 oranges. Place all fruit in deep nonaluminum kettle, add juices, and simmer until cooked and rinds look translucent, stirring often. Add small amount of water if needed to keep from getting too thick while cooking. Remove from heat and sprinkle gelatin over hot liquid, stirring to be sure it dissolves. Stir in pectin, then calcium solution and salt. Pour into hot, sterile $^1/_2$-pint jars, leaving $^1/_2$ inch at top. Cap with hot, sterile lids and process in boiling-water bath for 5 minutes after water returns to boiling. If any jars fail to seal, refrigerate and use within ten days or freeze for later use. Makes 6$^1/_2$ cups.

Nutritional value: 1 tablespoon contains 18 Calories (P0,F0,C4$^1/_2$). 1$^3/_4$ tablespoons = $^1/_2$ diabetic fruit exchange. If salt is omitted, 2 tablespoons contain less than 1 milligram sodium. Recipe contains 0 cholesterol. $^2/_3$ teaspoon may be used without diabetic replacement.

Frostberry Jam

Whole frozen berries   2 cups
White grape juice   1 cup
Lemon juice $2^1/_2$ tablespoons
Lemon rind $^1/_4$ teaspoon grated
Low-methoxy pectin solution $^1/_2$ cup
Unflavored gelatin   1 tablespoon (1 envelope)
Salt   dash (optional)
Calcium solution $2^1/_2$ teaspoons

Place frozen berries, juices, and rind in a deep nonaluminum kettle. Simmer until berries are barely cooked—about 5 minutes. Mash berries to break up any large pieces. Stir in pectin, gelatin, and salt. Return to heat, bring to a boil, then add calcium solution and remix. Skim and pour into hot, sterile pint jars, leaving $^1/_2$ inch at top. Cap with hot, sterile lids. Process in boiling-water bath for 5 minutes, after water returns to boiling. If any jars fail to seal, refrigerate and use within ten days or freeze for later use.

If you plan to freeze, omit boiling-water processing. Allow capped, filled jars to reach room temperature; then place in sharp-freeze section of freezer until hard. Store in main part of freezer. Thaw overnight in refrigerator before using. Makes $3^1/_2$ cups.

Note: Any frozen sweet berries (or mixtures of berries) can be used to make this jam. You may wish to add more lemon or some spice with some berries—taste after cooking and add whatever you prefer.

Nutritional value: 1 tablespoon contains 8 Calories (P0,F0,C2). $2^1/_2$ tablespoons = $^1/_3$ diabetic fruit exchange. If salt is omitted, $2^1/_2$ tablespoons contain less than 1 milligram sodium. Recipe contains 0 cholesterol. $1^1/_2$ teaspoons can be used without diabetic replacement.

Jam-Pot Jam

Odds and ends of fruit (canned peaches, apricots, pears, etc.) 3 cups
White grape juice 1 cup
Lemon juice 2 tablespoons
Lemon 1 slice, seeded and chopped
Whole cloves 6 to 8 (optional) **or Allspice (to taste)**
Low-methoxy pectin solution $^1/_2$ cup
Unflavored gelatin 1 tablespoon (1 envelope)
Calcium solution $2^1/_2$ teaspoons
Salt dash (optional)

Drain fruit and chop into small pieces, saving juice. Place fruit, juice drained from it before chopping, other juices, lemon, and cloves (or spice) in deep saucepan. Simmer until fruit is very soft and lemon pieces are translucent. Stir in pectin and gelatin, mix well, and return to heat. Bring to a boil; then remove from heat and add calcium solution and salt. Pour into hot, sterile $^1/_2$-pint jars, leaving $^1/_2$ inch at top. Cap with hot, sterile lids and process in boiling-water bath for 5 minutes after water returns to boiling. If any jars fail to seal, refrigerate and use within ten days or freeze for later use.

If you plan to freeze, pour into clean freezer containers or jars, cap with clean lids, and allow to cool to room temperature before placing in sharp-freeze section of freezer. When frozen, move to another section of freezer for storage. To use, thaw overnight in refrigerator. Makes 3 cups.

Note: Accumulate fruit in a jar in refrigerator, adding leftovers from various fruits until there is enough for a batch of jam. Each batch will be different and, of course, allspice, cinnamon, nutmeg, and other spices can be added to suit your taste.

Nutritional value: 1 tablespoon contains 8 to 12 Calories (P0,F0,C2–3) depending on fruits used. $^1/_2$ to $3^1/_2$ tablespoons = $^1/_3$ to $^1/_2$ diabetic fruit exchanges. If salt is omitted, 1 tablespoon will contain less than 1 milligram sodium. Recipe contains 0 cholesterol. 1–1$^1/_2$ teaspoons can be used without diabetic replacement.

Pineapple Jam

Crushed or chunk-style pineapple   1 cup (canned in own juice)
Canned pineapple juice $^3/_4$ cup
Lemon juice   1 tablespoon
Lemon rind $^1/_4$ teaspoon grated
Low-methoxy pectin solution $^1/_2$ cup
Unflavored gelatin   1–2 tablespoons* (1–2 envelopes)
Calcium solution   2 $^1/_2$ teaspoons
Salt   dash (optional)

Place pineapple in blender and blend until no large chunks are left. Combine with other juices and rind in a deep nonaluminum saucepan. Heat until boiling. Stir in pectin and half of the gelatin and bring to a boil again. Remove from heat and mix in calcium solution. Pour into hot, sterile $^1/_2$-pint jars, leaving $^1/_2$ inch at top. Cap with hot, sterile lids. Process in boiling-water bath for 5 minutes after water returns to boiling. If any jars fail to seal, refrigerate and use within ten days or freeze for later use. Makes 2 $^1/_2$ cups.

Nutritional value: 2 tablespoons contain 16 Calories (P0,F0,C4). 2$^1/_2$ tablespoons = $^1/_3$ diabetic fruit exchange. If salt is omitted, 2$^1/_2$ tablespoons contain less than 1 milligram sodium. Recipe contains 0 cholesterol. 1$^1/_2$ teaspoons can be used without diabetic replacement.

Pineapple Marmalade
Pineapple jam can be made into more of a marmalade by blending in $^1/_4$ minced, medium-sized seeded lemon (including peel).

---

*Use total amount for thick jam.

Cook this in the fruit juice called for plus an extra $\frac{1}{4}$ cup of pineapple juice until lemon is soft. Then add pineapple and other ingredients (except pectin and calcium solutions), including $\frac{1}{2}$ cup water. Process as directed. Makes $2\frac{1}{2}$ cups.

Nutritional value: 2 tablespoons contain 11 Calories (P0,F0,C3). $3\frac{1}{2}$ tablespoons = $\frac{1}{3}$ diabetic fruit exchange. If salt is omitted, 2 tablespoons = less than 1 milligram sodium. Recipe contains 0 cholesterol. 1 teaspoon can be used without diabetic substitution.

Tomato-Pineapple Jam

Canned whole peeled tomatoes with juice   2 cups chopped
Crushed pineapple   1 cup (in own juice)
Lemon juice   2 tablespoons
Concentrated apple juice   1 cup
White grape juice $\frac{1}{2}$ cup
Lemon slices   2, seeded and minced
Cream of tartar $\frac{1}{16}$ teaspoon

Place tomatoes with juice in deep nonaluminum kettle. Add pineapple, juices, and lemon slices. Boil for an hour or longer over low heat, until thickened. Stir often to prevent sticking. Remove from heat and add cream of tartar, stirring well. Skim and pour into hot, sterile $\frac{1}{2}$-pint jars, leaving $\frac{1}{2}$ inch at top. Cap with hot, sterile lids and process in boiling-water bath for 15 minutes after water returns to boiling. (Refer to page 137 for times to use at altitudes higher than 1,000 feet.) If any jars fail to seal, refrigerate and use within ten days. Makes $2\frac{1}{2}$ cups.
Note: This recipe does not freeze well.

Nutritional value: 1 tablespoon contains 16 Calories (P0,F0,C4). Scant 2 tablespoons = $\frac{1}{2}$ diabetic fruit exchange. If salt is omitted and salt-free tomatoes are used, 1 tablespoon contains 1 milligram sodium. Recipe contains 0 cholesterol. $^2/_3$ teaspoon can be used without diabetic replacement.

Cranberry Jelly

Cranberries   2 cups
Concentrated apple juice   1 cup
Lemon juice $^1/_4$ cup
Liquid pectin (regular)   3 ounces ($^1/_2$ package)
Glycerine   5 tablespoons
Unflavored gelatin   1–2 tablespoons* (1–2 envelopes)

Wash and pick over cranberries, discarding any that are soft. Place in a deep saucepan and add fruit juices. Cover and simmer for about 20 minutes, until fruit is soft. Mash to break up any berries left whole. Strain in food mill to remove seeds. Return to saucepan and heat to boiling. Add pectin, glycerine, and gelatin, stirring well. Boil for 1 minute. Remove from heat. Skim and pour into hot, sterile pint jars, leaving $^1/_2$ inch at top. Cap with hot, sterile lids. Process in boiling-water bath for 5 minutes after water returns to boiling. If any jars fail to seal, refrigerate and use within ten days or freeze for later use. Makes $3^1/_2$ cups.

Variation: You can substitute $^1/_2$ cup low-methoxy pectin solution and $2^1/_2$ teaspoons calcium solution for the liquid pectin and glycerine, but add calcium after removing from heat. If you plan to freeze the jelly, be sure to use the full amount of gelatin.

Nutritional value: 1 tablespoon contains 20 Calories (P0,F0,C5). $1^1/_2$ tablespoons = $^1/_2$ diabetic fruit exchange or $^1/_2$ bread exchange. If salt is omitted, $1^1/_2$ tablespoons contain less than 1 milligram sodium. Recipe contains 0 cholesterol. $^1/_2$ teaspoon can be used without diabetic replacement.

---

*Use full amount for very firm jam or for freezing.

Grape Juice Jelly

Unsweetened grape juice   3 cups (2 cups Concord plus 1 cup
   white grape juice)
Lemon juice   1 tablespoon
Low-methoxy pectin solution $^1/_2$ cup
Unflavored gelatin   1 tablespoon (1 envelope)
Calcium solution $2^1/_2$ teaspoons
Salt   dash (optional)

Simmer grape juice down to 2 cups; then stir in lemon juice,
pectin, and gelatin, mixing well. Bring to a boil, remove from heat,
and add calcium solution and salt. Pour into hot, sterile $^1/_2$-pint jars,
leaving $^1/_2$ inch at top. Cap with hot, sterile lids and process in boiling-water bath for 5 minutes after water returns to boiling. If any jars
fail to seal, refrigerate and use within ten days or freeze for later use.
Makes $2^1/_2$ cups.

Nutritional value: 1 tablespoon contains 16 Calories (P0,F0,C4).
Scant 2 tablespoons = $^1/_2$ diabetic fruit exchange. If salt is omitted, 2
tablespoons contain less than 1 milligram sodium. Recipe contains 0
cholesterol. $^2/_3$ teaspoon can be used without diabetic replacement.

Herb Jelly

Herb Infusion (see below)   *2 cups*
Cider vinegar $^1/_4$ cup
Concentrated apple juice   2 cups
Lemon juice   2 tablespoons
Low-methoxy pectin solution   1 cup
Calcium solution   5 teaspoons
Green vegetable coloring $^1/_4$ teaspoon (optional)

Place 2 cups herb infusion, vinegar, and juices in deep nonaluminum kettle. Stir in pectin and heat to boiling. Add calcium solution

and coloring; mix well. Pour into hot, sterile pint jars, leaving $1/2$ inch at top. Cap with hot, sterile lids. Process in boiling-water bath for 5 minutes after water returns to boiling. If any jars fail to seal, refrigerate and use within ten days. Makes $5^1/2$ cups.

Note: This jelly does not freeze well.

Nutritional value: 1 tablespoon contains 12 Calories (P0,F0,C3). $2^1/2$ tablespoons = $1/2$ diabetic fruit exchange. $1/2$ cup contains 1 milligram sodium. Recipe contains 0 cholesterol. 1 teaspoon can be used without diabetic replacement.

Note: This jelly is a nice accompaniment for meat, fish, or poultry.

Herb Infusion

Pour $2^1/2$ cups boiling water over 4 tablespoons dried or 1 cup fresh chopped herbs, leaves, and stems (use basil, marjoram, rosemary, thyme, or Italian herb mix). Let stand 15 to 20 minutes. Strain through fine strainer to remove herbs. Makes $2^1/2$ cups.

Note: This can be frozen but is much better made fresh. It will keep for several days in the refrigerator, stored in a sterile jar capped with a sterile lid.

Nutritional value: Negligible [maximum per $1/2$ cup = 2 Calories (P0,F0,C$1/2$), 0 milligram sodium, 25 milligrams potassium]. No diabetic replacement required. Recipe contains 0 cholesterol.

Mint Jelly

Apple juice 2 cups
Lemon juice 1 tablespoon
Mint extract $1/4$ teaspoon *or Fresh mint* 2 large sprigs
Green vegetable coloring $1/4$ teaspoon (optional)
Low-methoxy pectin solution $1/2$ cup
Calcium solution $2^1/2$ teaspoons

Place apple juice, lemon juice, and mint in saucepan and bring to a quick boil. Add green food color and pectin. Stir well to dissolve; return to heat and bring liquids to a boil. Remove from heat and add calcium solution. Stir well. Pour into hot, sterile $\frac{1}{2}$-pint jars, leaving $\frac{1}{2}$ inch at top. Cap with hot, sterile lids. Process in boiling-water bath 5 minutes after water returns to boiling. If any jars fail to seal, refrigerate and use within ten days. Makes $2\frac{1}{2}$ cups.

Note: This jelly does not freeze well.

Variations: This jelly can be flavored with other herbs as well. Try geranium leaves, or sprigs of thyme, or rosemary.

Nutritional value: 1 tablespoon contains 8 Calories (P0,F0,C2). $2\frac{1}{2}$ tablespoons = $\frac{1}{3}$ diabetic fruit exchange. If salt is omitted, $2\frac{1}{2}$ tablespoons contain less than 1 milligram sodium. Recipe contains 0 cholesterol. $1\frac{1}{2}$ teaspoons can be used without diabetic replacement.

Dried Apricot-Pineapple Preserves

Crushed pineapple   1 cup (canned in own juice), drained
Large lemon $\frac{1}{4}$ to $\frac{1}{3}$, seeded and finely chopped
   (including juice)
Canned pineapple juice   1 cup
Dried apricots $1\frac{1}{2}$ pounds, diced
Salt   dash (optional)

Drain pineapple, set aside; add pineapple juice to other juices and use to soak apricots, adding enough water to cover fruit. Soak at least 2 hours (overnight is even better), then place in deep saucepan and simmer for 20 minutes, stirring often. Add remaining ingredients and continue to cook until thick. Taste, adding more lemon if desired.

Remove from the heat and pack into hot, sterile $\frac{1}{2}$-pint or pint jars, leaving $\frac{1}{2}$ inch at the top. Cap with hot, sterile lids; process in boiling-water bath for 5 minutes after water returns to boiling.

To freeze, pour hot jam into clean containers or jars; top with clean lids and cool to room temperature before placing in sharp-freeze section. Move to other section for storage. To use, thaw overnight in refrigerator. Makes 4 cups.

Variations: Use mixtures of dried fruits to vary the flavor of these preserves; for example, dried peaches in place of half the apricots.

Nutritional value: 1 tablespoon contains 28 Calories (P0,F0,C7). 1 tablespoon = $^1/_2$ diabetic fruit exchange. If salt is omitted, 1 tablespoon contains less than $^1/_2$ milligram sodium. Recipe contains 0 cholesterol.

Dried Peach Preserves

Dried peaches   2 pounds, coarsely chopped
Apple-pear juice $3^1/_2$ cups
Lemon juice   3 tablespoons
Orange juice $^3/_4$ cup
Seedless raisins   1 cup chopped
Orange   1, sliced paper thin, seeded
Salt   dash (optional)
Walnuts or pecans   1 cup chopped

Soak dried peaches in juices overnight. In the morning, place in deep nonaluminum pan and add remaining ingredients except chopped nuts. Cook over low heat until thick, stirring frequently to prevent sticking. Add nuts and remove from heat. Pour into hot, sterile pint jars, leaving $^1/_2$ inch at top. Cap with hot, sterile lids. Process in boiling-water bath for 5 minutes after water returns to boiling. If any jars fail to seal, refrigerate and use within ten days or freeze for later use. Makes $8^1/_2$ to 9 cups.

Note: If apple-pear juice blend is not available, substitute $^2/_3$ apple juice and $^1/_3$ white grape juice.

Nutritional value: 1 tablespoon contains 27 Calories (P0,F$\frac{1}{2}$,C5$\frac{1}{2}$). Scant tablespoon = $\frac{1}{3}$ diabetic fruit exchange. If salt is omitted, 1 tablespoon contains less than 1 milligram sodium. Recipe contains 0 cholesterol. $\frac{1}{2}$ teaspoon can be used without diabetic replacement.

Extra Good Apricot Butter

Dried apricots   1 pound
White grape juice   1 cup
Concentrated apple juice   1 cup
Lemon juice   2 tablespoons
Large lemon   1, seeded and chopped
Cinnamon   1 teaspoon
Cloves $\frac{1}{2}$ teaspoon
Allspice $\frac{1}{4}$ teaspoon (optional)
Salt   dash (optional)

Soak dried fruit overnight in fruit juices with enough water added to cover. In morning, add chopped lemon and place in blender to soften hard pieces. Cook over low heat until fruit tastes cooked, about 8 minutes, stirring often. Add spices and simmer until thick, about 10 minutes longer. Pour into hot, sterile $\frac{1}{2}$-pint jars, leaving $\frac{1}{2}$ inch at top. Cap with hot, sterile lids; process in boiling-water bath for 5 minutes after water returns to boiling. If any jars fail to seal, refrigerate and use within ten days or freeze for later use.

If you plan to freeze, cool covered jars to room temperature; then place in sharp-freeze section of freezer. When hard, move to other area of freezer for storage. To use, thaw overnight in refrigerator. Makes 5 cups.

Nutritional value: 1 tablespoon contains 16 Calories (P0,F0,C4). Scant 2 tablespoons = $\frac{1}{2}$ diabetic fruit exchange. If salt is omitted, 1 tablespoon contains 2 milligrams sodium. Recipe contains 0 cholesterol. $\frac{2}{3}$ teaspoon can be used without diabetic replacement.

Lemony Prune Butter

Medium prunes $^3/_4$ cup
Concentrated apple juice   1 cup
Large lemon $^1/_4$, seeded, finely chopped or ground, with juice
Cinnamon $^1/_2$ (add $^1/_2$ more when cooking, if desired)
Salt   dash (optional)

Soak prunes overnight in apple juice. Drain, saving liquid. Remove pits. Place prunes in a deep nonaluminum saucepan; add remaining ingredients and reserved liquid. Simmer over low heat until thickened, mashing to break up any prune pieces, if needed. Taste. Add more cinnamon if stronger flavor is desired. When thickened, pour into hot, sterile $^1/_2$-pint jars, leaving $^1/_2$ inch at top. Cap with hot, sterile lids. Process in boiling-water bath for 5 minutes after water returns to boiling. If any jars fail to seal, refrigerate and use within ten days or freeze for later use.

If you planto freeze, cool filled jars to room temperature; then place in sharp-freeze section of freezer until hard, storing in regular section. To use, thaw overnight in refrigerator. Makes $2^1/_4$ cups.

Variations: Try the spice combination suggested for Applesauce or Apple Butter (see Recipe Index) but in reduced amounts, or try adding nutmeg.

Nutritional value: 1 tablespoon contains 24 Calories (P0,F0,C6). $2^1/_2$ tablespoons = 1 diabetic fruit exchange. If salt is omitted, $2^1/_2$ tablespoons contain 1 milligram sodium. Recipe contains 0 cholesterol. $^1/_2$ teaspoon can be used without diabetic replacement.

Raisin-Apple Spread

Seedless raisins   1 cup
Boiling water   2 tablespoons
Concentrated apple juice $^1/_4$ cup, boiling hot

Lemon juice   2 tablespoons
Unsweetened applesauce (see Recipe Index)   1 cup
Cinnamon $^1/_2$ teaspoon
Cloves $^1/_4$ teaspoon
Lemon rind $^1/_2$ teaspoon grated
Salt   dash (optional)

Soak raisins in water and juices for at least 15 minutes. Put into blender and run at medium speed until all are pureed. Combine with remaining ingredients and cook over low heat until quite thick, stirring often to prevent sticking. Taste. Add more spices if desired. Pour into hot, sterile $^1/_2$-pint jars, leaving $^1/_2$ inch at top. Cap with hot, sterile lids. Process in boiling-water bath for 5 minutes after water returns to boiling. If any jars fail to seal, refrigerate and use within ten days or freeze for later use. Makes 2 cups.

Nutritional value: 1 tablespoon contains 20 Calories (P0,F0,C5). 1$^1/_2$ tablespoons = $^1/_2$ diabetic fruit exchange. If salt is omitted, 1$^1/_2$ tablespoons contain less than 1 milligram sodium. Recipe contains 0 cholesterol. $^1/_2$ teaspoon can be used without diabetic replacement.

Delicious Pickled Vegetable Salad

Concentrated apple juice $^1/_4$ cup
Cider vinegar $^2/_3$ cup
Salt or salt substitute   1 teaspoon
Celery seed   1 teaspoon
Mustard seeds $^1/_2$ teaspoon
Cabbage   1 cup grated coarsely
Canned beets   1 cup minced
Onion $^1/_4$ cup minced
Green pepper $^1/_4$ cup minced
Celery $^1/_4$ cup minced

Combine juice, vinegar, salt, and seeds. Bring to a boil and cook 5 minutes. Stir in vegetables; lower heat and simmer for 10 minutes. Pour into hot, sterile pint jars, leaving $1/2$ inch at top. Cap with hot, sterile lids and process in boiling-water bath for 30 minutes after water returns to boiling. If any jars fail to seal, refrigerate and use within ten days. (Refer to page 137 for times to use at altitudes higher than 1,000 feet.) *Do not freeze!*

Note: Everyone who sampled this vegetable salad asked for a copy of the recipe. It's an excellent winter salad to serve for company.

Nutritional value: $1/2$ cup contains 28 Calories (P1,F0,C6). $1/2$ cup = 1 diabetic vegetable exchange. If salt is omitted and salt-free beets are used, $1/2$ cup contains 24 milligrams sodium. Recipe contains 0 cholesterol. $1^{1}/2$ tablespoons can be used without diabetic replacement.

Marinated Mushrooms and Zucchini Slices

Zucchini $1^{1}/2$ cups thinly sliced, ends discarded
Small mushrooms $1^{1}/2$ cups cut in half lengthwise
Marinade

Place zucchini and mushrooms in 1-quart plastic container with tight lid. Pour marinade over them, cover, and refrigerate at least 6 hours to chill and blend flavors. Stir often to ensure that all vegetables are well covered with liquid. Drain; serve with toothpicks. Makes 3 cups.

Do Not Freeze! These vegetables will lose crispness when frozen. **To can:** After standing as directed, drain off and heat liquid to boiling. Place vegetables in hot, sterile pint jars, pour boiling liquid over vegetables, leaving $3/4$ inch at top. Cap with hot, sterile lids, and process in boiling-water bath for 25 minutes after water returns to boiling. Serve well chilled. If any jars fail to seal, refrigerate and use within ten days. Makes 3 cups.

Marinade

Garlic clove   1, bruised
Vegetable oil   3 tablespoons
White vinegar $^1/_2$ cup
Honey $^1/_3$ teaspoon **or Concentrated apple juice** $1^1/_2$ teaspoons
Tabasco sauce   3 to 4 drops

Rub small bowl with garlic. Place garlic in bowl, add remaining ingredients, and mix well.

Nutritional value: $^1/_2$ cup contains 39 Calories (P0,F3,C3). $^1/_2$ cup = $^1/_2$ diabetic vegetable + $^1/_2$ fat exchange. $^1/_2$ cup contains 2 milligrams sodium. Recipe contains 0 cholesterol.

Mother's Beet-Cabbage Relish

Cabbage   4 cups chopped
Canned beets   4 cups chopped
Concentrated white grape juice   1 cup (simmered down
   from 3 cups)
Lemon juice   1 tablespoon
Horseradish   1 cup grated
Vinegar   1 cup
Pepper   1 tablespoon
Salt or salt substitute   1 teaspoon
Cayenne pepper $^1/_4$ teaspoon

Combine all ingredients; bring to a boil. Pack in hot, sterile jars, leaving $^1/_2$ inch at top. Cap with sterile lids. Process in boiling-water bath for 30 minutes after water returns to boiling. (Refer to page 137 for times to use at altitudes higher than 1,000 feet.) If any jars fail to seal, refrigerate and use within ten days. *Do not freeze.* Makes 9 cups.

Note: This is delicious with cold meat and makes a colorful and tasty garnish for luncheon or dinner dishes.

Nutritional value: 1 tablespoon contains 8 Calories (P0,F0,C2). $2\frac{1}{2}$ tablespoons = 1 diabetic vegetable exchange. If salt is omitted, 1 tablespoon contains 2 milligrams sodium. Recipe contains 0 cholesterol. $\frac{1}{2}$ tablespoon can be used without diabetic replacement.

Pickled Beet Slices

Canned beet slices 7 cups
Cider vinegar $1\frac{1}{2}$ cups
Concentrated apple juice $1\frac{1}{2}$ cups
Lemon juice 1 tablespoon
Whole cloves 2 tablespoons
Large cinnamon stick 1, broken into 4 pieces

Drain canned beets, discarding liquid. Fill 4 sterile $\frac{1}{2}$-pint jars with beet slices, leaving 1 inch at top. Combine other ingredients and bring to a boil. Divide spices evenly in hot, sterile pint jars and pour liquid over beets, adding boiling water if needed to fill jars leaving $\frac{1}{2}$ inch at top. Cap with hot, sterile lids and process for 30 minutes after water returns to boiling. (Refer to page 137 for times to use at altitudes higher than 1,000 feet.) If any jars fail to seal, refrigerate and use within ten days. *Do not freeze.* Makes 8 cups.

Nutritional value: $2\frac{1}{2}$ tablespoons contain 24 Calories (P1,F0,C5). $2\frac{1}{2}$ tablespoons = 1 diabetic vegetable exchange. If salt is omitted and salt-free beets are used, $2\frac{1}{2}$ tablespoons contain 18 milligrams sodium. Recipe contains 0 cholesterol.

Note: You can save the liquid from this recipe and use it for a new batch of beet slices (they will be a little less pickled) by pouring it over the slices, bringing to a boil, then bottling and leaving the mixture to stand in the refrigerator at least 24 hours. Use within ten days and do not freeze or can! Nutritional values will be very little changed.

Pickled "Deviled" Eggs

Apple juice   ³/₄ cup
Whole mixed pickling spices   ¹/₂ teaspoon
Salt or salt substitute   ¹/₂ teaspoon
Celery seed   ¹/₄ teaspoon
Mustard seed   ¹/₈ teaspoon
Cider vinegar   1 cup
Water   ¹/₂ cup
Garlic clove   ¹/₂, minced
Large eggs   6, hard-cooked, shelled

Combine all ingredients except eggs in deep nonaluminum saucepan. Simmer for 10 minutes. Prick eggs with fork to make design around middle and ends. Pour hot liquid over eggs and allow to stand at room temperature before placing in refrigerator. Let stand 48 hours or longer before using. Serve whole or halved as appetizer or salad garnish. Makes 6.

Note: These eggs, which taste like deviled eggs, are great to take on picnics.

Nutritional value: 1 egg contains 86 Calories (P7,F6,C1). 1 egg = 1 diabetic medium fat meat exchange. If salt is omitted, 1 egg contains 72 milligrams sodium. 1 large egg contains 274 milligrams cholesterol.

Pickled Green Beans

Frozen green beans, julienne cut   two 10-ounce packages
Large garlic cloves   2
Thin lemon slice   1, chopped
Onion   ¹/₂ cup thinly sliced
Cider vinegar   1 cup
Apple juice   ¹/₄ cup
Large bay leaf   1, broken into pieces
Salt or salt substitute   ¹/₂ teaspoon

Whole pickling spice $^1/_2$ teaspoon
Whole allspice $^1/_4$ teaspoon
Whole mustard seeds $^1/_4$ teaspoon

Cover beans with boiling water and cook 6 minutes. Drain, saving liquid. Pack into hot, sterile pint jars, leaving $^3/_4$ inch at top. Combine remaining ingredients with bean liquid and simmer for 8 minutes. Pour over beans, adding boiling water if needed to fill jars to $^1/_2$ inch of top. Cap with hot, sterile lids and process in boiling-water bath for 15 minutes after water returns to boiling. (Refer to page 137 for times to use at altitudes higher than 1,000 feet.) If any jars fail to seal, refrigerate and use within ten days. *Do not freeze.* Makes 4 cups.

Nutritional value: $^1/_2$ cup contains 24 Calories (P1,F0,C5). $^1/_2$ cup = 1 diabetic vegetable exchange. If salt is omitted, $^1/_2$ cup contains 51 milligrams sodium. Recipe contains 0 cholesterol.

Note: These beans can be made into Garlic Pickled Green Beans by omitting all the spices called for except the mustard seeds, and increasing the amount of garlic to 4 to 5 cloves. Process as directed. Nutritional values will be unchanged.

Hot Pickled Mushrooms

Small button mushrooms 1 pound
Large garlic cloves 3, peeled and sliced
Dried hot red pepper 1 tablespoon (2 tablespoons if you like them hot)
Whole peppercorns $^1/_4$ teaspoon
Large bay leaves 3, broken into pieces
Distilled vinegar 1 cup
Water 1 cup
Apple juice $^1/_4$ cup
Salt or salt substitute $^3/_4$ teaspoon

Wash mushrooms and slice off and discard stem ends. Cut into halves, quartering larger ones. Place in 3 hot, sterile $^1/_2$-pint jars, filling half full, then adding 1 sliced garlic clove, $^1/_3$ of red pepper, and $^1/_3$ of peppercorns to each jar. Fill to $^1/_2$ inch from top with mushrooms leaving $^1/_2$ inch at top. Combine remaining ingredients in saucepan and bring to a boil. Pour over mushrooms, adding boiling water if needed to cover mushrooms. Cap with hot, sterile lids and process in boiling-water bath for 20 minutes after water returns to boiling.   (Refer to page 137 for times to use at altitudes higher than 1,000 feet.) If any jar fails to seal, refrigerate and use within ten days. *Do not freeze.* Makes 4 cups, drained (3 pints before cooking).

Nutritional value: $^1/_2$ cup contains 40 Calories (P3,F0,C7). $^1/_2$ cup = $^1/_2$ diabetic bread exchange. If salt is omitted, $^1/_2$ cup contains 6 milligrams sodium. Recipe contains 0 cholesterol.

Pineapple Pickles

Distilled vinegar $^1/_2$ cup + 2 tablespoons ($^5/_8$ cup)
Concentrated apple juice $^1/_2$ cup
Lemon juice   1 tablespoon
Pineapple juice $^3/_4$ cup (juice drained from fruit, plus
    extra if needed)
Whole cloves $1^1/_2$ teaspoons
Cinnamon stick   1, broken into 4 pieces
Pineapple chunks   16-ounce can (canned in own juice),
    drained

Boil vinegar, juices, cloves, and cinnamon together for 10 minutes. Add drained pineapple and simmer for 20 minutes. Pack in hot, sterile pint jars.   Add extra boiling hot pineapple juice if needed to cover fruit, leaving $^1/_2$ inch at top. Cap with hot, sterile lids and process in boiling-water bath for 5 minutes after water returns to boiling. Refrigerate any jars that fail to seal and use within ten days. *Do not freeze.* Makes 2 pints.

Nutritional value: 3 tablespoons contain 20 Calories (P0,F0,C5). 3 tablespoons = 1 diabetic vegetable exchange or $^1/_3$ diabetic fruit exchange. 3 tablespoons contain 1 milligram sodium. Recipe contains 0 cholesterol.

Spiced Apples

Concentrated apple juice $1^1/_2$ cups
Distilled vinegar $^2/_3$ cup
Whole cloves   1 teaspoon
Cinnamon stick   1, broken into 4 pieces
Red food coloring $^1/_3$ teaspoon (optional)
Medium apples (sweet and firm, like Yellow Delicious)
    5, peeled, cored, and cut into eighths

Combine all ingredients except apples in saucepan and bring to a boil. Drop apples into hot solution and simmer until slightly soft, about 10 minutes at most. Pack in hot, sterile $^1/_2$-pint jars, leaving $^1/_2$ inch at top. Cap with hot, sterile lids and process in boiling-water bath for 5 minutes after water returns to boiling. If any jars fail to seal, refrigerate and use within ten days. *Do not freeze.* Makes $2^1/_2$ pints.

Note: These taste like old-fashioned crabapple pickles.

Nutritional value: 5 pieces contain 60 Calories (P0,F0,C15). 5 pieces = 1 diabetic fruit exchange. 5 pieces contain less than 3 milligrams sodium. Recipe contains 0 cholesterol.

Sweet-and-Sour Cabbage Pickle
(Cabbage Tsukemono)

Concentrated apple juice $1 ^1/_2$ cups
Cider vinegar   3 tablespoons
Coarse pickling salt   2 tablespoons
Sherry or dry white wine   3 tablespoons
Cabbage   12 cups cut into 1-inch pieces

Combine all ingredients except cabbage in nonaluminum saucepan; bring to a boil and boil until salt is dissolved. Cool slightly and pour over cabbage. Press cabbage down with plate on which a heavy weight is placed (glass jar filled with water will work). Allow to stand 24 hours. Drain and serve. Makes 6 cups.

Note: This does not can or freeze well; use fresh only.

Nutritional value: $^1/_4$ cup contains 28 Calories (P0,F0,C7). 3 tablespoons = 1 diabetic vegetable exchange. This recipe cannot be made satisfactorily without salt. Do not use on low-salt diet. Recipe contains 0 cholesterol.

Tangy Fruit Relish

Large apple   1, peeled, cored, and chopped
Medium lemon   1 cup sliced paper thin
Lemon juice   3 tablespoons
Bean sprouts   1 cup coarsely chopped
Dried apricots   1 cup cooked and chopped
Raisins $^1/_4$ cup
Salt   dash (optional)
Water $^1/_2$ cup
Unflavored gelatin   1–2 tablespoons (1–2 envelopes)
     (use the higher amount if planning to freeze relish)

Combine all ingredients except gelatin in saucepan and cook over low heat until fruit is tender and relish thickened. Add additional water while cooking if needed to prevent sticking. Remove from heat and sprinkle gelatin over hot relish, stirring rapidly to dissolve. Adjust seasonings to taste. Pour into hot, sterile $^1/_2$-pint jars, leaving $^1/_2$ inch at top. Cap with hot, sterile lids and process in boiling-water bath for 20 minutes after water returns to boiling. (Refer to page 137 for times to use at altitudes higher than 1,000 feet.) If any jars fail to seal, refrigerate and use within five days or freeze for later use. Makes 3 cups.

To freeze, pour hot mixture into clean containers or jars leaving $1/2$ inch at the top. Top with clean lids and cool to room temperature before placing in sharp-freeze section of freezer. When hard, move to other area of freezer for storage. To use, thaw overnight in refrigerator. Makes 3 cups.

Note: This relish does not keep well and should be canned or frozen if kept longer than a few days.

Nutritional value: $1/4$ cup equals 24 Calories (P1,F0,C5). $1/4$ cup = 1 diabetic vegetable exchange. If salt is omitted, $1/4$ cup contains 5 milligrams sodium. Recipe contains 0 cholesterol. 2 teaspoons can be used without diabetic replacement.

Uncooked Cucumber Relish

Large cucumbers   5, peeled and seeded
Green pepper $1/2$, seeded
Large onion   *1, peeled*
Medium apple (preferably tart)   1, peeled and cored
Distilled vinegar   1 cup
Salt or salt substitute $1^1/2$ teaspoons
Black pepper   1 teaspoon
Mustard seed   1 teaspoon
Celery seed $1/2$ teaspoon
Tabasco sauce   dash (optional)

Grind all vegetables and apple in meat grinder using medium blade. Mix with remaining ingredients and pack into hot, clean jars. Top with hot, clean lids. Refrigerate until used. This will keep for several weeks in the refrigerator, but it loses its crunchiness after a few days. *Do not freeze or can.* Makes $3^1/2$ cups.

Nutritional value: 3 tablespoons contain 24 Calories (P1,F0,C5). 3 tablespoons = 1 diabetic vegetable exchange. If salt is omitted, 3 tablespoons contain less than 8 milligrams sodium. Recipe contains 0 cholesterol. $1/2$ tablespoon can be used without diabetic replacement.

Winter Corn Relish

Frozen whole-kernel corn   4 cups
Green cabbage   1$^1/_2$ cups finely chopped
Medium white onions   3
Green peppers   2, seeded and stem removed
Dried hot red peppers   2 tablespoons
Pimiento $^1/_4$ cup minced
Cider vinegar   2$^1/_2$ cups
Concentrated apple juice $^1/_2$ cup
White grape juice $^1/_2$ cup (simmered down from 1 cup)
Salt   1 tablespoon (optional)
Celery seed $^2/_3$ teaspoon
Mustard seed $^2/_3$ teaspoon

Place corn in large nonaluminum kettle. Grind other vegetables, using coarse blade in meat grinder. Add with remaining ingredients to corn and bring to a boil. Turn down heat and simmer for 35 minutes. Skim and pack immediately in hot, sterile $^1/_2$-pint or pint jars, leaving $^1/_2$ inch at top. Cap with hot, sterile lids and process for 20 minutes in boiling-water bath after water returns to boiling. (Refer to page 137 for times to use at altitudes higher than 1,000 feet.) If any jars fail to seal, refrigerate and use within ten days or freeze for later use. Makes 8$^1/_2$ to 9 cups.

Nutritional value: 2 tablespoons with juice equal 16 Calories (P0,F0,C4). 2$^1/_2$ tablespoons = 1 diabetic vegetable exchange. If salt is omitted and corn is frozen without salt, 2 tablespoons contain 4 milligrams sodium. Recipe contains 0 cholesterol. 1$^1/_2$ teaspoons can be used without diabetic replacement.

All-Year-Round Chili Sauce

Canned whole tomatoes with liquid   4 cups, chopped
Onion   1 medium, chopped

Green pepper   1 large, seeded and chopped
Celery   2 large stalks, chopped fine
Concentrated apple juice $^1/_2$ to $^3/_4$ cup
Salt $^1/_2$ teaspoon (optional)
Black pepper $^1/_4$ teaspoon ground
Cinnamon $^1/_4$ teaspoon ground
Cloves $^1/_4$ teaspoon ground
Allspice $^1/_4$ teaspoon ground
Cumin $^1/_4$ teaspoon ground (optional)
Cider vinegar $^1/_2$ cup
Lemon juice   1 to 2 tablespoons (optional)

Combine first five ingredients in a deep, heavy nonaluminum kettle. Bring to a boil; then reduce heat and simmer until vegetables are very soft. Add remaining ingredients (except lemon juice); mix well and continue to simmer, uncovered, until thick. Cool; then taste and add more apple juice sweetening and/or lemon juice to suit. Return to heat and bring to boiling. Pour into hot, sterile pint jars, leaving $^1/_2$ inch at top. Cap with hot, sterile lids and process in boiling-water bath for 15 minutes after water returns to boiling. (Refer to page 137 for times to use at altitudes higher than 1,000 feet.) If any jars fail to seal, refrigerate and use within ten days or freeze for later use. Makes $5^1/_2$ cups.

Nutritional value: 1 tablespoon contains 7 Calories (P0,F0,C2). $2^1/_2$ tablespoons = 1 diabetic vegetable exchange. If salt is omitted, 1 tablespoon contains 19 milligrams sodium. Recipe contains 0 cholesterol. $1^1/_2$ teaspoons can be used without diabetic replacement.

Australian Tomato Sauce
(like catsup)

Canned whole tomatoes with juice   6 cups chopped
Onions $1^1/_4$ cups peeled and chopped or coarsely ground
Large garlic clove   1, peeled and minced or ground

White grape juice 1$^{1}/_{2}$ cups
Cider vinegar $^{1}/_{2}$ cup
Cloves, ground $^{1}/_{2}$ tablespoon
Ginger 1 teaspoon
Salt or salt substitute 1$^{1}/_{2}$ teaspoons

Place chopped or coarsely ground vegetables in deep nonaluminum kettle. Add remaining ingredients and cook over low heat until thick. Remove from heat, skim, and put through food mill. Return to heat and bring to a boil. Pack into hot, sterile pint jars, leaving $^{1}/_{2}$ inch at top. Cap with hot, sterile lids and process in boiling-water bath for 15 minutes after water returns to boiling. (Refer to page 137 for times to use at altitudes higher than 1,000 feet.) If any jars fail to seal, refrigerate and use within ten days or freeze for later use. Makes 6 cups.

Nutritional value: $^{1}/_{4}$ cup contains 20 Calories (P0,F0,C4). $^{1}/_{3}$ cup = 1 diabetic vegetable exchange. If salt is omitted, $^{1}/_{4}$ cup contains less than 3 milligrams sodium. Recipe contains 0 cholesterol. 1 tablespoon can be used without diabetic replacement.

Tomato Sauce

Medium onions 2, chopped
Green pepper 1, chopped
Tomato paste 4 cups **or Tomato puree** 8 cups
Water 4 cups (omit if using puree)
Large garlic clove minced
Concentrated apple juice 1 cup
Cider vinegar $^{2}/_{3}$ cup
Lemon juice 2 tablespoons
Salt 1 tablespoon
Black pepper $^{1}/_{4}$ teaspoon

Combine vegetables in large nonaluminum kettle. Add all other ingredients and cook over low heat until vegetables are very soft and volume is reduced by about one-third. Remove from heat and put through a food mill. Return to stove; heat to boiling. Pack in hot, sterile $\frac{1}{2}$-pint or pint jars, leaving $\frac{1}{2}$ inch at top. Cap with hot, sterile lids and process for 15 minutes in boiling-water bath, after water returns to boiling. (Refer to page 137 for times to use at altitudes higher than 1,000 feet.) If any jars fail to seal, refrigerate and use within ten days or freeze for later use.

To freeze, cool jars to room temperature and place in sharp-freeze section of freezer until hard. Store in main section of freezer. Thaw overnight in refrigerator before using. Makes 6 cups.

Nutritional value: 1 tablespoon contains 12 Calories (P0,F0,C3). $1\frac{3}{4}$ tablespoons = 1 diabetic vegetable exchange. If salt is omitted and salt-free tomato paste (or salt-free tomato puree) used, 1 tablespoon contains 1 milligram sodium. Recipe contains 0 cholesterol. 1 teaspoon can be used without diabetic replacement.

Winter Tomato Catsup

Use recipe for Tomato Catsup with Honey (see Recipe Index) but omit honey, substituting $\frac{3}{4}$ cup concentrated apple juice plus 2 tablespoons extra lemon juice.

Nutritional value: $1\frac{2}{3}$ tablespoons contain 20 Calories (P0,F0,C5). $1\frac{2}{3}$ tablespoons = 1 diabetic vegetable exchange. If salt is omitted, $1\frac{2}{3}$ tablespoons contain 3 milligrams sodium.

Winter Indian Chutney

Canned tomatoes   4 cups chopped with juice
Large onions   3, peeled
Large green pepper   1, seeded
Dried hot red pepper $1\frac{1}{2}$ to 2
Large, tart apples   4
Seedless raisins $\frac{7}{8}$ cup

Concentrated apple juice $^1/_4$ cup (simmered down
from $^1/_2$ cup)
White grape juice $^1/_4$ cup (simmered down from $^1/_2$ cup)
Cider vinegar 1 to $1^1/_3$ cups
Salt or salt substitute $1^1/_2$ teaspoons
Curry powder 1 teaspoon (optional)

Grind all vegetables and fruit in meat grinder using medium blade. Place in deep nonaluminum kettle and add remaining ingredients. Simmer until thickened, approximately 1 hour, stirring often. Skim and pack in hot, sterile pint jars. Cap with hot, sterile lids and process in boiling-water bath for 20 minutes after water returns to boiling. (Refer to page 137 for times to use at altitudes higher than 1,000 feet.) If any jars fail to seal, refrigerate and use within ten days or freeze for later use. Makes 8 cups.

Nutritional value: 2 tablespoons contain 20 Calories (P0,F0,C5). 2 tablespoons = 1 diabetic vegetable exchange. If salt is omitted and salt-free tomatoes used, 2 tablespoons contain 2 milligrams sodium. 1 teaspoon can be used without diabetic exchange replacement.

OTHER RECIPES TO MAKE YEAR-ROUND

Jams, Jellies, and Preserves:
Apple-Berry Jam (frozen berries)
Apricot Marmalade (dried apricots)
Mixed Soft Fruit Jam (diet canned fruit)
Apple Jelly (frozen apple juice)
Orange Juice Jelly (frozen orange juice)
Apricot-Pineapple Jam (dried apricots, canned pineapple)
Orange-Blueberry Jam (frozen berries)
Strawberry Date Nut Preserves (frozen berries)
Frozen Blueberry Jam (frozen berries)
Lazy Person's Plum Jam (dried prunes)
Grape Jelly (canned grape juice)
Meatless Mincemeat

Pickles, Relishes, and Seasoning Sauces:
Dilled Zucchini and Mushroom Pickles
Spicy Pears (winter pears)
Celery Chutney (canned tomatoes)
Cucumber Catsup

PRESERVING WITH HONEY

ADVANTAGES OF USING HONEY FOR CANNING

Honey is manufactured by bees from nectar gathered from flowers, flowering trees, and shrubs. It can taste mild or strong, depending on the nectar and its source—plants as different as cactus and columbine! Most useful for cooking is honey from clover or alfalfa. These are mild and will not divert attention from the foods they are used to sweeten.

Because it has the tendency to draw water to itself, foods made with honey may become sticky or runny. Use only enough to enhance the natural sweetness of the fruit without overpowering the flavor.

One tablespoon honey contains 16.5 grams sugar, whereas 1 tablespoon of refined sugar contains only 11.9 grams. This means that honey is almost 40 percent more concentrated than table sugar! Since the sweetening power of honey is greater than sugar, a little does a lot. *Honey should not be used by diabetics and hypoglycemics.* Although honey is a natural sugar, it can still overload the pancreas. Recipes in this section should not be used by anyone with either of these metabolic problems. On the basis of some recent research, some physicians recommend that honey not be consumed by infants less than one year of age because of risk of infant botulism.

Fruits canned without added sugar tend to lose color: Cherries or strawberries can fade almost to white after a year's storage. With honey, colors usually stay true, and there is little or no more fading than with refined sugar canning. *All foods canned with honey should be processed by water bath or pressure canner.* Honey-canned fruit will be sweeter than when preserved using only fruit juice, and honey-sweetened fruits, jams, and preserves will better suit a sugar-lover's taste. Honey isn't cheap, but it takes so little to sweeten, using these recipes, that it ends up costing less than fruit juice.

Fruit flavors are delicate; be sure to taste the fruit-honey combination you plan to use before making a whole batch. To can fruit with honey syrup, follow directions for selecting and preparing fruit (see General Index), and make syrup according to the following directions.

How to Make Honey-Sweetened Syrup

Light Syrup: 2 tablespoons honey plus 1$\frac{1}{2}$ to 2 teaspoons lemon juice (larger amount for sweet fruit) plus boiled water to make 1 cup syrup

Medium Syrup: 3 tablespoons honey plus 2 to 3 teaspoons lemon juice plus boiled water to make 1 cup syrup

Plan to add a few fruit pits to the fruit when using honey. This will add an almondlike taste that will blend well and help disguise the honey flavor. Do not use more honey than called for or the fruit flavor will be lost.

Converting Fruit Juice Sweetened Recipes to Honey Sweetened Recipes

You can convert fruit juice sweetened recipes to honey sweetened recipes, using Table 10. If you want to find the Calories in a converted recipe, you will find easy-to-follow directions in Table 11. Once you have converted a recipe, be sure to keep a copy of the changes you made, how much honey you used, and the new Calorie content so that you can repeat it at will.

Canning and Freezing Fruit with Honey

Process and pack fruit as directed in the chapter Selecting and Processing Fruit. All jam and jelly should be processed in a boiling-water bath for the times shown in the recipes. Use only the size jar that the recipe specifies (or smaller).

Applesauce with Honey

Apples   6 cups quartered with stem and blossom end removed
Water   1$^1/_4$ cups
Lemon juice   3 tablespoons
Honey $^1/_3$ cup to $^1/_2$ cup (use larger amount with tart apples)
Lemon rind $^1/_3$ teaspoon grated (optional)
Cinnamon $^3/_4$ teaspoon (optional)
Salt dash (optional)

Place apples and water in deep nonaluminum kettle. Cover and cook until very soft. Remove from heat and put through food mill. Return pureed material to kettle. Add remaining ingredients and reheat to boiling. Simmer for 5 minutes. Pour into hot, sterile jars, leaving $^1/_2$ inch at top. Cap with hot, sterile lids. Process in boiling-water bath for 20 minutes after water returns to boiling. (Refer to page 137 for times to use at altitudes higher than 1,000 feet.) If any jars fail to seal, refrigerate and use within ten days or freeze for later use. Makes 6 cups.

Nutritional value: $^1/_2$ cup contains 64 Calories (P0,F0,C16). *This should not be used by diabetics or hypoglycemics.* $^1/_2$ cup contains less than 2 milligrams sodium if no salt is added. Recipe contains 0 cholesterol.

Berry Applesauce with Honey

Raspberry or Strawberry puree   8 cups (see below)
Unsweetened applesauce   4 cups
Lemon juice   2$^1/_2$–3 tablespoons
Grated lemon rind (fresh)   1 teaspoon
Salt   2 dashes (optional)
Honey $^1/_2$ cup
Red food color $^1/_2$ teaspoon (optional)

Place puree and applesauce in deep nonaluminum pan. Mix well, then bring to a boil. Add remaining ingredients (except coloring). Mix and taste, adding more honey or lemon juice to suit. (Stir in coloring to give a pretty pink. Use more color if needed.) While still boiling hot, pour into hot, sterile pint jars leaving $\frac{1}{2}$ inch at top. Cap with hot, sterile lids and process in a boiling-water bath for 20 minutes after water returns to boiling. (Refer to page 137 for times to use at altitudes higher than 1,000 feet.) If any jars fail to seal, refrigerate and use within ten days or freeze for later use. Makes 12 cups.

Puree:

8 cups frozen berries
1 cup concentrated apple juice
1 cup water

Place in deep nonaluminum kettle, mashing berries as soon as thawed, then simmer until fruit is soft. Remove from heat and puree in a food mill to remove as many seeds as possible.

Nutritional value: $\frac{1}{2}$ cup serving contains 63 Calories (P0,F0,C16). *This should not be used by diabetics or hypoglycemics.* If salt is omitted, $\frac{1}{2}$ cup contains 2 milligrams sodium. Recipe contains 0 cholesterol.

JAM, JELLY, AND PRESERVES

Honey can precipitate pectin just as refined sugar does, provided enough is present. To convert other recipes, substitute honey at the rate of one-third the volume of sugar called for. Always use liquid (not powdered) pectin when cooking with honey; it mixes readily and eliminates sugar found in powdered pectin. Lemon juice is usually added to cut the honey taste (1 tablespoon lemon juice or more for each $\frac{1}{4}$ cup honey). With too little honey, regular pectin will not jell, and glycerine must then be added ($\frac{1}{2}$ to 1 tablespoon glycerine for each cup cooked fruit mixture). The amount of acid present also affects the jell; with too much acid, pectin will not jell, either.

Although it can be tricky to get honey jams and jellies to come out just right, when they do, they are delightful. Instead of making jelly or jam (other than with the tested recipes provided), why not omit pectin entirely and make preserves with honey? That way you don't have to worry about the pectin jelling and whether or not to use glycerine to help the jell.

The recipes that follow are samples of the good things that can be made with honey. To experiment with other recipes, just use the same amount of fruit/juice and pectin as usual, but add honey equal to one-third the amount of sugar. Make a small batch in case it doesn't thicken as you'd like. If it is too thin, reheat and add glycerine (2 teaspoons per cup jam) or unflavored gelatin (1 tablespoon [1 envelope] per 4 cups jam/jelly). Either should thicken jam/jelly satisfactorily.

While honey will jell regular pectin if used in adequate amounts, you can also use low-methoxy pectin with the calcium solution and sweeten with honey as you wish. I have included both regular and low-methoxy pectin recipes in this section. *Neither the USDA nor I recommend* that jams made with honey be preserved with paraffin, or be allowed to self-seal. All jars must be processed in a boiling-water bath according to the latest USDA recommendations (unless you freeze them when cooled). If any jars fail to seal, refrigerate and use within ten days or freeze for later use.

Basic Jam Recipe
(with Honey and Regular Pectin)

Fresh fruit   2 cups pitted and chopped
Water $^1/_4$ cup
Lemon juice   2 tablespoons
Honey $^1/_2$ cup
Lemon rind $^1/_2$ teaspoon (optional)
Liquid pectin (regular) $^1/_2$ cup

Salt dash (optional)
Spices (cinnamon, nutmeg, cloves, etc.) $^1/_2$ to 1 teaspoon
  (optional)
Gelatin 1 tablespoon (1 envelope) (optional)

Place fruit, water, juice, honey, and lemon rind in deep nonaluminum pan. Cook until fruit is soft, mashing for more uniform texture. Add pectin, return to heat, and bring to a rolling boil for 1 minute. Remove from heat; skim and add spices. If using gelatin, sprinkle over hot mixture, stirring well. Pour immediately into hot, sterile $^1/_2$-pint or pint jars, leaving $^1/_2$ inch at top. Cap with hot, sterile lids and process in boiling-water bath for 5 minutes after water returns to boiling. If any jar fails to seal, refrigerate and use within ten days or freeze for later use. Makes 3 cups.

Nutritional value: Depending on fruit used, 1 tablespoon contains from 12 to 40 Calories. *This should not be used by diabetics or hypoglycemics.* If no salt is added, 1 tablespoon contains less than 1 milligram sodium. Recipe contains 0 cholesterol.

JAMS WITH HONEY AND REGULAR PECTIN

Berry Jam with Honey

Whole berries* 4 cups
Water $^1/_2$ cup
Lemon juice 4 tablespoons
Honey 1 cup
Salt dash (optional)
Liquid pectin (regular) 1 cup
Gelatin 1 tablespoon (1 envelope) (optional)

---

*Note: If made with strawberries, reduce water to 2 tablespoons.

Place berries, water, lemon juice, honey, and salt in deep nonaluminum saucepan. Cook until berries are soft, mashing them for more uniform texture, if desired. Add pectin, return to heat, and bring to a rolling boil. If using gelatin, sprinkle over hot mixture, stirring well. Pour immediately into hot, sterile pint jars, leaving $1/2$ inch at top. Cap with hot, sterile lids. Process in boiling-water bath for 5 minutes after water returns to boiling. If any jar fails to seal, refrigerate and use within ten days or freeze for later use. Makes 6 cups.

Nutritional value: 1 tablespoon contains 15 Calories (P0,F0,C4). *This should not be used by diabetics or hypoglycemics.* If no salt is added, 1 tablespoon contains less than 1 milligram sodium. Recipe contains 0 cholesterol.

Rhubarb-Strawberry Jam with Honey

Rhubarb   6 cups cut into $1/2$-inch pieces
Water   1 cup
Strawberries   3 cups hulled and halved
Lemon juice   3 tablespoons
Salt   dash (optional)
Honey $1^1/2$ cups
Liquid pectin (regular)   6 ounces (1 package)

Place rhubarb and water in deep nonaluminum kettle. Bring to a boil, turn down heat, cover, and cook until rhubarb is almost soft. Add berries, lemon juice, and salt and cover and cook until fruit is very soft. Add honey, stir in pectin and return to heat, bringing to a rolling boil for 1 minute. Skim and immediately pour into hot, sterile pint jars, leaving $1/2$ inch at top. Cap with hot, sterile lids. Process in boiling-water bath for 5 minutes after water returns to boiling. If any jar fails to seal, refrigerate and use within ten days or freeze for later use. Makes $9^1/2$ to 10 cups.

Nutritional value: 1 tablespoon contains 12 Calories (P0,F0,C3). *This should not be used by diabetics or hypoglycemics.* If no salt is added, 3 tablespoons contain less than 1 milligram sodium. Recipe contains 0 cholesterol.

Tomato Jam with Honey

Tomatoes   2 pounds, skinned, chopped, with juice
Lemon $1^1/_3$ juiced, seeded, rind ground or finely chopped
Honey $^1/_2$ cup
Liquid pectin (regular) $^1/_2$ cup
Ginger $^1/_2$ teaspoon (optional)
Mace $^1/_2$ teaspoon (optional)
Salt   dash (optional)

Combine tomatoes, lemon rind and juice, and honey in deep non-aluminum pan. Simmer, stirring often, until lemon pieces are tender and jam is fairly thick. Add pectin and reheat to rolling boil. Boil for 1 minute. Add spices, stir, and pour into hot, sterile $^1/_2$-pint jars, leaving $^1/_2$ inch at top. Cap with hot, sterile lids and process in boiling-water bath for 5 minutes after water returns to boiling. If any jars fail to seal, refrigerate and use within 1 week or freeze for later use. Makes 5 cups.

Nutritional value: 1 tablespoon contains 12 Calories (P0,F0,C2$^1/_2$). *This should not be used by diabetics or hypoglycemics.* If no salt is added, 2 tablespoons contain 1 milligram sodium. Recipe contains 0 cholesterol.

Tomato Relish with Honey

To make this as a relish, add $^1/_4$ cup vinegar to the tomato-lemon mixture and omit the pectin and suggested seasonings, replacing with $^3/_4$ to 1 teaspoon ground allspice. Process as directed. Makes $4^1/_2$ cups.

Nutritional value: 1 tablespoon contains 10 Calories (P0,F0,C2$^1/_2$). *This should not be used by diabetics or hypoglycemics.* If no salt is added, 1$^1/_2$ tablespoons contain 1 milligram sodium. Recipe contains 0 cholesterol.

JAMS WITH HONEY AND LOW-METHOXY PECTIN

Basic Jam Recipe
(with Honey and Low-Methoxy Pectin)

Whole berries   4 cups, washed, hulled and mashed
 or soft fruit   4 cups, peeled, pitted and chopped
Lemon juice   2 to 3 tablespoons*
Water $^1/_2$ to $^3/_4$ cup*
Honey $^1/_2$ to $^3/_4$ cup*
Salt   dash (optional)
Lemon rind, freshly grated $^1/_2$ to $^3/_4$ teaspoon
Low-methoxy pectin solution   1 cup
Calcium solution   5 teaspoons

Combine first six ingredients in deep nonaluminum pan. Simmer over low heat until fruit is soft. Add more water if mixture gets thick before softening. Add pectin solution and reheat. Taste and add more honey or lemon juice if desired. Pour into hot, sterile $^1/_2$-pint or pint jars leaving $^1/_2$ inch at top. Cap with hot, sterile lids. Process in boiling-water bath for 5 minutes after water returns to boiling. If any jars fail to seal, refrigerate and use within ten days or freeze for later use.

If you prefer to freeze your jam, pour boiling hot jam into clean freezer containers or jars leaving $^1/_2$ inch at top. Cap with clean lids and cool to room temperature before placing in sharp-freeze section of freezer. When hard, move to other section for storage. Makes 5 $^1/_2$ cups.

Nutritional value: 1 tablespoon will contain between 15 and 18 Calories (P0,F0,C4). *This should not be used by diabetics and*

---

*Use smaller amounts to start, adding remainder during cooking if needed.

hypoglycemics due to its honey content. If salt is omitted, 1 table-spoon contains less than 1 milligram sodium. Recipe contains 0 cholesterol.

Strawberry or Raspberry Jam with Honey

Strawberries or raspberries, washed and hulled   4 cups
Lemon juice   2 tablespoons
Water $^1/_2$ to $^3/_4$ cup*
Honey $^1/_2$ to $^3/_4$ cup*
Salt   dash (optional)
Lemon rind, freshly grated $^1/_2$ teaspoon (optional)
Low-methoxy pectin solution   1 cup
Calcium solution   5 teaspoons

Combine first 6 ingredients in deep nonaluminum pan. Mash fruit to speed cooking. Simmer over low heat until fruit is soft. Add more water if mixture gets too thick. Add pectin solution and reheat. Remove from heat and add calcium solution, mixing well. Taste and add more honey or lemon juice to suit. While still boiling hot, pour into hot, sterile jars leaving $^1/_2$ inch at top. Cap with hot, sterile lids and process in boiling-water bath for 5 minutes after water returns to boiling. If any jars fail to seal, refrigerate and use within 10 days or freeze for later use.

If you prefer to freeze your jam, pour hot jam into clean freezer containers or jars, cap with clean lids and allow to cool to room tem-perature before placing in sharp-freeze section of freezer. When hard, move to other section for storage. Makes about 5 cups.

Nutritional value: 1 tablespoon contains 15 Calories (P0,F0,C4). *This recipe should not be used by diabetics and hypoglycemics due to the honey content.* If salt is omitted, $^1/_4$ cup contains 1 milligram sodium. Recipe contains 0 cholesterol.

---

*Use smaller amounts to start, add remainder during cooking, if needed.

JELLIES

Basic Jelly Recipe
(with Honey and Regular Pectin)

Fruit juice   2 cups
Lemon juice   1$^1/_2$ to 2 tablespoons
Honey $^1/_2$ cup
Salt   dash (optional)
Liquid pectin (regular)   2 ounces ($^1/_3$ package)
Gelatin   1 tablespoon (1 envelope) (optional)

Place juices, honey, and salt in saucepan. Bring to a boil. Add pectin and sprinkle gelatin over hot mixture; stir and return to a rolling boil for 1 minute. Pour immediately into hot, sterile pint jars, leaving $^1/_2$ inch at top. Cap with hot, sterile lids. Process lidded jars in boiling-water bath for 5 minutes after water returns to boiling. If any jars fail to seal, refrigerate and use within ten days or freeze for later use. Makes 2$^1/_4$ cups.

Nutritional value: 1 tablespoon contains from 30 to 40 Calories depending on juice used (P0,F0,C8–10). *This should not be used by diabetics or hypoglycemics.* If no salt is used, 1 tablespoon contains less than 1 milligram sodium. Recipe contains 0 cholesterol.

Grape Jelly with Honey

Concord grape juice   3 cups *or Concord grape juice*   2 cups
    and *White grape juice*   1 cup
Lemon juice   1$^1/_2$ tablespoons
Honey $^1/_2$ cup
Salt   dash (optional)
Liquid pectin (regular)   2 ounces ($^1/_3$ package)
Gelatin   1 tablespoon (1 envelope) (optional)

Simmer grape juice down to 2 cups; then add lemon juice, honey, and salt. Bring to a boil and stir in pectin and gelatin; bring to a rolling boil for 1 minute. Remove from heat and pour immediately into hot, sterile $1/2$-pint or pint jars, leaving $1/2$ inch at top. Cap with hot, sterile lids. Process in boiling-water bath for 5 minutes after water returns to boiling. If any jars fail to seal, refrigerate and use within ten days or freeze for later use. Makes $2^1/2$ cups.

Variation: Use white grape juice only and add $3/4$ to 1 teaspoon dried marjoram or thyme to the juice as you simmer it down. Strain to remove herbs and continue as directed. Nutritional value remains unchanged.

Nutritional value: 1 tablespoon contains 32 Calories (P0,F0,C8). *This should not be used by diabetics or hypoglycemics.* If no salt is added, 4 tablespoons contains less than 1 milligram sodium. Recipe contains 0 cholesterol.

Honey-Lemon Jelly

Lemon rind   1 teaspoon grated (optional)
Honey $1^1/4$ cups
Water $3/4$ cup
Lemon juice   2 tablespoons
Ginger   1 teaspoon (optional)
Liquid pectin (regular)   2 ounces ($1/3$ package)

Simmer lemon rind with honey and water for 10 minutes; allow to stand for 20 minutes to emphasize the lemon flavor. Combine honey, water, lemon juice, and lemon rind in deep nonaluminum saucepan. Bring to a boil. Add ginger and pectin, return to heat, and bring to a rolling boil for 1 minute. Pour into hot, sterile $1/2$-pint jars, leaving $1/2$ inch at top. Cap with hot, sterile lids. Process jars in boiling-water bath for 5 minutes after water returns to boiling. If any jars fail to seal, refrigerate and use within ten days or freeze for later use. Makes 2¼ cups.

Note: Double recipe for larger batch.

Nutritional value: 1 tablespoon contains 40 Calories (P0,F0,C10). This should not be used by diabetics or hypoglycemics. If no salt is added, 1 tablespoon contains less than 1 milligram sodium. Recipe contains 0 cholesterol.

JELLIES WITH HONEY AND LOW-METHOXY PECTIN

Basic Jelly Recipe
(with Honey and Low-Methoxy Pectin)

Unsweetened concentrated fruit juice   1½ cups
Water   1¼ cups
Honey   2½ to 3 tablespoons
Lemon Juice   3 to 4 tablespoons
Low-methoxy pectin solution   1½ cups
Salt   ¹⁄₁₆ teaspoon (optional)
Calcium solution   6½ teaspoons

Combine first four ingredients in deep nonaluminum pan. Simmer for 5 minutes or a little longer. Stir in pectin solution (and salt), mixing well before tasting. Add more honey (and/or lemon juice) to taste. Reheat to boiling. Remove from heat and stir in calcium solution. Pour into hot, sterile ½-pint or pint jars, leaving ½ inch at top. Cap with hot, sterile lids and process in boiling-water bath for 5 minutes after water returns to boiling. If any jars fail to seal, place in refrigerator and use within 10 days, or freeze for later use.

If you prefer to freeze jelly, pour into clean freezer containers or jars, cap with clean lids leaving ½ inch at top. Allow to cool to room temperature before placing in sharp-freeze section of freezer. When frozen, remove to another freezer section for storage. Makes 5 cups.

Nutritional value: Depending upon which fruit juice is used, 1 tablespoon contains between 15 and 20 Calories (P0,F0,C4–5). 1 tablespoon of jelly (regardless of which juice is used) will contain less than 1 milligram sodium. Recipe contains 0 cholesterol. *This recipe should not be used by diabetics or hypoglycemics due to the honey content.*

Orange Juice Jelly with Honey and Low-Methoxy Pectin

Concentrated frozen orange juice $1^1/_2$ cups
Water $1^1/_4$ cups
Honey $2^1/_2$ to $3^1/_2$ tablespoons
Lemon juice   3 to 4 tablespoons
Low-methoxy pectin solution $1^1/_2$ cups
Salt $^1/_{16}$ teaspoon (optional)
Calcium solution $6^1/_2$ teaspoons

Combine first four ingredients in a deep nonaluminum kettle. Simmer for 5 to 7 minutes, stirring occasionally. Stir in pectin solution (and salt). Mix well. Taste and add remaining honey or lemon juice if desired. Reheat to boiling. Remove from heat and stir in calcium solution. Pour into hot, sterile $^1/_2$-pint or pint jars leaving $^1/_2$ inch at top. Cap with hot, sterile lids, and process in boiling-water bath for 5 minutes after water returns to boiling. If any jars fail to seal, refrigerate and use within ten days or freeze for later use.

To freeze the jelly, pour into clean freezing containers, leaving $^1/_2$ inch at top. Cap with clean lids and allow to cool to room temperature before placing in sharp-freeze section of freezer. Move to another section for storage. Makes 5 cups.

Nutritional value: 1 tablespoon contains 15 Calories (P0,F0,C4). 1 tablespoon jelly contains less than 1 milligram sodium. Recipe contains 0 cholesterol. *This recipe should not be used by diabetics or hypoglycemics because of its honey content.*

Preserves

Basic Fruit Preserves with Honey

Fresh fruit   6 cups pitted and chopped
Other fruit   1 cup pitted or seeded and chopped
Water $^1/_2$ cup
Honey $^3/_4$ to 1 cup
Lemon juice   3 tablespoons
Spices (cinnamon, nutmeg, cloves, ginger, etc.)   (optional)
Salt   dash (optional)

Combine fruit, water, honey, and juice in large nonaluminum kettle. Bring to a boil; then simmer until thickened, stirring often. Taste, and add spices toward end of cooking time, if desired. Skim and pour into hot, sterile $^1/_2$-pint or pint jars, leaving $^1/_2$ inch at top. Cap with hot, sterile lids and process in boiling-water bath for 5 minutes after water returns to boiling or freeze for later use. If any jar fails to seal, refrigerate and use within ten days or freeze for later use. Makes 6 cups.

Nutritional value: 1 tablespoon contains from 28 to 40 Calories, depending on fruits used. *This should not be used by diabetics or hypoglycemics.* If no salt is added, 1 tablespoon contains less than 1 milligram sodium. Recipe contains 0 cholesterol.

Apple-Plum Conserve with Honey

Sweet plums   6 cups pitted and chopped or ground
Sweet apples   2 cups cored and chopped or ground
Seedless raisins   1 cup chopped or ground
Medium lemon $^1/_2$, seeded and chopped, or ground, with peels
Medium orange   1, seeded and chopped, or ground, with peels
Concentrated orange juice (frozen)   1 cup
Water   1 cup
Honey $^1/_2$ to $^2/_3$ cup

Combine all ingredients in deep nonaluminum kettle. Stir well; then bring to a boil before turning down heat and simmering until thickened (about 1 hour) stirring frequently. Taste and add more sweetening or some lemon juice to taste. While hot, pour into hot, sterile jars, leaving $1/2$ inch at top. Top with hot, sterile lids. Process for 5 minutes in boiling-water bath after water returns to boiling. If any jars fail to seal, refrigerate and use within ten days or freeze for later use. Makes 9 to $9^1/2$ cups.

Nutritional value: 1 tablespoon contains 16 Calories (P0,F0,C4). *This should not be used by diabetics or hypoglycemics.* 3 tablespoons contain 1 milligram sodium. Recipe contains 0 cholesterol.

Apricot-Orange Butter with Honey

Fresh apricots   6 cups pitted ***or Dried apricots*** $1^1/2$ pounds
  (6 cups after soaking)
Water $1/2$ cup
Concentrated orange juice $1/2$ cup
Honey $1/4$ cup for each cup puree
Cinnamon   1 teaspoon
Nutmeg $1/2$ teaspoon
Ginger $1/4$ teaspoon (optional)
Salt   dash (optional)

If using dried apricots, soak overnight in recipe's water and juice plus enough additional water to cover. In the morning, place in deep nonaluminum kettle and simmer until tender. Puree in food mill or blender, sieving afterward to remove pieces (reblend and add to rest). Measure puree volume and add $1/4$ cup honey for each cup puree. Add spices and salt and continue to simmer until thick, stirring often to prevent sticking. Skim and pour immediately into hot, sterile $1/2$-pint or pint jars, leaving $1/2$ inch at top. Cap with hot, sterile lids. Process in boiling-water bath for 5 minutes after water returns to boiling. If any jars fail to seal, refrigerate and use within ten days or freeze for later use. Makes 5 cups.

Nutritional value: 1 tablespoon contains 42 Calories (P^1/$_2$,F0,C10). *This should not be used by diabetics or hypoglycemics.* If no salt is added, 2 tablespoons contain 1 milligram sodium. Recipe contains 0 cholesterol.

Blueberry-Pineapple Preserves with Honey

Blueberries   4 cups, washed, stems removed
Water   2 tablespoons
Lemon juice   3 tablespoons
Crushed pineapple   2 cups (canned in own juice)
Honey   1^1/$_2$ cups
Lemon rind   1 tablespoon grated
Salt   dash (optional)
Cinnamon   1^1/$_2$ teaspoons (optional)

Place berries in deep nonaluminum kettle. Add water and juice. Cook until tender, mashing to break up whole berries. Add pineapple, honey, rind, salt, and cinnamon. Cook until thick. Skim and pack immediately in hot, sterile ^{1}/$_2$-pint or pint jars, leaving ^{1}/$_2$ inch at top. Cap with hot, sterile lids. Process in boiling-water bath for 5 minutes after water returns to boiling. If any jars fail to seal, refrigerate and use within ten days or freeze for later use. Makes 4 cups.

Nutritional value: 1 tablespoon contains 36 Calories (P0,F0,C9). *This should not be used by diabetics or hypoglycemics.* If no salt is added, 1 tablespoon contains less than 1 milligram sodium. Recipe contains 0 cholesterol.

Purple Plum Conserve with Honey

Purple plums, prune-type   6 cups chopped, pitted
Medium orange   1, seeded, chopped, including peel
Medium lemon   1, seeded, chopped, including peel
Water ^{3}/$_4$ cup

Honey $1^1/_2$ cups
Seedless raisins 2 cups
Salt dash (optional)
Pecans or walnuts $^3/_4$ cup chopped

Place plums, orange, lemon, and water in a deep nonaluminum kettle. Cover and simmer for 25 minutes. Add honey, raisins, and salt and continue to cook until thick, stirring often. Add nuts, mix well, skim, and pack immediately into hot, sterile $^1/_2$-pint or pint jars, leaving $^1/_2$ inch at top. Cap with hot, sterile lids. Process in boiling-water bath for 5 minutes after water returns to boiling. If any jars fail to seal, refrigerate and use within ten days or freeze for later use. Makes $9^1/_2$ cups.

Nutritional value: 1 tablespoon contains 25 Calories (P0,F$^1/_2$,C5). *This should not be used by diabetics or hypoglycemics.* If no salt is added, 1 tablespoon contains less than 1 milligram sodium. Recipe contains 0 cholesterol.

FREEZER JAM OR PRESERVES WITH HONEY

To make freezer jam with honey, you must use much more honey than is really needed. To reduce the excessive sweetness, you may want to add extra lemon juice. If the frozen-jam recipes given are not usable directly from the freezer, they should be thawed in the refrigerator for a short time before using.

Basic Frozen Preserves with Honey

Fruit 4 cups chopped or sliced, including juice
Lemon juice 3 tablespoons
Water $^1/_4$ cup (may omit if fruit is juicy)
Orange or lemon rind 1 teaspoon to 1 tablespoon grated
Honey $1^1/_2$ to 2 cups
Salt dash (optional)

Spices (cinnamon, nutmeg, cloves, ginger, etc.) to taste
(optional)

Place fruit, juice, and water in deep nonaluminum kettle. Bring to a boil and simmer until fruit is tender, stirring often. Add remaining ingredients and return to heat. Simmer until thickened. Add small amount of spices and taste after a few minutes, adding more if desired. Skim and pack immediately in clean $1/2$-pint or pint jars, leaving $1/2$ inch at top. Cap with clean lids. Cool to room temperature. Place in sharp-freeze section of freezer until hard. Store in regular section. If necessary, thaw in refrigerator before using. Makes 5 cups.

Nutritional value: 1 tablespoon contains from 28 to 40 Calories depending on fruit used (P0,F0,C7–10). *This should not be used by diabetics or hypoglycemics.* If no salt is added, 1 tablespoon contains less than 1 milligram sodium. Recipe contains 0 cholesterol.

Frozen Strawberry Preserves with Honey

Strawberries   4 cups washed and hulled
Lemon juice   3 tablespoons
Water $1/4$ cup
Honey $1 1/2$ cups
Salt   dash (optional)
Lemon rind $1/2$ teaspoon grated (optional)

Place berries, lemon juice, and water in saucepan; cover and simmer until tender. (Mash berries to release more juice if desired.) Add honey and salt and continue to cook until thick, stirring often. Taste, add lemon rind, if desired, and heat 1 minute longer. Skim and pour immediately into clean $1/2$-pint or pint jars, leaving $1/2$ inch at top. Cap with clean lids and cool to room temperature. When cool, place in sharp-freeze section of freezer until hard. Store in regular section. If necessary, thaw in refrigerator. before using. Makes $4 1/2$ cups.

Nutritional value: $1^1/_2$ tablespoons contain 40 Calories (P0,F0,C10). *This should not be used by diabetics or hypoglycemics.* If no salt is added, 2 tablespoons contain 1 milligram sodium. Recipe contains 0 cholesterol.

FRUIT SYRUPS WITH HONEY

Excellent fruit syrups may be made with honey by using only half the amount of pectin called for in the recipe. These syrups are *so* tasty on pancakes or waffles, and best of all, they contain no refined sugar!

Basic Fruit Juice Syrup with Honey

Follow recipe for Basic Fruit Juice Syrup (see Recipe Index) but make the following changes:

Add: **Honey** 1 tablespoon

Follow directions as given, adding honey just before adding pectin solution. Taste to see if you want more sweetening or lemon juice. Mix well, then add pectin solution and follow remaining directions as given.

Nutritional value: Apple juice syrup: $^1/_4$ cup contains 61 Calories (P0,F0,C15). *Grape juice syrup:* $^1/_4$ cup contains 64 Calories (P0,F0,C16). *Orange juice syrup:* $^1/_4$ cup contains 59 Calories (P0,F0,C14). All variations of sauce contain less than 2 milligrams sodium. Recipe contains 0 cholesterol.

BLUEBERRY-ORANGE SYRUP WITH HONEY

Blueberries   5 cups washed and stemmed
Concentrated orange juice (frozen, undiluted) $^1/_3$ cup
Lemon juice   2 to $2^1/_2$ tablespoons

Lemon rind $^1/_4$ teaspoon grated
Salt $^1/_4$ teaspoon (optional)
Liquid pectin (regular) *3 tablespoons*
Honey 2 to 3 tablespoons

Place fruit, juices, rind (and salt) in deep nonaluminum kettle. Simmer over low heat, stirring frequently, until berries are soft (may mash when softened to make a smoother syrup). Add pectin and honey. Return to heat and bring to a rolling boil for 1 minute. Remove from heat. Taste. Add more honey or lemon juice if desired. When still boiling hot, pour into hot, sterile $^1/_2$-pint or pint jars, leaving $^1/_2$ inch at top. Top with hot, sterile lids. Process in boiling-water bath for 5 minutes after water returns to boiling. If any jars fail to seal, refrigerate and use within ten days or freeze for later use. (If the syrup is thicker than you like, thin with boiling water before canning.) Makes about 5 cups.

Nutritional value: $^1/_4$ cup contains 36 Calories. *This should not be used by diabetics or hypoglycemics.* If salt is omitted, $^1/_4$ cup contains $2^1/_2$ milligrams sodium. Recipe contains 0 cholesterol.

Strawberry Syrup

Strawberries 4 cups, stemmed and halved
Lemon juice 4 tablespoons
Water $^3/_4$ cup
Salt dash (optional)
Liquid pectin (regular) 3 ounces ($1^1/_2$ package)
Honey $^3/_4$–1 cup

Place berries, lemon juice, water (and salt) in deep nonaluminum kettle. Simmer over low heat until berries are soft (may mash to make a smoother jam). Remove from heat; stir in pectin and honey. Return to heat and bring to a rolling boil for 1 minute. (If this is a little thick, thin with boiled water before packing.) Makes $4^1/_2$ cups.

Note: May be made with raspberries, boysenberries, etc., and lemon juice adjusted to taste.

Nutritional value: $^1/_4$ cup contains 54 Calories (P0,F0,C14). *This recipe should not be used by diabetics or hypoglycemics.* If salt is omitted, $^1/_4$ cup contains 1 milligram sodium. Recipe contains 0 cholesterol.

PICKLES, RELISHES, AND SEASONING SAUCES

Pickle, relish, and sauce recipes can be made with honey instead of sugar, but the amount used is half or less. It is hard to keep honey flavor from intruding, so in some recipes a degree of sweetness has been sacrificed to avoid this. Pickle and relish recipes in the section using fruit juices for sweetening (see Recipe Index) can be made with honey instead (see Table 10). Make a small trial batch to be sure the sweetness is right.

Pickles made with honey must be processed in a water bath or pressure cooker after water returns to boiling (see below). Check seal when cool, refrigerate any that are not sealed, and use within ten days. *Do not freeze!* Most pickles that have been frozen are mushy. You can freeze relish (try one jar) and seasoning sauces successfully.

IMPORTANT: READ BEFORE STARTING TO MAKE PICKLES!

The time required to process pickles increases with altitude. The times given in these recipes are for heights up to 1,000 feet. For altitudes from 1,001 to 3,000 feet, add 5 minutes to processing time (20 minutes); for those from 3,001 to 6,000 feet, add 5 minutes for quart-sized jars (other sizes need not be processed longer). At altitudes higher than 6,000 feet, add 5 minutes longer for all sizes (25 minutes for size smaller than quarts, 30 minutes for quarts). This timing is essential to ensure safe canning. *Do not use jars larger than those specified without increasing processing time.*

Be sure to use vinegar with at least 5 percent acidity (read the label on the container). Cider vinegar has a milder taste than white distilled vinegar and should be used for all pickles except light-colored ones, such as onions.

Do not use zinc, copper, brass, galvanized metal, iron, or aluminum kettles for making pickles. These metals may react with acid (vinegar) and/or salt and affect the quality and safety of home-canned pickles. As with all home-canned products, look for spoilage before using. *If in doubt, throw it out!*

Corn Relish with Honey

Whole kernel corn   4 cups (cut from ears or frozen)
Green cabbage $1^1/_4$ cups chopped
Medium white onions   3, chopped
Green peppers   2, seeded, stems removed
Small red peppers (hot or sweet)   2, seeded, stems removed
Pimiento   3 tablespoons minced
Celery seed $^2/_3$ teaspoon
Mustard seed $^2/_3$ teaspoon
Cider vinegar $2^1/_2$ cups
Salt or salt substitute   1 tablespoon
Honey $^1/_2$ cup

Place corn in large nonaluminum kettle. Grind other vegetables in meat grinder using coarse blade. Add with remaining ingredients to corn and bring to a boil. Turn down heat and simmer for 35 minutes. Skim and pack immediately into hot, sterile pint jars, leaving $^1/_2$ inch at top. Cap with hot, sterile lids and process in boiling-water bath for 15 minutes after water returns to boiling. (Refer to page 207 for times to use at altitudes higher than 1,000 feet.) If any jars fail to seal, refrigerate and use within ten days or freeze for later use. Makes $8^1/_2$ to 9 cups.

Nutritional value: *This should not be used by diabetics or hypo-glycemics.* 2 tablespoons contain 20 Calories (P0,F0,C5). If salt is omitted and fresh corn used, 2 tablespoons contain 4 milligrams sodium. Recipe contains 0 cholesterol.

Diabetic variation: A diabetic version of this recipe can be made by omitting honey and substituting 1$\frac{1}{4}$ cups concentrated apple juice and 1 to 2 tablespoons lemon juice.

Nutrional value: 2 tablespoons contain 18 Calories (P0,F0,C4$\frac{1}{2}$). 2 tablespoons = 1 diabetic vegetable exchange. If salt is omitted and fresh corn used, 2 tablespoons contain 12 milligrams sodium. Recipe contains 0 cholesterol, 2 teaspoons may be used without diabetic replacement.

Indian Chutney with Honey

Large, ripe tomatoes   5
Large onions   3, peeled and chopped
Green pepper   1, seeded and chopped
Hot or sweet red pepper   1, seeded
Large tart apples   4, seeded and cored
Seedless raisins $\frac{3}{4}$ cup
Honey $\frac{1}{3}$ cup
Cider vinegar   1$\frac{1}{3}$ cups
Salt or salt substitute   1$\frac{1}{2}$ teaspoons
Curry powder   1 teaspoon

Grind all fruits and vegetables in meat grinder using medium blade. Place in deep nonaluminum kettle and add honey, vinegar, salt, and curry. Simmer until thickened, about 1 hour. Skim and pour into hot, sterile pint jars, leaving $\frac{1}{2}$ inch at top. Cap with hot, sterile lids and process in boiling-water bath for 20 minutes after water returns to boiling. (Refer to page 207 for times to use at altitudes higher than 1,000 feet.) If any jars fail to seal, refrigerate and use within ten days or freeze for later use. Makes 8 cups.

Nutritional value: This should not be used by diabetics or hypoglycemics. 2 tablespoons contain 20 Calories (P0,F0,C5). If salt is omitted, 2 tablespoons contain 2 milligrams sodium. Recipe contains 0 cholesterol.

Diabetic variation: A diabetic version of this recipe could be made by omitting honey and substituting $1/2$ cup concentrated apple juice and 2 tablespoons lemon juice.

Nutritional value: $2^1/_2$ tablespoons contain 20 Calories (P0,F0,C5). $2^1/_2$ tablespoons = 1 diabetic vegetable exchange. If salt is omitted, 2 tablespoons contain 2 milligrams sodium. Recipe contains 0 cholesterol. 2 teaspoons can be used without diabetic replacement.

Mother's Beet-Cabbage Relish with Honey

Follow recipe for Mother's Beet-Cabbage Relish with Fruit Juice (see Recipe Index) but make the following changes:

Omit: Concentrated white grape juice   1 cup
Add: Honey $1/_4$ cup + $3/_4$ cup water

Follow directions as given, omitting the juice and substituting the honey water. Stir thoroughly, taste and determine if you wish to add more honey or more lemon juice. Follow remaining directions as given.

Nutritional value: 1 tablespoon contains 8 Calories (P0,F0,C2). If salt is omitted, 1 tablespoon contains 2 milligrams sodium. Recipe contains 0 cholesterol.

Pickled Beets with Honey

Tiny beets   12 cups
Whole allspice   1 teaspoon
Whole cloves $^1/_2$ teaspoon
Cinnamon sticks   2, broken into 4 pieces
Lemon juice   1 $^1/_2$ tablespoons
Honey   1 cup
Cider vinegar   2 cups
Water   2 cups plus water to cook beets

Wash beets and cut off tops, leaving at least 1 inch to prevent bleeding. Cover with water and cook until tender. Drain and cool sufficiently to handle easily. Remove skin and trim tops and roots uniformly. If any are too large, slice and pack separately. Make a bag for spices and place in deep saucepan along with lemon juice, honey, vinegar, and 2 cups of water. Bring to a boil, add beets, and cook for 10 minutes. Remove spice bag and pack beets immediately into hot, sterile pint jars, leaving $^1/_2$ inch at top. Cap with hot, sterile lids and process in boiling-water bath for 30 minutes after water returns to boiling. (Refer to page 207 for times to use at altitudes higher than 1,000 feet.) If any jars fail to seal, refrigerate and use within ten days. *Do not freeze.* Makes 6 pints.

Nutritional value: $^1/_4$ cup contains 28 Calories (P0,F0,C7). *This should not be used by diabetics or hypoglycemics.* If fresh beets are used, $^1/_4$ cup contains 21 milligrams sodium. Recipe contains 0 cholesterol.

Sweet Hot Pepper Relish with Honey

Large red peppers   6, seeded and chopped
Large green peppers   6, seeded and chopped
Medium onions   6, peeled and chopped
Salt or salt substitute   2 tablespoons

Pickling vinegar $1^1/_2$ cups
Lemon juice   2 tablespoons
Cayenne pepper $^1/_2$ teaspoon
Honey $^1/_2$ to $^3/_4$ cup
Tabasco sauce   dash (optional)

Grind vegetables in meat grinder using medium-coarse blade. Mix with salt and let stand 4 hours or overnight. Drain and discard liquid. Put drained vegetables in large nonaluminum kettle and add remaining ingredients. Cook over low heat until thickened, $^3/_4$ hour or more. Taste and add more cayenne (or Tabasco sauce) and honey if desired. Pour into hot, sterile $^1/_2$-pint or pint jars, leaving $^1/_2$ inch at top. Cap with hot, sterile lids and process in boiling-water bath for 15 minutes after water returns to boiling. (Refer to page 207 for times to use at altitudes higher than 1,000 feet.) If any jars fail to seal, refrigerate and use within ten days or freeze for later use. Makes 7 cups.

Nutritional value: 1 tablespoon contains 12 Calories (P0,F0,C3). If the larger amount of honey is used, 1 tablespoon contains 14 Calories (P0,F0,C3$^1/_2$). *This should not be used by diabetics or hypoglycemics.* If salt is not used, 1 tablespoon contains fewer than 3 milligrams sodium. Recipe contains 0 cholesterol.

Sweet Tomato Pickles with Honey

Green or unripe tomatoes   8 cups
Large onions   2, peeled and sliced
Large apple   1, peeled and cored
Salt or salt substitute $^1/_4$ cup
Cider vinegar   1 cup
Honey $^1/_2$ cup
Cloves $1^1/_2$ teaspoons
Dry mustard $1^1/_2$ teaspoons
Cinnamon $1^1/_2$ teaspoons
Cayenne pepper $^1/_8$ teaspoon

Peel and slice tomatoes, slice onions and apple, and place all in large bowl. Add salt, mix, and let stand at least 12 hours. Drain and discard liquid. Add vinegar and cook for 45 minutes. Add remaining ingredients and cook for 20 to 30 minutes longer until thick. Skim and pack in hot, sterile pint jars, leaving $1/2$ inch at top. Cap with hot, sterile lids and process in boiling-water bath for 15 minutes after water returns to boiling. (Refer to page 207 for times to use at altitudes higher than 1,000 feet.) If any jars fail to seal, refrigerate and use within ten days or freeze for later use. Makes 8 cups.

Nutritional value: 1 tablespoon contains 12 Calories (P0,F0,C3). *This should not be used by diabetics or hypoglycemics.* If salt is not used, 1 tablespoon contains less than 1 milligram sodium. Recipe contains 0 cholesterol.

Fruit Relish with Honey

Unsweetened applesauce (see Recipe Index)   2 cups
Honey   1 to $1^1/2$ teaspoons
Lemon juice $1^1/2$ tablespoons
Prepared horseradish   2 tablespoons
Lemon rind $1/4$ teaspoon grated (optional)
Salt   dash (optional)

Place applesauce in mixing bowl and add smaller amount of honey and remaining ingredients. Mix well. Taste. Add remaining honey if desired. Pack into hot, sterile $1/2$-pint jars, leaving $1/2$ inch at top. Cap with hot, sterile lids and freeze or process in boiling-water bath for 15 minutes after water returns to boiling. If any jars fail to seal, refrigerate and use within ten days or freeze for later use.

To freeze, place cooled jars in sharp-freeze section of freezer until hard. Store in regular section. Thaw overnight in refrigerator before using. Makes 2 cups.

Nutritional value: 1 tablespoon contains 12 Calories (P0,F0,C3). *This should not be used by diabetics or hypoglycemics.* If no salt is added, 1 tablespoon contains 1 milligram sodium. Recipe contains 0 cholesterol.

MEATLESS MINCEMEAT WITH HONEY

Follow recipe for Basic Sugarless Vegetarian Mincemeat (see Recipe Index), but instead of date sugar, substitute $^1/_4$ to $^1/_2$ cup honey. If the same volume honey as date sugar is used, the nutritional value does not change significantly. If the honey is increased to $^1/_2$ cup, the values are as follows:

Regular date sugar recipe, 116 Calories per $^1/_4$ cup
**With $^1/_4$ cup honey substituted for date sugar, 124 Calories
    per $^1/_4$ cup**
**With $^1/_2$ cup honey substituted for date sugar, 144 Calories
    per $^1/_4$ cup**

Sodium content is not altered by substituting honey for date sugar. $^1/_4$ cup contains 7 milligrams sodium.

Variation: To make Green Tomato Mincemeat with Honey, follow recipe for Green Tomato Mincement (see Recipe Index), but omit date sugar and substitute $^1/_2$ cup honey.

Nutritional value: $^1/_4$ cup contains 90 Calories, $^1/_4$ cup contains 5 milligrams sodium. *Diabetics or hypoglycemics should not use these recipes with honey.* Recipe contains 0 cholesterol.

WINTER RECIPES USING HONEY

All-year-round recipes made from nonseasonal fruits and vegetables follow. Be sure that winter recipe ingredients are as choice as those available "in season." Choose only eating-ripe fruits and vegetables. Many of the recipes presented in preceding sections can also be made during the winter or off-season: Try "Applesauce with Honey," "Mincemeat," "Fruit Relish" (see Recipe Index), or others adaptable to ingredients available during winter months.

WINTER JAMS, JELLIES, AND PRESERVES

Applesauce Apple Butter with Honey

White grape juice   2 cups
Unsweetened applesauce   4 cups
Apple juice   2 cups
Cinnamon   2 teaspoons ground
Cloves $^1/_3$ teaspoon ground
Allspice $^1/_3$ teaspoon ground
Lemon rind   1 teaspoon grated fresh
Lemon juice   2 tablespoons
Honey $^1/_4$ to $^1/_2$ cup (use larger amount for sweeter jam)

Simmer grape juice over low heat in deep nonaluminum kettle until reduced to half volume. Add next two ingredients, stirring to mix. Return to heat and bring to a boil; then turn down heat and simmer until slightly thickened, stirring frequently. Remove from heat, stir in remaining ingredients, and continue to simmer, stirring often. After 5 minutes, taste and add additional honey and/or lemon juice if desired. Continue to cook until jam reaches the desired thickness, stirring frequently. Pour into hot, sterile $^1/_2$-pint or pint jars, leaving $^1/_2$ inch at top. Cap with hot, sterile lids. Process in boiling-water bath for 15 minutes after water returns to boiling. If any jars fail to seal, refrigerate and use within ten days or freeze for later use. Makes 5¹/₂ cups.

Nutritional value: 1 tablespoon contains 13 Calories (P0,F0,C3). *This should not be used by diabetics or hypoglycemics.* 1 tablespoon contains 3.5 milligrams sodium. Recipe contains 0 cholesterol.

Apricot-Pineapple Jam with Honey

Dried apricots   1 pound
Water
Crushed pineapple   2 cups (in own juice)
Lemon   ¹/₄, seeded and chopped
Lemon juice   ¹/₄ cup
Honey   ³/₄ cup
Salt   dash (optional)

Soak apricots overnight in warm water (just enough to cover). In morning, place in deep nonaluminum kettle; add pineapple, lemon, and juice. (Add more water for cooking if all was absorbed into the dried fruit.) Cook slowly until fruit is tender and mixture thickened. Add honey and cook for 3 minutes longer, stirring to prevent sticking. Remove from heat, skim, and pour into hot, sterile ¹/₂-pint or pint jars, leaving ¹/₂ inch at top. Cap with hot, sterile lids. Process in boiling-water bath for 5 minutes after water returns to boiling. If any jars fail to seal, refrigerate and use within ten days or freeze for later use. Makes 5 cups.

Nutritional value: 1 tablespoon contains 20 Calories (P0,F0,C5). *This should not be used by diabetics or hypoglycemics.* If no salt is used, 1 tablespoon contains less than 1 milligram sodium. Recipe contains 0 cholesterol.

Winter Pear Jam with Honey

Ripe winter pears   3 pounds, peeled and cored
Medium orange   1, seeded
Medium lemon   1, seeded
Crushed pineapple   1 cup (canned in own juice)
Honey   3/4 cup
Fresh ginger root   1 inch, peeled and thinly sliced
Whole cloves   6
Cinnamon sticks   2, broken into 3 pieces
Salt   dash (optional)

Using coarse blade of meat grinder, grind fruits. Place in deep nonaluminum kettle, adding pineapple and juice. Add remaining ingredients and simmer until fruit is tender and mixture thick, stirring often. Skim and pour into hot, sterile pint jars, leaving 1/2 inch at top. Cap with hot, sterile lids. Process in boiling-water bath for 5 minutes after water returns to boiling. If any jars fail to seal, refrigerate and use within ten days or freeze for later use. Makes 3 pints.

Nutritional value: 1 tablespoon contains 20 Calories (P0,F0,C5). *This should not be used by diabetics or hypoglycemics.* 1 tablespoon contains 2 milligrams sodium. Recipe contains 0 cholesterol.

Prune Conserve with Honey

Medium prunes   1 pound, pitted
Seedless raisins   1 cup
Water   2 cups
Crushed pineapple   1 cup (canned in own juice)
Medium orange   1, seeded, with juice and chopped rind
Medium lemon   1/2, seeded, with juice and chopped rind
Honey   1/2 cup
Walnuts or pecans   1/2 cup chopped
Lemon rind   1 teaspoon grated (optional)
Salt   dash (optional)

Soak prunes and raisins overnight in the water plus any juices from the orange and lemon. In the morning, place in deep nonaluminum saucepan with all other ingredients except nuts. Simmer until thick, stirring often to prevent sticking. When thick, add nuts and heat 1 minute more. Skim and pack immediately in hot, sterile $1/2$-pint or pint jars, leaving $1/2$ inch at top. Cap with hot, sterile lids. Process in boiling-water bath for 5 minutes after water returns to boiling. If any jars fail to seal, refrigerate and use within ten days or freeze for later use. Makes 7 cups.

Nutritional value: 2 tablespoons contain 61 Calories (P0,F1,C13). *This should not be used by diabetics or hypoglycemics.* If no salt is added, 2 tablespoons contain 2 milligrams sodium. Recipe contains 0 cholesterol.

Frozen Blueberry-Pineapple Preserves with Honey

Frozen blueberries   4 cups
Crushed pineapple   2 cups (canned in own juice)
Water $1/4$ cup
Lemon juice   3 tablespoons
Lemon rind   2 teaspoons grated
Honey $1^1/2$ cups
Cinnamon or nutmeg $1/2$ teaspoon
Unflavored gelatin   1 tablespoon (1 envelope)
Salt   dash (optional)

Place berries, pineapple, water, lemon juice, and lemon rind in deep nonaluminum kettle. Cook slowly until berries are tender, stirring often. Remove from heat; add honey, spices, gelatin, and salt. Return to heat and cook until thick. Skim and pour into hot, sterile $1/2$-pint jars, leaving $1/2$ inch at top. Cap with hot, sterile lids. Process in boiling-water bath for 5 minutes after water returns to boiling. If any jars fail to seal, refrigerate and use within ten days or freeze for later use.

To freeze, cool jars to room temperature; then place in sharp-freeze section of freezer until hard. Store in regular section. To use, thaw overnight in refrigerator. Makes 4 cups.

Nutritional value: 1 tablespoon contains 36 Calories (P0,F0,C9). *This should not be used by diabetics or hypoglycemics.* If no salt is added, 1 tablespoon contains less than 1 milligram sodium. Recipe contains 0 cholesterol.

Variation: This recipe makes a wonderful fruit syrup if gelatin is omitted and mixture cooked for a shorter time and thinned with 1 to $1\frac{1}{2}$ cups boiling water before freezing or canning. Makes 5 to $5\frac{1}{2}$ cups.

Nutritional value: $1\frac{1}{4}$ to $1\frac{1}{2}$ tablespoons will contain same nutritional value as jam, depending on how thin the syrup is.

Winter Marmalade with Honey

Carrots   3 large bunches (approximately 4 pounds)
Water
Large grapefruit   1
Large lemons   2
Large orange   1
Large tangerines   2
Honey   4 cups

Peel or scrape carrots, cover with water, and cook until tender. Drain and discard water (or save to use; it is rich in vitamins and minerals). Mash to make uniform pieces. Squeeze juice from fruit and add to carrots. Cut rinds into chunks, cover with water, and cook for 15 minutes. Drain and add liquid to carrots. Chop rinds into very narrow strips. Add to carrots, along with honey. Refrigerate overnight. Boil in deep nonaluminum pan until thick, stirring often. Remove from heat; skim and pack immediately in clean pint jars, leaving $1/2$ inch at top. Cap with clean lids. Refrigerate and use within ten days or freeze for later use. *Do not can this marmalade.* Makes 10 cups.

Nutritional value: 1 tablespoon contains 34 Calories (P0,F0,C8$1/2$). *This should not be used by diabetics or hypoglycemics.* 1 tablespoon contains 16 milligrams sodium. Recipe contains 0 cholesterol.

Preserved Orange Slices with Honey

Large, thin-skinned oranges   6
Lemon slices   2, seeded and diced
Water   1 quart (approximately)
Lemon juice $1/4$ cup
Honey   1 cup

Wash and dry oranges. Cut off and discard ends; then cut about 3 slices per inch, including rind, but removing seeds. Place in deep nonaluminum saucepan, adding lemon and juice plus enough water to cover. Cover pan and simmer until rind is tender and translucent. Add honey and simmer 5 minutes more. Place slices in wide-mouth hot, sterile pint jars, leaving $1/2$ inch at top. Cover with hot liquid and cap with hot, sterile lids. Process in boiling-water bath for 5 minutes after water returns to boiling. If any jars fail to seal, refrigerate and use within ten days. *Do not freeze.* Makes 6 cups.

Nutritional value: 2 slices contain 64 Calories (P0,F0,C16). *This should not be used by diabetics or hypoglycemics.* 2 slices contain less than 1 milligram sodium. Recipe contains 0 cholesterol.

Note: These orange slices are wonderful to serve at a buffet meal. They blend well with any entrée or salad.

WINTER RELISHES AND SEASONING SAUCES WITH HONEY

Barbecue Sauce with Honey

Tomato puree   2 cups *or Tomato paste*   1 cup *and*
    Water   1 cup
Honey   1 tablespoon or more
Onion powder $1/2$ teaspoon
Allspice $1/8$ teaspoon
Garlic powder $1/8$ teaspoon
Cider vinegar $1/2$ cup
Worcestershire sauce $1/2$ teaspoon

Mix all ingredients and stir well. Place in nonaluminum kettle and heat to boiling; then simmer for 5 minutes. Pack in hot, sterile $1/2$-pint jars, leaving $1/2$ inch at top. Cap with hot, sterile lids and process in boiling-water bath for 15 minutes after water returns to boiling. (Refer to page 207 for times to use at altitudes higher than 1,000 feet.) If any jars fail to seal, refrigerate and use within ten days or freeze for later use.

To freeze, allow to cool after packing; then place in sharp-freeze section of freezer until hard. Store in regular section of freezer. Thaw overnight in refrigerator before using. Makes $2^1/2$ cups.

Variation: For hot barbecue sauce, add $1/2$ teaspoon Tabasco sauce and $1/4$ to $1/2$ teaspoon cayenne pepper.

Nutritional value: $1/2$ cup contains 40 Calories (P2,F0,C8). *This should not be used by diabetics or hypoglycemics.* If no salt is added and salt-free puree or paste is used, 2 tablespoons contain 14 milligrams sodium. Recipe contains 0 cholesterol.

Diabetic variation: This can be made into a diabetic recipe by omitting honey and substituting 2 tablespoons concentrated apple juice instead.

Nutritional value: $^1/_2$ cup contains 36 Calories (P2,F0,C7). $^1/_2$ cup = $^1/_2$ diabetic bread exchange. If salt is omitted and salt-free puree or paste is used, $^1/_2$ cup contains 56 milligrams sodium. Recipe contains 0 cholesterol. 1 tablespoon can be used without diabetic replacement.

Tomato Catsup with Honey

Ripe tomatoes or whole canned, drained   8 cups, peeled and quartered (with sauce)
Medium onions   2, peeled and chopped
Large green pepper   1, seeded and chopped
Small garlic cloves   4, minced
Large celery stalks   2, diced
Cider vinegar   1 cup
Honey $^1/_2$ cup
Cloves $^1/_2$ teaspoon
Dry mustard   1 teaspoon
Mace $^1/_2$ teaspoon
Allspice   1 teaspoon
Tabasco sauce $^1/_4$ teaspoon (optional)
Lemon juice   2 tablespoons
Salt or salt substitute   1 tablespoon
Black pepper $^1/_2$ teaspoon

Combine all ingredients in large nonaluminum kettle. Cook slowly over low heat, stirring often, until vegetables are very soft, being careful to prevent mixture from boiling. Remove from heat and put through food mill. Return to heat and bring to boil. Pour into hot, sterile pint jars, leaving $^1/_2$ inch at top. Cap with hot, sterile lids and process in boiling-water bath for 15 minutes after water returns to boiling. (Refer to page 207 for times to use at altitudes higher than 1,000 feet.) If any jars fail to seal, refrigerate and use within ten days or freeze for later use. Makes 4 pints.

Nutritional value: 1 tablespoon contains 16 Calories (P0,F0,C4).If made with honey, *this should not be used by diabetics or hypo-*

glycemics. If fresh tomatoes are used and no salt is added, 1 tablespoon contains 1 milligram sodium. Recipe contains 0 cholesterol.

Diabetic variation: This can be made into a diabetic recipe by omitting honey, substituting $^3/_4$ cup concentrated apple juice, and increasing lemon juice to 4 tablespoons.

Nutritional value: 1 tablespoon contains 12 Calories (P0,F0,C3). 2 tablespoons = 1 diabetic vegetable exchange. If salt is omitted and fresh tomatoes used, 1 tablespoon contains 1 milligram sodium. Recipe contains 0 cholesterol. $1^1/_2$ teaspoons can be used without diabetic replacement.

Tomato Sauce for Tacos with Honey

Ripe tomatoes   6 cups, peeled, cored, and finely chopped
Large garlic clove   1, minced
Onion $2^1/_2$ cups, finely chopped
Jalapeño peppers $1^1/_4$ to $1^1/_2$, seeded and finely chopped*
Long green chilies   1, finely chopped
Cider vinegar   1 cup
Salt $^1/_4$ to $^1/_2$ teaspoon (optional)
Black pepper $^1/_4$ teaspoon ground
Honey $^1/_2$ teaspoon
Dried oregano   1 tablespoon
Cumin   pinch (optional)

Combine all ingredients (using smaller amounts of seasonings where there is an option) in deep nonaluminum kettle. Mix well and bring to a boil. Reduce heat and simmer until thick, stirring often. Taste; add remaining ingredients, if desired. Reheat to boiling if additions are made. Pour into hot, sterile pint jars, leaving $^1/_2$ inch at top. Cap with hot, sterile lids and process in boiling-water bath for 15

*For mild sauce, use $1^1/_4$ peppers. For hotter sauce, increase to $1^1/_2$. For really hot sauce, use 2 and add $^1/_2$ teaspoon Tabasco sauce.

minutes after water returns to boiling. (Refer to page 207 for times to use at altitudes higher than 1,000 feet.) If any jars fail to seal, refrigerate and use within ten days or freeze for later use. Makes about 8 cups.

Nutritional value: 2 tablespoons contain 6 Calories (P0,F0,C1^1/$_2$). *This should not be used by diabetics or hypoglycemics.* If no salt is added, 2 tablespoons contain 2 milligrams sodium. Recipe contains 0 cholesterol.

All-Year-Round Chili Sauce

Canned whole tomatoes, with liquid   4 cups, chopped
Medium onion   1, peeled and chopped
Large green pepper   1, seeded and chopped
Celery   2 large stalks, chopped fine
Apple juice ^{3}/$_4$ cup
Honey ^{1}/$_8$ to ^{1}/$_4$ cup
Salt ^{1}/$_2$ teaspoon (optional)
Black pepper ^{1}/$_4$ teaspoon ground
Cinnamon ^{1}/$_4$ teaspoon ground
Cloves ^{1}/$_4$ teaspoon ground
Allspice ^{1}/$_4$ teaspoon ground
Cumin ^{1}/$_4$ teaspoon ground (optional)
Cider vinegar ^{1}/$_2$ cup
Lemon juice   1 to 2 tablespoons

Combine first five ingredients in a deep, heavy nonaluminum kettle. Bring to a boil; then reduce heat and simmer until vegetables are very soft. Add remaining ingredients (lower amounts of honey and lemon juice), mix well, and continue to simmer, uncovered, until thick, stirring often. Taste and add more honey and/or lemon juice to suit. Return to heat and bring to boiling. Pour into hot, sterile ^{1}/$_2$-pint or pint jars, leaving ^{1}/$_2$ inch at top. Cap with hot, sterile lids and process in boiling-water bath for 15 minutes after water returns to boiling. (Refer to page 207 for times to use at altitudes higher than

1,000 feet.) If any jars fail to seal, refrigerate and use within ten days or freeze for later use. Makes about 5$\frac{1}{2}$ cups.

Nutritional value: 1 tablespoon contains 6 Calories (P0,F0,C1$\frac{1}{2}$). 1 tablespoon contains 19 milligrams sodium. Recipe contains 0 cholesterol.

Salsa for Nachos (Mild or Hot)

Trial recipe:

Green pepper   1 cup, seeded and chopped fine
Large raw tomato   1, cored and chopped fine
Jalapeño or green chile peppers   1$\frac{1}{2}$ cored, seeded and chopped fine
Onion $\frac{1}{4}$ cup, chopped fine
Cider vinegar   1$\frac{1}{2}$ tablespoons
Honey $\frac{1}{2}$ to 1 teaspoon
Salt $\frac{1}{2}$ teaspoon (optional)
Black pepper $\frac{1}{4}$ teaspoon, ground
Chili powder $\frac{1}{2}$ teaspoon

For hot salsa, add:
   Cayenne pepper $\frac{1}{4}$ to $\frac{1}{2}$ teaspoon ground
   Tabasco sauce $\frac{1}{8}$ to $\frac{1}{4}$ teaspoon

Combine ingredients (using lesser amounts where there is a choice) and mix well. Cover and refrigerate for 1 to 2 hours before tasting. If desired, add more of any of the seasonings, honey, or additional chopped onion to taste. Makes about 2 cups.

When you have modified the recipe to suit you, multiply ingredients by 6 to 8 times to make a large batch for processing. Place ingredients in a deep nonaluminum kettle. Bring to a boil; then pour into hot, sterile pint jars, leaving $\frac{1}{2}$ inch at top. Cover with hot, sterile lids and process in boiling-water bath for 15 minutes after water returns to boiling. (Refer to page 207 for times to use at altitudes higher than

1,000 feet.) If any jars fail to seal, refrigerate and use within ten days or freeze for later use.

Nutritional value: $^1/_4$ cup contains 14 Calories (P1,F0,C3). *This should not be used by diabetics or hypoglycemics.* If salt is omitted, $^1/_4$ cup contains 4 milligrams sodium. Recipe contains 0 cholesterol.

Winter Indian Chutney with Honey

Canned tomatoes, canned with juice   4 cups, chopped, with juice
Large onions   3, peeled
Large green pepper   1, seeded
Dried hot red pepper $1^1/_2$ to 2 tablespoons
Large tart apples   4, seeded and cored
Seedless raisins $^7/_8$ cups
Honey $^1/_2$ cup
Cider vinegar $1^1/_3$ cups
Salt or salt substitute $1^1/_2$ teaspoons
Curry powder   1 teaspoon (optional)

Grind all vegetables and fruit in meat grinder using medium blade. Place in deep nonaluminum kettle and add remaining ingredients. Simmer until thick, approximately 1 hour, stirring often. Skim and pack in hot, sterile pint jars, leaving $^1/_2$ inch at top. Process in boiling-water bath for 15 minutes after water returns to boiling. (Refer to page 20 7 for times to use at altitudes higher than 1,000 feet.) If any jars fail to seal, refrigerate and use within ten days or freeze for later use. Makes 8 cups.

Nutritional value: 2 tablespoons contain 20 Calories (P0,F0,C5). *This should not be used by diabetics or hypoglycemics.* If salt substitute and diet-pack tomatoes are used, 2 tablespoons contain 2 milligrams sodium. Recipe contains 0 cholesterol.

SPECIAL INFORMATION FOR DIABETICS AND HYPOGLYCEMICS

Canning and Freezing with Artificial Sweeteners

Unless you or some member of your family is on an extremely low-calorie diet, the fruit packed in this book's light syrup can be used. If you study the tables at the end of this book, you will see that there is very little carbohydrate added by this light syrup. At most, you would have to decrease a diabetic fruit exchange by 1 tablespoon in a half-cup serving. If you really *want* to use artificial sweetening, read the following sections.

Artificial Sweetening—Yes? or No!

Until the cyclamate scare of the late sixties, nobody had ever thought about any undesirable side effects from using artificial sweeteners. Saccharine had been used for over 60 years without any known bad results, and cyclamates had also been in use for 20 years or more with no problems that anyone was aware of. As some of you will remember, all products with cyclamate were removed from the market after some tests indicated that they might be involved in causing cancer with massive use. (Canada removed cyclamates at the same time as the United States did but continued to do further extensive testing. Following the testing they put cyclamates back on their market but banned saccharine.)

The next sweetener to be approved for American use was aspartame (brand names: Equal and Nutrasweet), which was not satisfactory for food processing that involved prolonged heating—including all canning.

This means that no artificial sweetener on the U.S. market is completely free of problems at present—either the manufacturer does not recommend its use for canning and processing, or it may have some undesirable side effects, or just plain not taste good when processed.

Many still feel concerned about using cyclamates (available worldwide, outside of the United States) or saccharine, so the remaining choices are to use water-packed fruit (directions elsewhere in this section), or use slightly smaller portions of fruit juice sweetened, as I suggest.

EVALUATING ARTIFICIAL SWEETENERS

In the coming years there will doubtless be new products that will be safe to use and suitable for processing fruits. With this in mind, I have included some guidelines for evaluating new products as they are available, if you choose to try them.

To be suitable for canning and processing fruit, any new artificial sweetener needs to meet the following criteria:

1. Product does not change when heated for times used in canning.

2. Product does not change when combined with acid or alkaline foods.

3. Product is either a liquid or a solid that dissolves easily in water.

4. Product has no distinctive color or flavor.

GUIDELINES FOR USING ARTIFICIAL SWEETENERS

A. Use only half the amount of sweetening that the label indicates should replace a given volume of sugar. (Example: Label shows 1 teaspoon product = 2 teaspoons sugar. Assume it really equals 3 or 4 teaspoons sugar to your not-using-sugar taste!) Make your trial batch (see Recipe Index), let cool, and taste. You can then add more sweetening if you wish, or you may find that the reduced amount is sufficient. Be sure to cool before you make your taste test so that sweetener has had time to permeate the fruit. *Use boiled water to dissolve the sweetener, allowing the amount of sweetener in 1 cup of water sufficient to sweeten 1 quart fruit.*

I recommend using a light syrup for sweet, ripe fruit. Determine how much artificial sweetener you will need by using the sweetener equivalent of $1/2$ teaspoon sugar for 1 cup processed fruit. If you've been avoiding sugar for some time, this may be amply sweet. Make a trial batch with the fruit, adding $^1/_4$ teaspoon lemon juice for each cup of fruit. Taste after cooling. Once you find how much you want per cup, you then multiply by how many cups you expect to use (1 cup liquid is enough for 1 quart packed fruit). Make your syrup with boiling water, adding $^1/_4$ teaspoon lemon juice (or more) per cup fruit.

B. Be sure fruit is at the *eating-ripe* stage—its natural sugar is at its highest level and it is at its tenderest—so that you need the least amount of supplemental sweetening.

C. Cut fruit into slices or small pieces so that it will pack solidly in the jar, thus allowing its own juice to form part of the liquid. You will then need only a small amount of the sweetened liquid to bring the level up over the fruit, leaving $^3/_4$ to 1 inch for expansion at the top. Top with sterile lids and process (can or freeze) according to the directions in the chapter Selecting and Processing Fruit.

Note: Fruit processed with artificial sweeteners will fade in color even more than that processed with fruit juice. Be sure to keep in a cool, dark place to reduce the amount of fading.

WATER-PACK CANNING DIRECTIONS

If you feel that processing fruit with fruit juice and other natural sweeteners makes the sugar content of the foods too high, you may choose to pack without sweetening (water-pack). Here are the recommendations for you to follow to get best results:

1. Use fruit that is eating-ripe. Slice thin for such fruits as peaches and pears, or quarter plums, halve cherries, etc., so that a minimum of liquid is needed to fill the jar and the juice from the fruit will be diluted as little as possible.

2. Pack the hot, sterile jar as full of fruit as you can without damaging the fruit. Try inserting a small spatula along the sides of the jars to

help eliminate air spaces. When you think it is as full as you can get (leaving 1 inch at top for fluid expansion), gently shake the jar to further pack down the fruit. Then, add boiling hot water to within $^3/_4$ inch of top (completely covering fruit) and process as directed for jar size and variety of fruit (see Table 5).

Freezing Fruit with Artificial Sweeteners

I have found that as long as you cover the frozen fruit completely with liquid, you can as successfully use syrup made with boiled water and artificial sweeteners as with syrup made with fruit juice.

Make your syrup according to the guidelines I've included, making 1 cup with sufficient sweetening for $^1/_2$ quart of fruit. If you have packed the fruit into the freezing container as I have suggested for water-pack canning (see preceeding section), $^1/_2$ cup of this artificially sweetened syrup should be adequate to cover 1 pint of fruit, leaving $^3/_4$ inch at top when packing fruit and $^1/_2$ inch at top with clean lids after syrup is added. Use clean freezing containers or jars, and top with clean lids before placing in sharp-freeze section of freezer until hard. Move to another section of freezer for storage.

Thaw overnight in refrigerate before using, as with other syrup. If it isn't sweet enough when you taste it, you may add more artificial sweetening, recover the jar, and refrigerate for at least 4 hours to let the sweetener permeate the fruit. Or you may just sprinkle more sweetener on top, which won't sweeten the fruit all the way through, but will make it taste all right when eaten.

Water-Pack Freezing Fruits

Follow same directions as given for artificially sweetened syrup.

APPENDIX

RECIPE CONVERSION TABLES

How to Convert Honey-Sweetened Recipes to Fruit Juice-Sweetened
How to Convert Fruit Juice-Sweetened Recipes to Honey-Sweetened
How to Find Calorie Content of Converted Recipes

TABLE 9

SUGGESTED FRUIT JUICE REPLACEMENT FOR HONEY SWEETENING

Amount	Item	Fruit Juice Replacement
1 tablespoon honey		= $2^1/_3$ tablespoons concentrated apple juice
		= $2^1/_2$ tablespoons concentrated orange juice
		= $1^7/_8$ tablespoons concentrated pineapple juice
		= $8^1/_3$ tablespoons regular apple juice
		= $6^1/_4$ tablespoons regular grape juice
		= 3 tablespoons grape juice simmered down from 6 tablespoons
		= $15^1/_4$ tablespoons lemon juice
		= $8^3/_4$ tablespoons regular orange juice
		= $7^1/_2$ tablespoons regular pineapple juice
		= $5^1/_2$ tablespoons regular prune juice

You must consider two things when replacing honey with fruit juice:

1. You must find replacement volume for the juice you add or plan to cook the product longer before adding pectin to allow the extra liquid to evaporate.

2. You should taste before adding pectin and possibly modify the amount of lemon juice and/or spice called for in the recipe. Most recipes using honey have extra lemon juice to balance the honey taste and with fruit juice sweetening, you will not need as much (try cutting amount in half, then taste and add more to suit).

3. If the taste without honey is not to your liking, consider adding a small amount of one of the "sweet" spices (see General Index), and/or extra salt (try $1/8$ teaspoon and add more if desired), and/or use additional concentrated juice (use whatever you've used before). Always do your taste-testing before you add the pectin!

How to Figure Replacement:

1. Find amount of honey to be replaced in the recipe.

2. Decide on the juice you want to use and locate the amount for one tablespoon honey in the table opposite.

3. Multiply the amount of juice by the number of tablespoons of honey you plan to replace.

4. Although honey is approximately 17 percent water ($1^1/3$ teaspoons water in 2 tablespoons honey), it's a small enough amount to usually ignore. You need to look at the recipe to find if there is water or other liquid in the recipe that can be omitted and replaced with the volume of juice to be added. (Replace this liquid with juice at the appropriate place in recipe.) If the recipe calls for regular fruit juice, you may substitute 1/4 the amount in concentrated juice and use the difference in volume as added liquid in the sweetening juice.

If there is no place where you can reduce the liquid without making a major change in the recipe, plan to cook the product longer to reduce the volume before you add the pectin. If you simmer over very low heat, this extra cooking will not alter the taste.

Example: Prune Conserve with Honey (see Recipe Index)

1. Recipe calls for $1/2$ cup honey (8 tablespoons). You decide to use concentrated orange juice to replace that sweetening since orange is already in the recipe.

2. This table shows that it takes $2^1/2$ tablespoons concentrated orange juice to replace 1 tablespoon honey. You need 8 times that since the recipe calls for 8 tablespoons honey. $2^1/_2$ x 8 = 20 tablespoons concentrated orange juice ($1^1/_4$ cup) to replace $^1/_2$ cup honey.

3. The recipe also calls for 2 cups water. Omit approximate volume of concentrated orange juice ($1^1/_4$ cup), and use remaining volume as water. If there is no water or concentrated juice to replace the fruit juice volume, plan to simmer down longer before adding pectin to get a satisfactorily thick product.

You may also combine juices to replace the honey. In this recipe, which contains prunes, you could use part of the sweetening as regular prune juice. To do this, decide proportions of each you wish to use and find replacements in the table that add up to the original sweetening.

How to Convert Fruit Juice-Sweetened Recipes to Honey-Sweetened

Honey tastes at least one third sweeter than does the comparable amount of carbohydrate found in fruit juice. Honey's taste can alter the results of a recipe, and it is best disguised by the addition of lemon juice.

It's tricky to balance the honey sweetening and the natural sweetness of the fruit. Table 10 gives replacements that take into consideration honey's increased sweetening capacity and the differences in sweetening found in the various juices. This table is based on what works best when replacing juice sweetening with honey.

It is best to make a trial batch ($^1/_4$-$^1/_2$ usual amounts) using the amounts of honey and lemon juice shown in Table 10. Follow the example and directions given at the end of the table. Mix well, then taste. If not sweet enough, add proportionately more honey and lemon juice, mixing and tasting after each addition. The cooked product will taste sweeter after it has cooled, so it's best to undersweeten slightly when tasting hot. If you've added too much honey, gradually add lemon juice, tasting after each addition. Write down what you did, as you did it, for future reference.

TABLE 10
WHAT TO START WITH WHEN REPLACING FRUIT JUICE WITH HONEY

Amount	Item	Honey Replacement	Lemon Juice
1 cup	conc.* apple juice	$4^1/_2$ tbsp.	$1^1/_8$ tsp.
1 cup	conc.* orange juice	$4^1/_4$ tbsp.	$1^1/_{16}$ tsp.
1 cup	conc.* pineapple juice	$5^3/_4$ tbsp.	$1^1/_3$ tsp.
1 cup	white grape juice (simmered down from 2 cups)	$3^1/_3$ tbsp.	$^7/_8$ tsp.
1 cup	regular apple juice	4 tsp.	$^1/_3$ tsp.
1 cup	regular orange juice	$3^3/_4$ tsp.	scant $^1/_3$ tsp.
1 cup	regular pineapple juice	$4^2/_3$ tsp.	scant $^1/_2$ tsp.
1 cup	regular white grape juice	5 tsp.	scant $^1/_2$ tsp.

* frozen, undiluted

HOW TO FIGURE REPLACEMENT:

a. Find amount of juice to be replaced.

b. Find equivalent amount of honey to be used (see example below).

Example: Plum Marmalade (juice sweetened, see Recipe Index) calls for two juices—1 cup concentrated orange juice and 1 cup white grape juice. The orange juice is definitely a major ingredient and should not be omitted. Replace only the white grape juice in this recipe.

a. From the table above you'll find that 1 cup regular white grape juice = 5 teaspoons honey + scant $^1/_2$ teaspoon lemon juice.

b. Place 5 teaspoons honey + scant $^1/_2$ teaspoon lemon juice in measuring cup. Fill to 1 cup with warm water. Stir well to dissolve the honey. Use in recipe when it calls for adding the replaced fruit juice.

c. If adding more honey/lemon juice, remove $1/2$ cup liquid from the recipe mixture, add the honey/juice, stir well, and add back to the total mixture. Taste-test, and, if satisfactory, continue with directions. If more sweetening is needed, repeat as necessary.

TABLE 11

CALORIE CONTENT OF JUICES* COMPARED TO HONEY

Amount	Calories
1 tablespoon honey (= 4 teaspoons sugar)	61.0
1 tablespoon concentrated apple juice	29.0
1 tablespoon concentrated orange juice	28.0
1 tablespoon concentrated pineapple juice	32.0
1 tablespoon apple juice	7.3
1 tablespoon grape juice	9.7
1 tablespoon lemon juice	4.0
1 tablespoon orange juice	7.0
1 tablespoon pineapple juice	8.1

*Values used for concentrated juices are for frozen, undiluted unsweetened juice.

HOW TO FIND CALORIES IN RECIPES CONVERTED FROM FRUIT JUICE-SWEETENED TO HONEY-SWEETENED:

1. Find the Calories in the amount of fruit juice(s) called for (but omitted) in the recipe.

2. Find the Calories in the amount of honey added.

3. Subtract the fruit juice Calories from the honey Calories.

4. Divide by the number of servings the recipe makes (as given in the original recipe).

5. Add or subtract from Calories per serving given in original recipe.

6. The answer is the Calories per serving in your new recipe.

Example:

Boysenberry Jam with Fruit Juice Sweetening (see Recipe Index):

Recipe calls for: 1 cup concentrated apple juice + 1 cup white grape juice (you simmered it down to half). You used $^3/_4$ cup honey instead of both the concentrated apple juice and grape juice.

1. From the chart find the Calories in 1 tablespoon concentrated apple juice (29), multiply by amount used (16 tablespoons per cup) = 29 x 16 = 464. Now find the Calories in 1 tablespoon grape juice (9.7), multiply by amount used (16 tablespoons per cup) = 9.7 x 16 = 155. Add these figures together: 464 + 155 = 619.

2. Find the Calories in 1 tablespoon honey: 66 x 12 (tablespoons in $^3/_4$ cup) = 792. Subtract: 792 - 619 = 173 additional Calories.

3. Figure the number of servings in recipe (serving = 1 tablespoon). Recipe makes $10^1/_2$ cups x 16 (tablespoons per cup) = 168.

4. Divide the additional Calories by the number of servings: 173 ÷ 168 = 1.1 Calories additional per tablespoon (1 serving).

A lot of work, isn't it! But you don't have to do this! To save you work, I've figured out the replacements for you so that if you replaced fruit juice with honey using Table 10, the Calories will be almost identical with those in the original recipe! (If you use more sweetening than suggested, figure the actual amount you used, find the equivalent Calories and follow the directions above to get the actual Calories in a serving. Then divide this number by 4 to find the grams of carbohydrate for replacement if you used more than recommended.)

NUTRITIONAL INFORMATION

TABLE 12

NUTRITIONAL VALUE OF CANNED FRUIT IN VARIOUS SYRUPS

Fruit	Diabetic Fruit Exchange Equivalent	Water Pack Carb.	Cal.
Applesauce	$^3/_5$ cup	C15	60
Apple slices	$^3/_5$ cup	C15	60
Apricots	6 halves + 3 T. juice	C14	56
Apricot/Apple Slices	(3 apricot halves) $^3/_4$ cup	C16	64
Cherries	12 cherries + $^1/_3$ cup juice	C16	64
Berries: (all with juice)			
Blackberries	$^3/_4$ cup	C16	64
Blueberries	$^7/_8$ cup	C15	60
Boysenberries	$^3/_4$ cup	C16	64
Red Raspberries	$^3/_4$ cup	C16	64
Strawberries	$^3/_4$ cup	C14	56
Berry/Applesauce	$^3/_4$ cup	C16	64
Fruit Cocktail (Mixed fruits)	$^2/_3$ cup	C16	64
Grapes	15 + 2 T. juice	C18	72
Nectarines	$^3/_4$ medium + $1^1/_2$ T. juice	C16	64
Peaches halves or slices	$^3/_4$ cup (2 lg. halves) + 2 T. juice	C15	60
Pear halves	3 small + 3 T. juice	C17	68
Pineapple chunks	$^1/_2$ cup + $1^1/_2$ T. juice	C17	68
Pineapple Slices	2 small + $1^1/_2$ T. juice	C17	68
Prune Plums	3 + 3 T. juice	C16	64

Sources:
1. Catherine Adams. *Nutritive Value of American Foods, in Common Units,* U.S. Department of Agriculture, Agriculture Handbook No. 456. U.S. Government Printing Office, 1975.
2. *Composition of Foods,* Agriculture Handbook No. 8 U.S. Department of Agriculture, Human Nutrition Service, U.S. Government Printing Office, Washington, D.C., Revised 1982–8.
3. Pennington, Jean A. T., and Church, Helen N., *Bowes & Church's Food Values of Portions Commonly Used,* 14th ed. New York: Harper & Row, 1985.

TABLE 12 (continued)

Light Syrup		Medium Syrup*		Sodium**
Carb.	Cal.	Carb.	Cal.	Cont. (Mg.)
C17	68	C19	76	3
C17	68	C19	76	2
C16	64	C18	74	3
C18	72	C20	80	3
C19	76	C21	84	3
C18	72	C20	80	0
C16	64	C18	74	1
C18	72	C20	80	2
C18	72	C20	80	1
C16	64	C18	74	2
C18	72	C20	80	2
C18	72	C20	80	6
C20	80	C22	88	7
C18	72	C20	80	0
C18	72	C20	80	7
C19	76	C21	84	8
C19	76	C21	84	2
C19	76	C21	84	2
C19	76	C21	84	3

*Must reduce portion for diabetics to $^2/_3$ amount shown = 1 fruit exchange
**Sodium content given is for commercially packed juice pack. Home canned will be lower since no sodium is used in processing.

TABLE 13

NUTRITIONAL VALUE OF FRUIT PACKED IN FRUIT JUICE

Fruit	Amount	Un-sweetened Carb.	Cal.	Medium Syrup Carb.	Cal.	Pure Juice Carb	Cal.
Apple slices	$1/_2$ cup	C8	32	C9	36	C10	40
Apricots	$1/_2$ cup	C10	40	C11	44	C12 (Apple juice)	48
Grapefruit sections	$1/_2$ cup	C9	36	C10	40	C10$1/_2$ (Grapefruit juice)	42
Melons Cantaloupe	$1/_2$ cup	C6$1/_2$	28	C7$1/_2$	32	C8 (Orange juice)	34
Watermelon	$1/_2$ cup	C5	21	C6	25	C7 (Apple juice)	29
Nectarines	$1/_2$ cup	C12	48	C13	52	C13$1/_2$ (Orange juice)	54
Orange sections	$1/_2$ cup	C11	44	C12	48	C12$1/_2$ (Orange juice)	50
Peach slices	$1/_2$ cup	C8$1/_2$	36	C9$1/_2$	40	C10$1/_2$ (Apple juice)	44
Pear quarters	$1/_2$ cup	C12$1/_2$	50	C13$1/_2$	54	C15 (Apple-Pear juice)	60

*1 ounce (2 tablespoons) juice allowed per $1/_2$ cup fruit.

TABLE 14

NUTRITIONAL VALUE OF FROZEN FRUITS IN SYRUP*

Fruit	Amount	Liquid Used	Grams Carbo-hydrate	Calories	Sodium mg.
Apple slices	$\frac{1}{2}$ cup	Medium syrup	16	62	2
Applesauce	$\frac{1}{2}$ cup	(recipe given)	16	62	2
Apricots	$\frac{1}{2}$ cup	Medium syrup	12	50	10
Cherries	$\frac{1}{2}$ cup	Medium syrup	12.5	50	1
Grapefruit sections	$\frac{1}{2}$ cup	Grapefruit juice	14.5	58	2
Nectarines	$\frac{1}{2}$ cup	Orange juice	15.5	62	4
Orange sections	$\frac{1}{2}$ cup	Orange juice	14.5	58	1
Peach slices	$\frac{1}{2}$ cup	Medium syrup	13	54	1
Pear slices/ quarters	$\frac{1}{2}$ cup	Medium syrup	15.5	62	2
Plums	$\frac{1}{2}$ cup	Medium syrup	14	57	1
Mixed fruits	$\frac{1}{2}$ cup	Medium syrup	15	60	6

*This assumes liquid is eaten along with fruit.

TABLE 15

NUTRITIONAL VALUE OF
HONEY-SYRUP CANNED FRUITS*

Fruit	Serving Size
Applesauce	$^1/_2$ cup
Apple slices	$^1/_2$ cup
Apricot	4 halves plus 2 Tablespoons juice
Apricot-Apple slices	$^1/_2$ cup
Cherries	8 cherries plus $^1/_4$ cup juice
Berries:	
Blackberries	$^1/_2$ cup
Boysenberries	$^1/_2$ cup
Raspberries, red	$^1/_2$ cup
Strawberries	$^3/_4$ cup
Berry-Applesauce	$^1/_2$ cup
Nectarines	$^1/_2$ cup plus 1 Tablespoon juice
Peach halves	2 halves plus 2 Tablespoons juice
Peach slices	$^1/_2$ cup with 1 Tablespoon juice
Pear halves	2 halves plus 2 Tablespoons juice
Pear slices	$^1/_2$ cup
Pineapple chunks	$^1/_2$ cup with juice
Pineapple slices	1 slice plus 1 Tablespoon juice
Purple (Prune) Plums	2 plums plus 2 Tablespoons juice
Fruit Cocktail (Mixed fruits)	$^1/_2$ cup with 1 Tablespoon juice

*Not for use by diabetics or hypoglycemics.

TABLE 15 (*continued*)

| Light Syrup | | Medium Syrup | | Sodium |
Carb.	Cal.	Carb.	Cal.	Mg.
C18$^1/_2$	72	C19$^1/_2$	76	2
C18$^1/_2$	72	C19$^1/_2$	76	2
C14$^1/_2$	60	C15$^1/_2$	64	1
C16$^1/_2$	66	C17$^1/_2$	70	2
C15	60	C16	64	1
C16$^1/_2$	70	C17$^1/_2$	74	1
C16$^1/_2$	70	C17$^1/_2$	74	1
C16	65	C17	69	1
C15$^1/_2$	66	C16$^1/_2$	70	1
C17$^1/_2$	71	C18$^1/_2$	75	1
C17$^1/_2$	70	C18$^1/_2$	74	4
C15$^1/_2$	64	C16$^1/_2$	68	2
C15$^1/_2$	64	C16$^1/_2$	68	2
C18	72	C19	76	1
C18	72	C19	76	1
C16$^1/_2$	67	C17$^1/_2$	71	1
C15$^1/_2$	65	C16$^1/_2$	69	1
C16$^1/_2$	67	C17$^1/_2$	71	1
C17$^1/_2$	70	C18$^1/_2$	74	1

U.S. AND METRIC MEASUREMENTS

Approximate conversion formulas are given below for commonly used U.S. and metric kitchen measurements.

Teaspoons	x	5	= milliliters
Tablespoons	x	15	= milliliters
Fluid ounces	x	30	= milliliters
Fluid ounces	x	0.03	= liters
Cups	x	240	= milliliters
Cups	x	.024	= liters
Pints	x	0.47	= liters
Dry pints	x	0.55	= liters
Quarts	x	0.95	= liters
Dry quarts	x	1.1	= liters
Gallons	x	3.8	= liters
Ounces	x	28	= grams
Ounces	x	0.028	= kilograms
Pounds	x	454	= grams
Pounds	x	0.45	= kilograms
Milliliters	x	0.2	= teaspoons
Milliliters	x	0.07	= tablespoons
Milliliters	x	0.034	= fluid ounces
Milliliters	x	0.004	= cups
Liters	x	34	= fluid ounces
Liters	x	4.2	= cups
Liters	x	2.1	= pints
Liters	x	1.82	= dry pints
Liters	x	1.06	= quarts
Liters	x	0.91	= dry quarts
Liters	x	0.26	= gallons
Grams	x	0.035	= ounces
Grams	x	0.002	= pounds
Kilograms	x	35	= ounces
Kilograms	x	2.2	= pounds

TEMPERATURE EQUIVALENTS

Fahrenheit $- 32 \times 5 \div 9 =$ Celsius
Celsius $\times 9 \div 5 + 32 =$ Fahrenheit

U.S. EQUIVALENTS

1 teaspoon	$= \frac{1}{3}$ tablespoon
1 tablespoon	= 3 teaspoons
2 tablespoons	= 1 fluid ounce
4 tablespoons	$= \frac{1}{4}$ cup or 2 ounces
$5\frac{1}{3}$ tablespoons	$= \frac{1}{3}$ cup or $2\frac{2}{3}$ ounces
8 tablespoons	$= \frac{1}{2}$ cup or 4 ounces
16 tablespoons	= 1 cup or 8 ounces
$\frac{3}{8}$ cup	$= \frac{1}{4}$ cup plus 2 tablespoons
$\frac{5}{8}$ cup	$= \frac{1}{2}$ cup plus 2 tablespoons
$\frac{7}{8}$ cup	$= \frac{3}{4}$ cup plus 2 tablespoons
1 cup	$= \frac{1}{2}$ pint or 8 fluid ounces
2 cups	= 1 pints or 16 fluid ounces
1 liquid quart	= 2 pints or 4 cups
1 liquid gallon	= 4 quarts

METRIC EQUIVALENTS

1 milliliter	= 0.001 liter
1 liter	= 1000 milliliters
1 milligram	= 0.001 gram
1 gram	= 1000 milligrams
1 kilogram	= 1000 grams

BIBLIOGRAPHY

Adams, Catherine. *Nutritive Value of American Foods, in Common Units.* U.S. Department of Agriculture, Agricultural Handbook No. 456, Washington, D.C.: U.S. Government Printing Office, 1975.

Berto, Hazel. *Cooking with Honey.* New York: Crown Publishing Co., 1972.

Borella, Anne. *The How-To Book, Canning, Freezing and Drying.* Rev. Ed. New York: The Benjamin Co., Inc., 1976.

Composition of Foods, Agriculture Handbook No. 8, U.S. Department of Agriculture, Human Nutrition Service, U.S. Government Printing Office, Washington, D.C., Revised 1982–8.

Dawson, Elsie H.; Gilpin, Gladys L.; and Fulton, Lois H. *Average Weight of a Measured Cup of Various Foods.* U.S. Department of Agriculture, Agricultural Research Service ARS 61-6. Washington, D.C.: U.S. Government Printing Office, 1969.

Fulwiler, Kyle D. *The Apple Cookbook.* Seattle: Pacific Search Press, 1980.

Gibbons, Euell, and Gibbons, Joe. *Feast on a Diabetic Diet.* Rev. Ed. Greenwich, Connecticut: Fawcett Publications, Inc., 1974.

Griswold, Ruth M. *The Experimental Study of Foods.* Boston: Houghton Mifflin Co., 1962.

Hillers, Val. *Canning Fruits,* PNW 199. A Pacific Northwest Cooperative Extension Publication, Washington/Oregon/Idaho, 1990.

Hillers, Val. *Canning Vegetables,* PNW 172. A Pacific Northwest Cooperative Extension Publication, Washington/Oregon/Idaho, 1989.

Hillers, Val, and Dougherty, Richard. *Salsa Recipes for Canning,* PNW 395. A Pacific Northwest Cooperative Extension Publication, Washington/Oregon/Idaho, 1992.

Lesem, Jeanne. *The Pleasures of Preserving and Pickling.* New York: Knopf Publishing Co., 1975.

Lowe, Belle. *Experimental Cookery.* 4th Ed. New York: John Wiley & Sons, Inc., 1961.

Raab, C. A. *Pickling Vegetables,* PNW 355. A Pacific Northwest Cooperative Extension Publication, Washington/Oregon/Idaho, 1990.

Pennington, Jean A. T., and Church, Helen N. *Bowes & Church's Food Values of Portions Commonly Used.* 14th Ed. New York: Harper & Row, 1985.

Walnut Acres Bulletin: "Low Sugar Jams and Jellies." Walnut Acres, Penns Creek, Pennsylvania. (Product information sheet)

Note: PNW 199 and PNW 172 are available from the Cooperative Extension, Washington State University, Pullman, Washington.

PNW 395 and PNW 355 are available from the Cooperative Extension, Oregon State University, Corvallis, Oregon.

Software used for calculating recipes: *The Food Processor II.* Salem, Ore: ESHA Research, 1990.

General Index

RECIPE INDEX

NOTES